ABOVE TH
AN ANTIRACIST LITERACY
ARGUMENT FROM
A BOY OF COLOR

PERSPECTIVES ON WRITING
Series Editors, Rich Rice, Heather MacNeill Falconer, and J. Michael Rifenburg
Consulting Editor, Susan H. McLeod | Associate Series Editor, Jonathan P. Hunt

The Perspectives on Writing series addresses writing studies in a broad sense. Consistent with the wide ranging approaches characteristic of teaching and scholarship in writing across the curriculum, the series presents works that take divergent perspectives on working as a writer, teaching writing, administering writing programs, and studying writing in its various forms.

The WAC Clearinghouse, Colorado State University Open Press, and University Press of Colorado are collaborating so that these books will be widely available through free digital distribution and low-cost print editions. The publishers and the Series editors are committed to the principle that knowledge should freely circulate. We see the opportunities that new technologies have for further democratizing knowledge. And we see that to share the power of writing is to share the means for all to articulate their needs, interest, and learning into the great experiment of literacy.

Recent Books in the Series

Alexandria Lockett, Iris D. Ruiz, James Chase Sanchez, and Christopher Carter. *Race, Rhetoric, and Research Methods* (2021)

Kristopher M. Lotier, *Postprocess Postmortem* (2021)

Ryan J. Dippre and Talinn Phillips (Eds.), *Approaches to Lifespan Writing Research: Generating an Actionable Coherence* (2020)

Lesley Erin Bartlett, Sandra L. Tarabochia, Andrea R. Olinger, and Margaret J. Marshall (Eds.), *Diverse Approaches to Teaching, Learning, and Writing Across the Curriculum: IWAC at 25* (2020)

Hannah J. Rule, *Situating Writing Processes* (2019)

Asao B. Inoue, *Labor-Based Grading Contracts: Building Equity and Inclusion in the Compassionate Writing Classroom* (2019)

Mark Sutton and Sally Chandler (Eds.), *The Writing Studio Sampler: Stories About Change* (2018)

Kristine L. Blair and Lee Nickoson (Eds.), *Composing Feminist Interventions: Activism, Engagement, Praxis* (2018)

Mya Poe, Asao B. Inoue, and Norbert Elliot (Eds.), *Writing Assessment, Social Justice, and the Advancement of Opportunity* (2018)

Patricia Portanova, J. Michael Rifenburg, and Duane Roen (Eds.), *Contemporary Perspectives on Cognition and Writing* (2017)

ABOVE THE WELL: AN ANTIRACIST LITERACY ARGUMENT FROM A BOY OF COLOR

By Asao B. Inoue

The WAC Clearinghouse
wac.colostate.edu
Fort Collins, Colorado

Utah State University Press
upcolorado.com/utah-state-university-press
Logan, Utah

The WAC Clearinghouse, Fort Collins, Colorado 80523

University Press of Colorado, Louisville, Colorado 80027

ISBN 978-1-64215-124-4 (PDF) | 978-1-64215-125-1 (ePub) | 978-1-64642-224-1 (pbk.) 978-1-64642-237-1 (ebook)

DOI: 10.37514/PER-B.2021.1244

Produced in the United States of America

Library of Congress Cataloging-in-Publication Data

Names: Inoue, Asao B., author.
Title: Above the well : an antiracist literacy argument from a boy of color / by Asao B. Inoue.
Description: Fort Collins, Colorado ; Logan, Utah : The WAC Clearinghouse | Utah State
   University Press, [2021] | Series: Perspectives on writing | Includes bibliographical references.
Identifiers: LCCN 2021016038 (print) | LCCN 2021016039 (ebook) | ISBN 9781646422241
   (Paperback) | ISBN 9781646422371 (eBook) | ISBN 9781642151244 (PDF) | ISBN
   9781642151251 (ePub)
Subjects: LCSH: Language arts—United States. | Language awareness. | Racism in language. |
   Violence in language. | Discourse analysis—United States.
Classification: LCC LB1576 .I634 2021 (print) | LCC LB1576 (ebook) | DDC 372.6—dc23
LC record available at https://lccn.loc.gov/2021016038
LC ebook record available at https://lccn.loc.gov/2021016039

Copyeditor: Karen Peirce
Designer: Mike Palmquist
Series Editors: Rich Rice, Heather MacNeill Falconer, and J. Michael Rifenburg
Consulting Editor: Susan H. McLeod
Associate Editor: Jonathan P. Hunt
Cover Photos: Asao B. Inoue. Used with permission.

The WAC Clearinghouse supports teachers of writing across the disciplines. Hosted by Colorado State University, and supported by the Colorado State University Open Press, it brings together scholarly journals and book series as well as resources for teachers who use writing in their courses. This book is available in digital formats for free download at wac.colostate.edu.

Founded in 1965, the University Press of Colorado is a nonprofit cooperative publishing enterprise supported, in part, by Adams State University, Colorado State University, Fort Lewis College, Metropolitan State University of Denver, University of Colorado, University of Northern Colorado, University of Wyoming, Utah State University, and Western Colorado University. The University Press of Colorado partners with the Clearinghouse to make its books available in print.

In 2012, University Press of Colorado merged with Utah State University Press, which was established in 1972. USU Press titles are managed as an active imprint of University Press of Colorado, and the Press maintains offices in both Louisville, Colorado, and Logan, Utah.

CONTENTS

ANTIRACIST ENDOWMENT

In the past, I have made it a practice to provide my books for free online and refuse any royalties. I've said I'd rather be read than bought. My rationale was that knowledge belongs to everyone, that it is more ethical and antiracist to make my scholarship openly accessible, at least online. Even when my books have been published in print, I have not taken any royalties. I wanted it to be clear that my motive and agenda for writing a book and offering it to others was not tainted by profit, at least from my end.

I could have this philosophy due to Mike Palmquist and the WAC Clearinghouse's innovative model of academic publishing that offers their books free and open source for anyone to download in PDF or ePub editions. The printed editions of the books are priced low, with the goal of covering the cost of copyediting and production. Most don't cover those costs. Some do. And a few, including my other books with the Clearinghouse, actually make a profit. Those profits are put toward the cost of publishing new books.

This book, however, is not provided free or open source initially. This is so that a profit can be made and used to fund an endowment for antiracist teaching and assessment purposes. All of my profits (Asao Inoue) and all of those of the WAC Clearinghouse will be directed to this endowment, the **Asao and Kelly Inoue Antiracist Teaching Endowment**, which we have started at our alma mater, Oregon State University, the place where my wife and I met and where I started teaching writing. I want as much as possible of the money made from this book to be used to further antiracist educational goals, which may be training for new teachers, scholarships, establishing conferences, or other projects. Time will tell what antiracist educational work we can do through the endowment.

This is why this book has a monetary price, but only for a few years, then the electronic versions will be free, just like my books before this. And, of course, all profits from printed versions at that time will always go to the antiracist endowment. To be clear, after the costs of printing each book are recouped, 50% of the profits will be retained by the University Press of Colorado, while the other 50% will go the Antiracist Teaching Endowment. My hope is that this practice will offer not only a way to create an endowment for antiracist educational purposes but also a model for other academics and writers to accomplish other social justice work in the world.

Please know that your money paid, or donated separately, to access this book goes to a good cause. It does not go to me, the author, or to the WAC Clearinghouse. We make no profits from the sale of this book. Instead, I use this book as a way to give back, to move forward, to write our mutual antiracist future together as antiracist educators and students.

To learn more about the Asao and Kelly Inoue Antiracist Teaching Endowment, for details and links see the WAC Clearinghouse page (wac.colostate.edu /books/perspectives/above), my website (www.asaobinoue.com), or the direct donation page at www.osufoundation.org/Inoue. The endowment is managed by and housed at the Oregon State University Foundation.

ACKNOWLEDGMENTS

Writing a book requires the help of many people. I'm grateful to many who have contributed in a variety of ways in my life so that I might spend my time and labors on this book. All the people in my life are important, and I doubt I can recognize everyone. My apologies for missing many. First and foremost, I am grateful and humbled by my wife and partner, Kelly Inoue, for all that she does each day to give me the freedom to write, read, and think. She feeds my belly, my soul, and my heart. I am also grateful for my twin brother, Tadayoshi L. Inoue. I am lucky to have had a brother like him in my life from the very beginning. Not many people can say they have such a steadfast life-partner, confidant, and twin. I'm also deeply grateful for my mother, Dixie Peterson. My mom is the hero in my childhood story; she is strong, determined, loving, kind, and often sacrificing for her family. She was and is the strongest person I know, and she gave me wonderful gifts of heart, mind, and words. I have no way to repay her. I love you, mom.

I am thankful for the blind reviewers who took the time to read an earlier draft of this book and give me copious feedback. I'm humbled by not only their time but the praise they offered and the ideas that contributed toward the final version. I want to thank Mara Grayson for her reading and encouraging words. I thank Mark Blaauw-Hara for his thoughtful and compassionate feedback on the earlier draft; his insightful remarks were encouraging and offered critical considerations that helped me think through a few ideas. His feedback is the kind I strive to give to others.

Of course, the later chapters are a kind of acknowledgement to two mentors in my life, Chris Anderson and Victor Villanueva, both important to my story and to this book. I am thankful to Chris for opening the door to the academy to me, encouraging me in my nascent moments as a scholar and teacher. I am also thankful to my academic dad, Victor, for his reading of an earlier draft that helped me shape the manuscript for review and for his indefatigable guidance along my journey, which continues today. I strive to be like him in all my work and mentoring, turtles on posts.

I have been lucky to have a small group of former graduate students, all of whom now are successful high school teachers and university professors. They come from my days at Fresno State, and I'm honored and grateful to have their confidence. I'm thankful for their reading and feedback of an earlier draft of this book. Thank you to Donny Garcia, a wonderful teacher and thoughtful reader; Andy Dominguez, aka. "Pirate Andy," who always has smart and interesting insights to offer; Tyler Richmond, a soft-spoken, careful, and smart reader; Matt

Gomes, a little quirky at times but always has interesting ideas to contribute; and Shane Wood, a hard-working, honest, and compassionate man who gave me copious feedback on an earlier occasion too. These are the "Rhet-Comp Dudes," a group that re-formed after years apart. During the pandemic summer of 2020, the Rhet-Comp Dudes Zoomed together to talk teaching, research, and our writing. We started with this manuscript. I'm grateful for them and the time they gave to my draft.

Finally, I thank the editors at the WAC Clearinghouse, Rich Rice, Heather Falconer, and Michael Rifenburg, for their good work and continued confidence in me. In particular, I'm grateful to Michael Rifenburg's careful reading of the reviewers' comments and thoughtful synthesizing of that feedback, which helped me prioritize my revisions. And last but by no means least, I am humbled and grateful for the labors and support of Mike Palmquist, the founding editor and publisher of the WAC Clearinghouse. I cannot imagine publishing a book without him and his unfailing support and keen judgement. He's a friend, a colleague, and just about the best publisher around that I know of.

FOREWORD

Thoughts upon reading *Above the Well.*

Wake up in the middle of the night. A bathroom run. Don't turn on the lights, stub a toe against one of the bed's legs, bump a shoulder against the door jam, even though the doorway is four-foot wide and I'm not.

I've got stereoscopic vision, yet I'm not always conscious of using this gift. And I bang up against the edge of the door.

And then there's the light switch.

Forget about why I didn't turn on the light. Might have been a good reason (not wanting to disturb my mate in the middle of the night). Here, I'm thinking about how that light switch came to be.

~~~

We've been told about Benjamin Franklin and a key and a kite, harnessing electric power (and leading to the lightning rod). And we've been told about Thomas Edison and the electric lightbulb. And there were others, of course (but of course, we mainly learn of the Americans). But consider the conversations that led to General Electric, the first electric company. It took folks we would think of as scientists and engineers and manufacturers agreeing to work together, to be convinced, to cooperate. And it would take convincing a wealthy man, J.P. Morgan, to invest in the making of General Electric.

What I'm getting at with all of this is that we have a biological predisposition for language, the gift of language, maybe greater than the gift of stereoscopic vision, since no other creature uses language the way we humans do, but we're not always conscious of our uses of language. When we do become conscious of those language abilities we enter the world of rhetoric. Without our ability to cooperate through the negotiations made possible by the conscious use of language, by rhetoric, none of the great wonders of the world, the wonders of architecture, science, technology—none of it—would be possible. It all begins by our working together through language.

But in saying that, there is the presumption of cooperation. Yet "cooperate" is a tricky word, because it assumes equal power. Neither Edison nor his friend Henry Ford despite their abilities to create and to convince others of the value of their creations still needed the power of money. They had to sell their ideas to those of great wealth. And less recognized would be the women and the folks of color who helped to produce the lightbulb, motion pictures, the auto industry's assembly line.

What Dr. Inoue provides is some ways to think about rhetoric and power and the languages that come into play in the creation of workable rhetorics. His is not a linguistic study, it is a rich rhetorical study.

~~~

Another thought.

There was a time when Martin Joos's *The Five Clocks* (1967) was commonly read as an introduction to linguistics and as a discussion on "usage" (the ways language is used by native speakers of that language). Using the metaphor of clocks, he places the "norm" in English as "Central Standard Time," and he questions it. He writes,

> English-usage guilt-feelings have not yet been noticeably
> eased by the work of linguistic scientists, parallel to the work
> done by the psychiatrists. It is still our custom unhesitatingly
> and unthinkingly to demand that the clocks of language all
> be set to Central Standard Time. And each normal American
> is taught thoroughly, if not to keep accurate time, at least to
> feel ashamed whenever he notices that a clock of his is out of
> step with the English Department's tower-clock. Naturally,
> he avoids longing aloft when he can. Then his linguistic guilt
> hides deep in subconscious mind there secretly gnaws away
> at the underpinnings of his public personality. . . . [I]n his
> social life he is still in uneasy bondage to the gospel accord-
> ing to Webster as expounded by Miss Fidditch [the English
> teacher]. (4)

That was written in the nineteen sixties. Dialects and racism don't enter into his writing. He is busy saying that there's nothing natural about the language of power. So that since Joos, we have espoused the viability of various dialects and have argued the "Students' Right to Their Own Language" (*College Composition and Communication*, vol. 25 Special Issue, 1974). Yet that gnawing away of "correctness" lingers—maybe even especially among students of color and the bilingual (more than the polylingual) attempting college. And the good-hearted tutors at the writing center reinforce the mentality, even if kindly, and the good professor, wanting his and her students to succeed will reinforce it, even as speaking of dialects and the like. We recognize that standing before a wave with our hand up yelling "Stop!" cannot stem the tide of standardized conventions. We can't help but recognize the power at play. Inoue recognizes that if there is power, that power cannot help but be racialized. It's not simply the conventions of a disassociated dialect of prestige, but that prestige and power belongs to a certain class and its racial power. Not just a standard, but a symbolic imposition of what he calls a "white language supremacy."

~ ~ ~

Dr. Fidditch—two instances.

A graduate student and teacher, a woman of color, emails. A student had asked if the southern dialect is also an instance of white language supremacy. I respond:

> The answer to your student (great question!) is yes and no.
> No. The regional dialect of the South and even the southern
> Midwest (which is different) and the Southwest (especially
> Texas) are not the prestige dialect (which is how linguists
> have described it for years). And historically, the dialect of
> the southeast came from Black folks (who raised the wealthy
> white folks as "mammies" and "aunties" and "uncles"). And
> those Black folks got their dialect from a mix of their native
> tongues, mixed with the lingua franca of slave trade, West
> African English Pidgin, and the "accent" of the task masters
> (not the Masters who lived in the Big House, but the guy
> who was like a foreman in a factory, the guy with the whip).
> The task masters were Irish (when they were still considered
> racially inferior though above the Black slaves). BUT since
> regionally there is a middle-class white southern dialect, it
> becomes a localized white language of supremacy. We've had
> presidents with a Texas accent (Johnson) or a Southern accent
> (Carter), so the power is the power even if the northerners
> wouldn't recognize their dialects as the dialect if white lan-
> guage supremacy. See? . . . I prefer Standardized American
> English—not "standard," which is the linguistic term for the
> oral, but since it's a social construct, standardized. Now, one
> last complication. There is no southern accent in written
> discourse. If it weren't for a few words (like *colour* or *honour*
> or referring to a *lorry* instead of a truck), we wouldn't know
> a southerner from a northerner or a Canadian or a Brit or an
> Australian from an American. So in written discourse, what
> linguists call Edited American English, the written "stan-
> dard," there sure is a discourse of power (which is what Asao
> is getting at). But even that gets messy. EAE doesn't have to
> be academic discourse. Asao is using that language. I use that

language. So do you—and we ain't white. But we recognize the power in the prestige dialect.

So—yes, in the south, the white southern dialect would be a "language" of white supremacy (you know, the language is English, more a matter of Imperialism). But outside of the south, no, not really (northerners and midwesterners and westerners denigrate the dialect). But in writing there is no "southern dialect." There's only the standardized and its conventions, which have been imposed by those in power—white folks. That help?

I got pedantic. Couldn't help it somehow. The thing is, what Asao provides and demonstrates and discusses isn't really a matter of linguistics. It's a matter of power. It's a rhetoric—it's the stories of accommodating and of resisting the rhetoric of power, white language supremacy.

Example two.

I read Asao's manuscript—more than once. I had a habit—each time and over many years—of pointing to his spelling: *judgement*. As you will read in what follows, Asao talks back. He has his logic. It makes sense. And after all, the British *standardisation* (with an -s rather than a -z) does spell it as *judgement*.

But here's where bilingualism (even as what is known as a "heritage speaker," someone able to hear with a ready bilingualism but feels anxiety in speaking the first language, which is my case) comes into play as the "gnawing away of 'correctness'."

⌐⌐⌐

Our writing system (and I mean the alphabetic system) is based on the oral. It's what is termed a *phoneme-grapheme* correspondence. The sound effects the graphic, the writing. Now, in English the correspondence sometimes falls apart because of English's long written history, so that *knight* is pronounced *nite* rather than its original kuh-nikt. The first sounds that met my ears were Spanish, but the first writing I did was in English, when I entered school. I had to learn the sounds of English (a New York and Black English until I was sixteen and very consciously learned Central Standard Time). I learned the sounds and was taught spelling using phonics. The phoneme-grapheme correspondence was rigid for me. Since I knew that the spoken dropped the final -r (in New York), I would write that a thought was an *idear* (which when I was twelve, the president of the U.S. would say too, John F. Kennedy's Boston dialect). Even when it came to the language of the streets, I would not hear *gonna* (the written convention for *going to*) but *gone* ("I gone tell ya *what!*" when pushing back against a challenge). I was in my twenties when I discovered (or, more precisely, was mockingly told) that the brow was not pronounced for-eh-head. So I cannot see *judgement* and not say in my head judg-eh-ment. I still subvocalize as I read. And that is *my* problem, a problem with usage from which Asao breaks free. He owns his language, does not kowtow.

Because of the imperative to learn English, imposed by my parents (who gave me the duty of teaching them English), imposed by the school (Sister Fidditch), and imposed by society, I am compelled by the need for a kind of precision. I remain subject to "English-usage guilt-feelings." Asao, throughout the book, and in the example of this one word, *judgement*, breaks free of any guilt, and in so doing allows us all to break free.

I have to be very conscious to resist white language supremacy, to the degree that that's possible, more so than Dr. Inoue, apparently. I very rarely turn to dialect in my writing. My youth was Spanish and Spanglish and what linguist Ana Celia Zentella calls Puerto Rican Black English. But if TV can be a guide (and I think it can in this case), that dialect sounds very different now, nearly sixty years later. I fear I'd sound like someone mimicking a dialect that I no longer own. But I can and do turn to the rhetoric of my upbringing and my ancestry. In the language of rhetoric, as Asao will explain, I employ the rhetoric of the Sophists more than Aristotle. The language might be the language of the power of those in power, but my use of it pushes back against that power. And that is true of Asao's writing.

~~~

All this brings us back to what we will discover and learn as we enter this work by Asao Inoue. His history is not mine. We might both be what Asao calls *languagelings,* but we arrived at our ways with words differently, even with different commonalities, given differences in time and place and "color." His is the history of the working class, the history of an American of color, a mixed-race Asian American. And just like even an octaroon (someone one-eighth Black) remains Black or a "high yella" or a "redbone," what is clear to those who come in contact with Asao is that he is not white, confused, as he tells us, with a Latino. Even as he is a champion reader in elementary school, he is a champion reader who is nevertheless regarded as having a language deficiency. What folks see affects what they hear. We will learn of the ways in which racism is never not tied to language, its use, its power—even when the power is on his side, as in the "language" he shares with his twin brother Tad (who sounds so much like Asao, even down to Asao's linguistic idiosyncrasies, that it's uncanny). "Twin Language" still becomes subject to white language supremacy. We travel with

Asao through grade school, the southwest, the Pacific Northwest, colleges, the Midwest and the ways in which racism is always vying for power and must be challenged. Autobiography, theory, teaching, philosophy, theology—all are beautifully interwoven. And always there is power.

Enjoy the journey in the pages ahead. And with Asao Inoue consider how we might assume our own power.

Victor Villanueva
Pullman, Washington
22 November 2020

ABOVE THE WELL: AN ANTIRACIST LITERACY ARGUMENT FROM A BOY OF COLOR

AN INTRODUCTION

Our language participates in racial violence. That is, we are all enlisted, whether we like it or not, into an invisible and very deadly racial war waged around us daily. That's too much to tell you this soon. Let me come back to this in a few pages.

Years ago, I was introduced to an elder's wife in a church that my wife, two sons, and I were visiting. We thought we might join that church. We had just moved to town. It was my first professor job after getting my Ph.D. We were in an unfamiliar place, southern Illinois. The elder's wife, an older, White woman who spoke loudly, was greeting us in the foyer. It was our first visit to the church. She asked our names. I said, "My name is Asao Inoue. This is my wife, Kelly, and my sons, Kiyoshi, and Takeo." She replied, "Well, you don't make it easy." I didn't know what to say, except to smile awkwardly at her and never go back to that church again.

In many ways, this anecdote is symbolic of my literacy journey, of what you may find in the following pages. I know that the elder's wife did not mean to be unkind or unwelcoming, but she was. She didn't mean to insult me or my name or my heritage, but she did. She didn't mean to open a wound of mine that was inflicted when I was seven or eight years old, but she did that, too. Should I have given her and that all-White church another chance? Maybe, but why is it that in such exchanges that involve race and language, it is the person of color who must always do the forgiving, who must always overlook the faults and missteps of the White people around them?

I don't mean to lay all of the blame on that White woman's shoulders. She wasn't trying to be mean or racist. She's really just a symptom of racism in our society, not the cause. She likely lived her entire life in the Midwest, in southern Illinois, in communities of mostly, if not completely, White people like her. She most likely had never confronted her own racial positioning or considered how her words were tied to the community she came from. Her environment never asked her to, never showed her clearly her own Whiteness. She likely was always an insider. She was a product of a culture that allowed her to think that making fun of someone's Japanese name was okay, that jokes are just jokes, words just words, that race and our histories of racism don't factor into her words or our names. She didn't mean to be racist in conditions that make racism.

Race is a set of structures that make up our lives. Language is one of those structures. Language and names are conjured in groups of people who use their language together. In this seemingly innocent exchange that was ostensibly about being welcoming and learning our names, this White lady could not see how salient race is to our use of language and the judgements that language is interlaced with.[1] In one sense, this book attempts to illustrate just how salient race is to language, judgement, and our attitudes towards language and people around us who use it.[2]

Let me be clear. This book is for students of language. I don't mean just for school purposes, but for anyone who wants to learn about the connections between language and racism and who are not researchers or scholars of language, just regular people interested in this thing we do together, language, and in stopping the racial violence in our world. In many ways, I envisioned a first-year college student audience or a high school senior as I wrote this book. I try to open up the kinds of discussions about language, judgement, and racism that I have with first-year college students in my writing courses.

I am not offering a memoir. This book is not a straight narrative of a boy's coming to his own literacy. In fact, I resist rehearsing a coherent or chronological narrative of my schooling or of my learning to read and write, so you may resist how I've written this book. We have plenty of books about Brown and Black kids who made it or didn't. You don't get to pity me or be amazed at all that I have done. That's not my story here.

In my experience, those kinds of literacy narratives, as useful as they are in many ways, also too often are an excuse for White readers to wallow in the exotic, to feel pity and sadness for the poor Brown kid, then feel good about how they feel about racism because they felt good about sympathizing with the Brown or Black author. Those narratives often mingle the pathos of the writer of color with what that writer is offering as analysis, critique, or solutions to racism or White supremacy. And when it comes to race and Whiteness, White readers often have difficulty with all these things for some valid reasons, which I'll get into.

White readers too often act as if rooting for the Brown kid, being on his side, is enough. It is not. You must *do* antiracist work, as Ibram X. Kendi has explained.[3]

---

1   I spell this word "judgement," realizing that the more common way to spell it is "judgment," with only one "e." I do this because, well, it looks better to me, complete. It's my languaging. It also preserves in a visual way the operative word, "judge," with the implications of an agent who has their own perspective, a judge with a singular view of things. Judgements do not just happen. They come from a judge who "judges." A judgement is the end of an action. I'm preserving the noun and verb in my word. I like to keep all of these meanings visualized and represented in the word on the page. And if it bothers you to read it this way, that's one of my points in this book. It should also be noted that this is the common British spelling of the word, but I'm not using this spelling to favor that standardized spelling over an American one.

2   I take this idea of saliency from Robin DiAngelo. She says: "We all occupy multiple and intersecting social positionalities. I am White, but I am also a cisgender, woman, able-bodied, and middle-aged. These identities don't cancel out each other; each is more or less salient in different contexts." See, Robin DiAngelo, *White Fragility: Why It's So Hard for White People to Talk About Racism* (Boston: Beacon Press, 2018), xvi.

3   Ibram X. Kendi, *How To Be An Antiracist* (New York: One World, 2019).

It's not enough to just feel for others' misfortunes and abstain from racism. We must act in different ways and change the structures in our lives that enable us to act or stand by and watch. The structures I mean in this book are those that maintain acceptable language in schools and public spaces—that is, what we often call, "Standard American English," "Dominant American English," and what I call "Standardized American English." More on this later in the book, too.

Our habits are often strong, comforting, even when they hurt us, or do not help us. It's hard to give up a habit—say smoking, or eating too many sweets, or saying "like" in front of every other sentence, or smiling when you are nervous. In many ways, this book is about habits of language that become our ways of communicating and judging words and people. This book is also my literacy story. It describes some of the important things that made me into the language-ling I am today.

But this book is not simply a story about a poor Brown kid from the ghetto who made it out and up. It cannot be. It is also about the ways we all participate in the White language supremacist systems and conditions that we work, live, and do language in. It is about our names for things and people, about the race-judgements we make in and through our language that we may not know we are doing. It's about the economics of race that affect our languaging. It's about the Whiteness in language and how I'm not a good example of how great our systems are.

This book will not give you a linear narrative or chronological story of my life or education, yet paradoxically you can find that chronology in these pages if you wish to piece it together. I will not always engage in the habits of language that you likely expect in stories like this one. Even if you can't say exactly what those expectations are, I guarantee that you will feel them when they are broken in books like this. I'm hoping many of my readers will notice this about their own expectations and habits of language. I hope you will feel your expectations broken. This is one small stone in the path to antiracist languaging.

For instance, I ain't gonna always write whatcha call Standard American English all the time. I will not always give you an experience about myself then interpret that experience or make sense of it for you. I may reverse that order or skip one part, or I may use it. I am not going to tell you a story about me only, as if doing that would explain my languaging.

These kinds of common expectations in books like this one are the habits of the English language that I'm trying to critique, trying to understand with you as I tell my literacy story. So I may use them, because that's my training in school, but that ain't the only way I language. Like you and many others, I too have a hard time imagining what language is like—or what it could be—outside of these standardized ways of doing it. I'm not above these common habits of language, these habits of White language (more on that later, too). No one is. But I'm trying to work around them as much as with them.

So, what is my method in this book? There is a scene that I'm trying to show, one that has no central actor, and yet I am the subject of this literacy narrative. But it ain't just my literacy narrative. It cannot be. To understand my literacy, I need to drop myself onto a landscape with lots of other interesting people, ideas, and topography that I want you to know next to me. You should know about Freire and Western and Taoist dialectic differences in habits of language, know about the economics of racism, about textbooks and my experiences, about naming in other places I've never been, and about Horatio Alger. I want you to know all these things so you can simulate an orientation to language like mine, so you can come close to knowing me and my languaging as I do. You'll miss too much if you focus just on my schooling, or my reading history, or my story. Furthermore, why should I talk just about me, yet how can I talk about anyone else?

My opening scene above is a good example of this tension. It seems so natural to start a book about my literacy journey in this way. So many other books start in similar ways. I start with me and my name, an experience you, my reader, can see and connect with. A good way to start a story about literacy is with a story about names and language, right? Now, what I'm describing is a set of language habits that are so ingrained in English language users that they can seem natural and right. If I did something else, you may not find my book worth continuing past the first page. You may think I'm not a good writer. You may think I got bad editorial advice. You may wonder: How is this a story about this guy's literacy or education? These judgements come out of White, middle- and upper-class, monolingual English language habits that I want to call attention to in this book. Why? Because they make up many of our literacy stories and they hurt so many, particularly when they are used in society as universal standards and used to withhold opportunities and rewards.

So, part of my reasoning for how I have written this book is to help readers escape from a false sense of knowing about "good" language and its "appropriate" standards. Another part is about understanding our feelings about language that influence our judgements and expectations of people and their words. And another part is about understanding racism and the White supremacy in our literacy practices. What I aim to do is disrupt your expectations about how such stories of literacy like mine are told by disrupting what you think learning English means and what it takes to understand it in any of us.

In many places, then, my discussion will sound less like a story of my experiences and more like an exposition of other things, an argument. In those places, it may sound like a discussion of education, history, language, testing, economics, or race in the US. And that is because it is. I don't think I can tell my story of learning to read and write without telling a larger story of language and judgement in the US, even if only in parts. Who I am, and how I use language, what I think of that language, is connected to many other things in the world, in my life, in history. And most of these larger things, I do not control. And for many of us, they are invisible. I want to make them more visible.

Some of these things, these structures, are economic and governmental systems. Others are narratives and ideas in U.S. culture that are interlaced with language and ideas about language, which often seem to be about other things, not race. For instance, the notions we have about how a smart person talks—that's a set of structures, narratives, and ideas that we use to make decisions about things and people. And those structures about what smart sounds like are connected to lots of other structures, like economic, geographic, and educational systems, all of which no single individual controls. So my literacy story, like everyone's, is also a story about larger systems in place that we all live in and shape us in different ways. My story of literacy, like yours, is really a story of structures, of systems that make me, and that now I try to remake.

It is often more comforting to believe that we are in full control of who we are and how we use the languages we do. This allows us, especially teachers and bosses, to blame others for not communicating in ways we think they should. Thinking you have full control of your languaging means that when someone else thinks you don't language well, it's your fault. And while I do believe we have a lot of control over who we are and what happens in our lives, I do not believe we control all of it, nor do I think just anything is possible for every person.

There are boundaries and limits to what we can do, and those limitations are not the same for everyone. I'm not saying that some people are inherently less than others. I'm saying people commune and live among other people in groups, and these groups have different relations to the systems we all work in. Those relations to systems matter because they create walls and doorways.

It is the systems in place, like schools, civic life, economic markets, governments, churches, even our systems of language and standards for language that make the conditions of our lives. These systems create and structure what is possible for us and how our own words will be valued or heard or understood by others. Thus, what is possible for any given person is not equal. That White elder's wife was a product of White supremacist systems just as much as I am, as we all are. And the question I want to ask through my own literacy narrative is this: *How do we come to understand the White language supremacist conditions in our lives in order to remake those conditions for a more equitable, antiracist, and better world?*

Now, let me come back to my opening statement. Language participates in violence. This is the reason I write this book now in this way. It's the exigency for this book. It's also a tacit argument for teaching languaging in writing classrooms in ways that matter to our lives, not just to arguments, to bodies in the street, but I won't make the explicit teaching argument here. Teachers will have to figure that out, just as other readers will have to figure out why this kind of book is important at this moment in our world. But in or out of the classroom, we all are fighting an invisible racialized war on the battlefield of words. And what's at stake is White language supremacy.

As I write this introduction, there are numerous protests, rallies, and activist groups across the US, even in other countries, demanding that police violence against Black bodies stop, that local governments defund their police departments, that they invest in community policing and programs that help and nurture Black people, not treat them as criminals first, which then justifies any violence done to them, including killing them. These widespread protests have come after the brutal and indiscriminate killing of George Floyd by a White Minneapolis police officer while other police officers stood guarding that officer as he slowly choked Mr. Floyd to death.

While Floyd was being killed in front of a group of people, some recorded it on their cell phones. One video captured Floyd begging in a weak choking voice, "Please, I can't breathe." The video quickly went viral and sparked the protests. It is traumatic for many Brown and Black people, like me, to watch. I have actually not watched it in its entirety. I can't. It's too painful. One reason is that this is just one of the many killings of Black citizens in the US by police for no reason. It is a synecdoche of many, many other police killings and violence against Black bodies in the US. It's one killing that reveals the many others before it. The protests wouldn't be so numerous, loud, and ubiquitous if this kind of racialized violence weren't a long, historical, and racialized pattern. It's one way White supremacy occurs.

How could a police officer, charged to protect and defend citizens, do such a thing? What conditions create such killing, such disregard for a human life? What orientation to the world and words must it take to ignore a begging, choking, dying Black man in front of you? How could his words not be heard by that White police officer, or any of the others? This book, my literacy story, aims to explain why. So I hope you will bear with me, sit in some discomfort (if you feel it at times), and take the full journey with me.

One of the central themes about language in this book is that words have real effects on us, emotionally, physically, even spiritually. They are more than logos, than reasoning, more than terms and ideas. The ancient, fifth century (BCE), pre-Hellenic (Greek) philosopher and teacher of orators, Gorgias, named this language phenomenon as magical. He said,

> Speech is a powerful lord, which by means of the finest and
> most invisible body effects the divinest works: it can stop fear
> and banish grief and create joy and nurture pity. . . . Fearful
> shuddering and tearful pity and grievous longing come upon
> its hearers, and at the actions and physical sufferings of others
> in good fortunes and in evil fortunes, through the agency of
> words, the soul is wont to experience a suffering of its own.
> . . . Sacred incantations sung with words are bearers of plea-
> sure and banishers of pain, for, merging with opinion in the
> soul, the power of the incantation is wont to beguile it and
> persuade it and alter it by witchcraft and magic.[4]

I think it is important to notice how words work on us, how they make us and our emotional responses to others and their words. Because language can have such magical effects on us, like witchcraft, beguiling us in various ways, it seems prudent to notice, to pay attention when it happens and that it does. I offer a short appendix essay at the end of this book that discusses a method for reading that I think may help you see the magic in words as you read. I call the practice *deep attentive reading*, and it can be an antiracist reading practice.

Furthermore, our emotions and understandings have a relationship to one another, often in ways we may not realize or want all the time. In his Pulitzer Prize winning novel, *House Made of Dawn*, N. Scott Momaday speaks of a grandmother and her languaging: "her regard for words was always keen in proportion as she depended upon them . . . for her words were medicine; they were magic and invisible. They came from nothing into sound and meaning. They were beyond price; they could never be bought nor sold. And she never threw words away."[5] If you have magic, you don't throw it away. You pay attention. You respect it, tend it, take special care of it, perhaps give it as a gift to others. We all do word magic. We just don't always realize it. We have a responsibility to pay attention.

But if we aim to be antiracist and anti-White supremacist in our actions and words, if we hope to stop the racial violence around us, then we should acknowledge the magic in words, how they are also tacitly racialized, how they work on us in invisible ways, how they limit and bind us, how they do violence as much

---

4   Gorgias, "Encomium of Helen," in *The Rhetorical Tradition: Readings from Classical Times to the Present*, 2nd ed., ed. Patricia Bizzell and Bruce Herzberg (Boston: Bedford/St. Martin's, 2001), 45.

5   N. Scott Momaday, *House Made of Dawn*, (New York: Harper & Row, 1968), 95–96, quoted in Thomas King, *The Truth About Stories: A Native Narrative* (Minneapolis: University of Minnesota Press, 2003), 100.

as attend to us in loving, compassionate, and medicinal ways. And of course, no one is above the magic of words, no one is above their own language conditions. If these conditions are White supremacist, then we all have responsibilities to attend to and tear down these systems and rebuild better ones.

CHAPTER 0.

LANGUAGE, POLITICS, AND HABITS

Why is there a chapter 0? I think it is important to establish a few definitions and key ideas that I draw on in the rest of this book. These terms may be triggers for some readers. I don't want them to be. I want them to be terms that help us engage together, perhaps engage through our disagreements. This chapter is important because it helps me tell my story better, and it must come first.

Let me give you an example to help explain. Imagine you are trying to have a conversation about going to Los Angeles with someone you care about, someone you respect, say your sister. You believe that both of you would have a great time, be enriched in a number of ways, if you both took a trip to L.A. Your sister, let's call her Angelica, doesn't like L.A., won't even talk about it. Now, every time you mention the topic, or even say "L.A.," you can see her face crinkle up, her eyes narrow, and her mood become sour and angry. She gets upset about it.

She had a really bad experience in L.A. ten years ago. She never wants to go back, and even talking about the city reminds her of that terrible event. But you have good reason to think this time will not be like that last one. Things are different, better. In fact, you have made extra efforts to ensure that your proposed L.A. trip with Angelica will be really great, nothing like her last one. But she just won't listen when you bring it up. You can't even get to the details. She turns and goes away or focuses in on how the details she does hear are just like the L.A ten years ago, the bad L.A.

So your job, if you really think that trip is worth it, is not to convince Angelica about how good the trip is or will be, or how her last trip to L.A. was a fluke, an unlucky set of occurrences, or simply a long time ago. Your best shot at convincing her likely will be to help her through her emotional response to the idea of L.A., not to change her mind, but to help her deal more productively with those emotions and see how they may be keeping her from hearing new details, a different L.A. You have to help her hear details that may be different from her initial ideas.

This kind of problem is what I think many people have with the terms that I explain in this chapter, like White language supremacy. Angelica is missing out on a really great trip and a great city, but she's also right. Her experiences were awful, a good reason not to go back. But if she can't confront at some point those past experiences and her emotions about them and find a way through it all—that is, if she can't sit with difference meaningfully—she is limited, and her limitations are self-imposed. She imposes a boundary on her life that excludes L.A., a place that is bound to offer her something rich, even if she never goes on the trip. This chapter, I hope, helps some readers who might be in Angelica's position around issues of racism and White language supremacy. These ideas are vital to my story in the rest of this book.

Now, should you find that you still have trouble reading, trouble accepting ideas, even just entertaining them long enough to hear what I'm saying, you might read my appendix, "An Argument and Method for Deep Attentive Reading," which I mentioned in the Introduction. That stand alone essay offers a compassionate reading practice that I think can help. I know it has helped me.

The essay also offers a more detailed discussion of several key ideas that I reference throughout the rest of this book, namely, the availability and WYSIATI heuristics, confirmation bias, and the halo effect, all of which Daniel Kahneman discusses and that keep many people from considering seriously different ideas or arguments from those they already hold.[1] These are mindbugs we all have that Banaji and Greenwald also explain.[2] They are ways our brains often think too fast and in the process make faulty judgements. And they are implicated in racism and my literacy story.

WHITE LANGUAGE SUPREMACY

"White language supremacy" is a term that can conjure up some ugly feelings. The words "White" and "supremacy" in the same phrase often trigger many people, particularly White people, because it can sound like I'm calling all White people racist, or I'm placing evil intentions on all White people, but I'm not. I'm not even referring to people's intentions or attitudes when I use this term. This misunderstanding is reasonable in the US today, since historically the phrase "White supremacy" is connected to bad people doing and saying bad or racist things, like enslaving and lynching Black Americans, imprisoning those of Japanese and Arab descent into "internment camps" or "detention centers," or turning high-powered water hoses onto innocent people.

While certainly the kind of White supremacy I'm speaking of in this book is historically related to that kind from the past in the US, it does not look the same today, is not accomplished in the same ways, nor is it experienced in exactly the same ways. But it is connected to our past. It is a legacy we live in.

---

1   Daniel Kahneman, *Thinking, Fast and Slow* (New York: Farrar, Straus and Giroux, 2011).

2   The concept of "mindbugs" comes from chapter 1 of Mahzarin R. Banaji and Anthony G. Greenwald, *Blind Spot: Hidden Biases of Good People* (New York: Bantam Books, 2016).

We must remember that who and what we are today is built on who and what we were yesterday. We don't escape our history because we are born from the material of history. We cannot say that we are only shaped by today's stuff or by just the good stuff of our past. We gots all of it—the good, the bad, and the other—in us. So White supremacy, as Robin DiAngelo tells us about racism, is "a structure, not an event."[3]

Dina Gilio-Whitaker, an indigenous scholar who studies native environmental justice, offers a good explanation of her use of the term "White supremacy" and of the anxiety around it for many people. She connects it to U.S. settler colonial history and the injustices done against native American tribes and nations and their homelands. It is worth reading her explanation at length:

> Americans like to think that since the civil rights era, we have achieved the postracial, meritocratic, multicultural state where color blindness and equal opportunity prevails. Both liberals and conservatives like to think that racism is defined only by hostile behavior from which individuals can excuse themselves because they have friends, employees, perhaps an old lover or two who are people of color. In this way of thinking, White supremacy is an ideology restricted only to rogue alt-right, neo-Nazis or White-nationalist fringe groups, and certainly not well-meaning everyday people, whether conservative or liberal. While White supremacy is most definitely at the root of those regressive social movements, as a foundational worldview constructed by centuries of White European settlement of the United States, it is far broader than that. It is the thread from which the American social fabric is woven. A few decades of laws promoting racial justice have failed to unravel the systemic forms that White supremacy has taken, reflected by range of social indicators from chronic wealth inequality to negative educational outcomes to disproportionate rates of violence (police, sexual, and domestic) and incarceration in communities of color. Centuries of dehumanization of American Indians, African Americans, and ethnic minority "others" has left its mark on the American mind and in its institutions, refusing to die.[4]

---

3   DiAngelo, *White Fragility*, 28.
4   Dina Gilio-Whitaker, *As Long As Grass Grows: The Indigenous Fight For Environmental Justice, From Colonization to Standing Rock* (Boston: Beacon Press, 2019), 99.

What Gilio-Whitaker highlights is a "range of social indicators" that help us see White supremacy in our world. These indicators are conditions that are the effects of White supremacy and its cause. In short, White supremacy can be seen in the *conditions* that we all live in and that disproportionately hurt people of color in the US.

These conditions typically help or privilege those deemed racially White, mostly through historically made structures that are connected to or associated with racial groups and the places each group tends to live in. Such structures consist of things like language practices, family wealth, different qualities of schools in particular neighborhoods, and the different levels of police engagement and crime rates in various areas of a city. Thus, my use of this term in this book is not meant to directly reference evil people, or bad intentions, or hooded figures burning crosses, even though it is historically connected to that kind of overt racism.

The term as I use it is meant to help us remember our history, not forget it. Race, while not biological or real in that sense, is an important factor in who we are, how we use and judge language, and what we believe. Race is so interlaced in our world that we often mistake it for something else.

The terms I use are meant to remind us that we are trying to *change conditions*, systems, not people's minds or hearts, although changing our conditions can change minds and hearts. It takes time, though, for the new antiracist structures to do their work on us. So it's important to use these words, even if they are initially shocking or jarring, even if they make us uncomfortable, or pause, or cringe.

When we were first married, my wife and I lived with her grandma in a home in Monmouth, Oregon. My wife's father and mother and I were sitting out on the patio in the back. We were talking about the wedding a year before, how nice it was, how many people showed up. One of them, I think her mom, a selfless and kind White woman who has worked very hard her whole life, mostly for those around her, said, "They thought you were *Mexican*." She said the last word, "Mexican," in a half-whisper, and I thought I saw her scrunch her nose just slightly on the word. She explained that others disapproved of her daughter's marriage to me at first, that they told her this at the wedding. "You allowed her to marry *him*?" they asked. She said to us, "We told them that you were Japanese, not Mexican." No whisper.

I remember how uncomfortable the conversation was, how quickly it turned, not just because race was referenced, or rather whispered, but that it was also deployed to show I was accepted into their family. I was glad she moved on quickly and politely. This was my new family. I loved them. I love them more today. I did not want to cause strife because I disapproved of how they defended me. I didn't want to call them out on the racist language they were likely trying to avoid and probably thought they were successful at avoiding.

This is often how White language supremacy operates in our daily lives. It is hard to see and hear and even harder to talk about, to investigate. This kind of work requires conscious compassion, suffering with others, like my misguided mother-in-law, whom I love dearly. We have so few words that can help us through our racism. And yet, our words make us and unmake us. They are all we have.

White language supremacy, therefore, can be defined as the condition in classrooms, schools, and society where rewards are given in determined ways to people who can most easily reach them, because those people have more access to the preferred embodied White language habits and practices. These White language habits are so because they historically have come from White racial groups in the US who have had the power to make such standards and enforce them in schools, civic spaces, governments, and businesses. Part of the conditions of White language supremacy is an assumption in most systems that what is reachable at a given moment for the normative, White, middle- and upper-class, monolingual English user is reachable for all.

This assumption is often cloaked in narratives or justifications that use meritocracy and "fairness," such as "everyone must be judged by the same standards," without examining who tends to be most advantaged by the use of such universal standards. It seems irrelevant to consider where those standards of expression come from, who made them, and who they tend to benefit most in the present context. This assumption is also justified in arguments about merit, bootstrapping, and the idea that anyone can achieve as long as they work hard and long enough, while ignoring who tends to end up achieving the most, who usually must work harder for the same benefits or opportunities, and what prior preparation is necessary in order for someone to be able to take advantage of those opportunities.

Here's how we know White supremacy and White language supremacy exist and are vigorously reproduced in our world: look to who controls things in our society and where they come from. In her discussion of White supremacy, Robin DiAngelo offers a list of facts about the U.S. society's systems that amount to White supremacy in the key areas of education, literacy, government, business, and entertainment. Each of these areas play an important part in determining which English language standards are used, what language is normal and acceptable, and how people think about that language. Here's a shortened version of DiAngelo's list:

- Ten richest Americans: 100% White
- U.S. Congress: 90% White
- U.S. governors: 96% White

- Top military advisors: 100% White
- People who decide which TV shows we see: 93% White
- People who decide which news is covered: 85% White
- People who decide which music is produced: 95% White
- People who directed the one hundred top-grossing films of all time, worldwide: 95% White
- Teachers: 82% White
- Full-Time college professors: 84% White[5]

These are the judges and decisions makers in our society. They make our structures and conditions, our society. We inherit these structures and conditions, often taking them for granted. We consider them normal and neutral. At face value, they do not appear to be about race or White racial superiority. They seem like objective, race-neutral policies about language use, or about standards for evaluation and grading in schools, or about practices of reading and judging words and people. But these structures are little machines that help us do things and make things with words, like communicate or make decisions. These little language machines can only make particular things in predetermined ways, because that is how machines work. They are designed to produce a particular thing in a particular way. This is to say, all machines have their biases. They cannot make something else or change the way they operate on their own. Our language habits are little machines.

To make something else or make something in a different way, we have to dismantle the machine and build a new machine. This is why my definition for White language supremacy centers on *conditions* and *assumptions*, both of which are structural in nature. That is, we may not realize we are in these conditions or have these assumptions, but we operate from them nonetheless. Assumptions are thought and judgement structures we take for granted, use unconsciously most of the time because it's more efficient to do so. This is Kahneman's fast thinking.[6] It's implicit racial and other biases, or the mind-bugs that Banaji and Greenwald discuss.[7] Thus, White language supremacy is not an intention or an expressed goal for anyone or any system; rather it is an inherited condition in society, schools, classrooms, courtrooms, boardrooms, everywhere, that determines the outcomes in these places as White language supremacist.

---

5   DiAngelo, *White Fragility*, 31.
6   Kahneman, *Thinking*.
7   Banaji and Greenwald, *Blind Spot*.

To see our world as White supremacist is not to say that White people have gotten things they have not worked for, that they are less than who they think they are. That's one of the paradoxes. I am making no comment on whether a particular White individual or group has earned all that they have, or are as good as the system seems to say they are. In fact, I'm willing to assume they are good and have earned all they have, but this does not negate the fact that the systems they have worked in and used to earn their rewards are White supremacist, that it helps them more than others, even as most White people have not asked for that help.

Just because you aren't to blame for the way the system works doesn't mean that you don't unfairly benefit from it. So it ain't enough to say, "well, I worked hard for what I have." White language supremacy ain't about how hard you worked to get what you got. It's about the fact that your hard work doesn't equate to the same rewards as others, that White people's hard work is worth more than people of color's, and that this fact is set up in our systems of rewards and punishments.

Meanwhile, the same systems make it more difficult for people of color to receive the same kinds of rewards with the same kinds of efforts and work. And these systems are overlapping. You cannot just get rid of one White supremacist set of structures and think you've solved the problem of White supremacy. These are the conditions of life in the US, and they are so ubiquitous, so normal, so dispassionate in the way they function, we often don't notice how racist they are.

The conditions of White language supremacy are those in which the environment is set up so that rewards move mostly in one direction—that is, they are given to particular people with particular linguistic and bodily dispositions or habits. These language habits historically have come from a White racial formation.[8] The assumptions about these language habits are that they are the best, clearest, and most effective ways to communicate. The rewards, opportunities, and privileges that these habits give people are not usually described or identified as racialized in nature, but because of the racialized outcomes that they produce

---

8   I use "racial formation" as well as "racial group," but racial formation preserves the dynamic and evolving nature of any group of people defined by a socially changing construct like race—race is "forming" always. This means that a racial formation such as a White racial formation is different today in New York than it was say in 1900 in the same place, or different from a White racial formation in London, England. What it means to be White is not static but changes depending on place and time. I take the term "racial formation" from Michael Omi and Howard Winant, *Racial Formation in the United States*, 3rd ed. (New York: Routledge, 2015), 109.

(like fewer African American and Latine[9] in certain key professions), they really are racist in practice, or *de facto*.

For instance, we say we just want our lawyers or nurses to speak clearly and effectively in order to do their jobs well, but what we mean by clear and effective speech is language that matches a dominant form of English that excludes Black English and other English varieties. The assumption is that other forms of English are less communicative, less effective, less professional, or less able to do the jobs of lawyering or nursing.[10] This dominant standard of English comes from a group of White, middle and upper class, monolingual men who speak English and often come from New England or the East Coast.

While we can say that African Americans are not inherently born predisposed to speaking Black English, many do, more do than White people, relative to each group's total numbers. There are lots of structural reasons for this linguistic phenomenon in society, which have to do with where many African Americans have lived or have been forced to live, where they go to

---

9   The terms Latino, Latina, Latinx, and Latine, which are various ways that many use to refer to those who come from Central and South America, are complicated and political. There has been much debate about the use of these terms. Latinx has been used as a gender inclusive term, but the "x" ending is not a Spanish language ending, and many consider it an Anglicized version of the root word, which has masculine (o) and feminine (a) ends depending on the reference. The "e" ending, which is a gender neutral ending in Spanish, is also used for a gender neutral reference; however, some point out that the "e" ending on "Latino" is illegitimate, since it has not been there historically. I am unsure. Language changes all the time. My mentor, Victor Villanueva, who is Puerto Rican and speaks English and Spanish, prefers "Latine" to refer to those from Central and South America, so I will use that term in this book for the gender inclusive term, realizing that this decision may be contested. For some discussion on these terms, see Ecleen Luzmila Caraballo, "This Comic Breaks Down Latinx vs. Latine for Those Who Want to Be Gender-Inclusive," Remezcla, October 24, 2019, https://remezcla.com/culture/latinx-latine-comic/; Raquel Reichard, "Latino/a vs. Latinx vs. Latine: Which Word Best Solves Spanish's Gender Problem?" *Latina*, March 30 2017, http://latina-1051845746.us-east-1.elb.amazonaws.com/lifestyle/our-issues/latinoa-latinx-latine-solving-spanish-gender-problem. And to see a comic strip that breaks down the term nicely, see Terry Blas, "'Latinx' is Growing in Popularity. I Made a Comic to Help You Understand Why," The Highlight by VOX, last updated October 23, 2019, https://www.vox.com/the-highlight/2019/10/15/20914347/latin-latina-latino-latinx-means.

10   While she doesn't explain the structural reasons for the phenomenon, Yolanda Young provides statistics from the American Bar Association on the number of Black and White lawyers, clerks, and judges in the U.S. She explains, "According to the American Bar Association, 88% of all lawyers are White and only 4.8% are Black, so for each of the 60,864 Black lawyers, there are 686 Black citizens needing assistance (compared with only 282 White citizens for each of the 1,117,118 White lawyers)." In actuality, the disparity is of course much greater because African Americans are disproportionately entangled in the criminal justice system—one in 15 Black men is incarcerated, compared to one in 106 White men. See Yolanda Young, "Why the U.S. Needs Black Lawyers Even More Than It Needs Black Police," *Guardian*, May 11, 2015, https://www.theguardian.com/world/2015/may/11/why-the-us-needs-black-lawyers.

school, and where and who they commune with in churches, schools, and neighborhoods.

The same historical and social dynamics that create the conditions for many Black Americans to use Black English also create conditions for many White Americans to use versions of English that share more language conventions with the dominant Standardized English.[11] The result is unsurprising: African Americans lose opportunities. But they do so not because they are Black, but because they use Black Englishes. This really means statistically that if you are Black, you ain't likely to be a lawyer or doctor. And as I'll show in my story, your English is you, and you are your English. Making decisions based on the kind of English a person uses is making decisions based on race.

Language standards are a way to be White supremacist without being White supremacist or using White supremacist language. In 1981, Martin Barker, a professor of media and cultural studies at the University of West England (and later at Aberystwyth University), identified a similar phenomenon in public children's comics and literature in the United Kingdom under the rule of Margaret Thatcher. Barker coined the term "new racism" that identified the way these language strategies maintained the same old racist policies, ideas, and outcomes.[12]

Similarly, Eduardo Bonilla-Silva's important sociological studies show how US students and others can be racist without being racist.[13] We can have good intentions, be good people, demand "clear and logical" writing from students in schools, yet through those standards we end up promoting White language supremacy because those standards and expectations come historically from a White racial formation in the Western world. I'll say much more about this in the rest of this book. When such standards are used to decide grades,

---

11   For a definitive study of Black English, see Geneva Smitherman, *Talkin and Testifying: The Language of Black America* (Detroit: Wayne State University Press, 1977). For discussions on the relationship between race and language attitudes, see H. Samy Alim, John R. Rickford, and Arnetha Ball, eds., *Raciolinguistics: How Language Shapes Our Ideas About Race* (New York: Oxford University Press, 2016).

12   Martin Barker, *The New Racism: Conservatives and the Ideology of the Tribe* (London: Junction Books 1981).

13   See Eduardo Bonilla-Silva, "Rethinking Racism: Toward a Structural Interpretation," *American Sociological Review* 62, no. 3 (1997): 465–480, https://doi.org/10.2307/2657316; Eduardo Bonilla-Silva, *White Supremacy and Racism in the Post-Civil Rights Era* (Boulder, CO: Lynne Rienner, 2001); Eduardo Bonilla-Silva, "'New Racism,' Color-Blind Racism, and the Future of Whiteness in America," in *White Out: The Continuing Significance of Racism*, ed. A. W. Doane and E. Bonilla-Silva (New York: Routledge, 2003), 271–284; Eduardo Bonilla-Silva, *Racism Without Racists: Color-Blind Racism and the Persistence of Racial Inequality in the United States* (Lanham, MD: Rowman and Littlefield, 2003).

opportunities, and preferred methods of communication for everyone, they privilege White people and disadvantage people of color and poor people. It's White language supremacy without White supremacists.

THE POLITICS OF LANGUAGE

In this book, when I speak of White language supremacy, I'm also talking about the politics of English languages. What do I mean by "politics"? I'm not referencing political parties or agendas in the typical sense of the word, "politics." That is, I'm not talking about whether someone is a Democrat or a Republican. It isn't those kinds of politics I am linking to standards and language usage. I'm referring to power relations in social and institutional settings, like schools, offices, churches, and public settings. And these power relations are always uneven or unequal. Some people have more power to do and say things than others in particular contexts. Some are more influential than others. Part of this phenomenon is due to the ways our Englishes are unequal.

And so in each setting, some ideas and words are more influential, attractive, and compelling than others. Conversely, there are other words and ideas that are less attractive, negative, or repellent than some. In short, politics means power relationships between people and between various language habits. So when I say that our use of language standards is political, I mean that not everyone gets to make judgements and decisions about language usage or standards that count and that not all words and ideas are considered equally, even when they should be. This means that not everyone gets to be heard or read as authoritative or compelling or persuasive for all kinds of reasons that have little to do with what they are saying and a lot more do with where they come from or who they are understood to be.

Let me give you an example that you likely have a lot of experience with. In classrooms, the teacher has more power to administer rewards and punishments, to make those in the class do things. Students usually have very little power to do this. We generally know why these politics work this way in schools. Teachers are trained in the subjects they teach and hired by schools to teach, thus their expertise is validated in many ways that we do not question. People with college degrees have knowledge and experiences that give them expertise in areas like teaching writing or history. They are granted more power to control things in classrooms because of their expertise.

Often, titles and positions—like teacher or professor, doctor or lawyer—as well as the money (salary) that goes along with such titles confirm to us that those people know things, that an institution or company has confirmed their knowledge and given them power to exercise. They are qualified to do their job and control things. They are often seen as knowledgeable and trustworthy in their areas of work and expertise. The teacher or doctor couldn't be hired to do their job otherwise, right? There are vetting processes that are competitive. So the most qualified end up with jobs, right?

But we can only accept the expertise of the teacher on these grounds if we accept the overlapping systems and institutions of education, commerce, training, and hiring in schools that create that expertise and in turn create the politics of the classroom. So the sources of power relations among people and their words are structural. Systems create power. And as DiAngelo's list of White dominated leaders and influencers shows, these systems currently reproduce authorities and experts who come from the same places as each other, White places. So really, our current systems create White power.

These same politics work in every language situation in our lives. Even sitting around our dinner table talking to our family members is created by conditions that affect the language we use and how it is heard and judged by those around us. I'm not suggesting that we question all authority, or that everyone with power should not have it. I'm saying that there is always a politics that constructs what we understand, how we understand it, who gets to make the rules and decisions, and what language and ideas end up being judged as acceptable and most compelling.

So, when we notice that an idea is very persuasive to many people, like the idea that "in the US, hard work always pays off," then we might ask: What political conditions help give that idea power? What conditions or systems make it compelling and persuasive in the present situation? We do not control a lot of the conditions we find ourselves in each day. For instance, none of us control the fact that in the US, most consider the language of business, education, commerce, politics, and everyday social life to be a particular kind of English.

We don't control the history of how that English has been used in any of those past settings in the US. We don't control who has been in control in those settings or what their biases and experiences with language, particular ideas, and people were. We just inherit these conditions. And these conditions shape further conditions, such as when we find ourselves sitting in a classroom or living room entertaining the idea that "in the US, hard work always pays off," or "my doctor or nurse should speak 'proper English.'"

But there are more overlapping factors that contribute to our language conditions and the politics inherent in them. Our own histories, biases, experiences, and idiosyncrasies also form language conditions. For example, we don't choose the particular brand of English, if that's your first language, that we speak and use. It is an inheritance, not a choice. It is a gift from our elders who nurtured us as children and adolescents. It evolves with those friends and others with whom we commune on a daily basis, a product of countless tiny decisions made each day in our lives, until what we say and how we say it all just seems natural to us.

Our own version of English is also a product of an incredible string of lucky circumstances that brought each of us to where we are today, regardless of who we are, what kind of English we speak, and what our pasts are. No one chooses where their family is from. And geography plays an important part in how languages are formed and evolve. That's why people in Atlanta speak and use English differently than those in Chicago, or New York, or Los Angeles.

But some locations, and the people who operate in them, are understood as more important than other locations and people. That is, New York is the center of publishing in the US. Los Angeles is the center of the entertainment industry. And the languages used by people in those places have dictated what is standard in them. If we are not thinking slowly enough, we may falsely assume that the languages of those two places are universal, that people in rural Kentucky should speak just like those in Los Angeles, California.

Politics, or the relations of power, is always a part of how we use language, how our languaging is judged, and how we judge others. When we pan back to see a larger swath of history, we find out that it's not hard to see who has had politics on their side. White people have controlled all of the systems and structures, the standards and practices, that create the version of English that has come to be acceptable and most valued in all areas of life.

In order to maintain White language supremacy, or deny that it exists and assume that language is neutral and universal, there are things about language that have to be ignored. The first is that language itself is political. Ignore this fact and it's easier to blame people for the language they speak, call them ignorant, lazy, or dumb, and deny them opportunities in society, all the while saying it's all fair because it's all neutral. We are just trying to put the most qualified and smartest people in the right places, and we are using language, not our racial biases and prejudices, to determine who gets into those places. If you do not ignore the politics of language, you cannot come to this conclusion. But remember, White language supremacy is a condition that has overlapping and redundant structures. There are lots of other things you have to ignore as well, which my story in this book will try to show you.

SIX HABITS OF WHITE LANGUAGE AND JUDGEMENT

Finally, in this book, I'll reference what I call *habits of White language and judgement*, or habits of White language, HOWL for short. These are the language habits usually assumed or promoted as universally appropriate, correct, or best in writing and speaking by those with power to do so. Historically, these habits of language have come out of elite White racial groups in Western, monolingual,

English speaking societies, as I'll illustrate in chapters 2, 3, 4, and 5 in various ways. There is nothing inherently racist about these habits of language. However, when they are used as universal standards for communication, used to bestow opportunities and privileges to people, then they become racist and produce White language supremacy.

Using the research on Whiteness, I've found at least six habits that often embody Whiteness as a privileged language position. These six habits of White language and judgement don't always exist at the same time in the same text or language expression, but the first one listed is almost always present in White supremacist expressions.

The presence of one habit in a text or judgement doesn't always equate to being White supremacist or producing White supremacy, but it often can. Usually the difference is in what that instance of language or judgement produces in the places it circulates. Is the outcome of the language or judgement a racially unequal or unfair distribution of resources, jobs, grades, etc.? Does it produce a racialized hierarchy in society? If so, then it is White supremacist.

Understanding when White language supremacy is happening not only helps us understand the consequences of a judgement or decision, but how that judgement or decision is made, how the habits are used to explain or think through language and other judgements. What ideas, values, competencies, or conditions of individuals or groups are assumed to be universal or accessible to all? Claims of universal fairness often fall into this category. They usually sound like: "I treat everyone the same," or "I try to be fair by giving everyone the same opportunity to get X or to do Y." But we are all not the same, nor do we come from the same conditions. We all don't get to run the same race, with the same training, or the same equipment. We don't use the same Englishes, not exactly. And these differences are patterned in groups, because our society has been racially and economically segregated into groups. While he does not frame White language and judgement as habits, nor use such terms, Ibram X. Kendi, in *Stamped From the Beginning*, offers a history of these habits in the racist ideas voiced by influential thinkers, religious leaders, and political figures such as Cotton Mather, Thomas Jefferson, Samuel Sewall, and John Saffin.[14]

Equally important to remember is that the intentions of writers, speakers, or institutions do not matter when determining whether something is White supremacist or racist. Because White language supremacy is a systemic and structural set of conditions that have been created historically, it is not an ethical

---

14   The first twelve chapters in Ibram X. Kendi, *Stamped From The Beginning: The Definitive History of Racist Ideas in America* (New York: Nation Books, 2016) are particularly illustrative of how all six habits of White language and judgement were established as common sense, neutral language practices, and compelling ways to use the English language.

blemish to say that someone is reproducing White language supremacy. When we determine that our judgements or decisions reproduce White language supremacy, we are not making any claims about the morality or goodness of people or institutions. We are identifying the way systems work and their biases in order to take responsibility and move forward, change, and make things better tomorrow.

Taking responsibility is an ethical imperative, something we do because we wish to act compassionately. Being to blame for perpetrating some injustice upon others is a judgement that is often understood as a moral failing. Taking responsibility for our world is what we do because it is our world, and the vast majority of us want to make it better for ourselves, for others, and those who come after us.

Here are the six habits of White language and judgement, or HOWL, that I'll reference throughout this book.[15]

- **Unseen, Naturalized Orientation to the World**—This is an orientation, a starting point, of one's body in time and space that makes certain habits, capacities, practices, languages, and ideas reachable. It assumes, or takes as universal, its own proximities or capabilities to act and do things that are inherited through one's shared space. It can be understood as an "oxymoronic haunting,"[16] leaving concepts and ideas unsaid or unstated for those in the classroom or other place to fill in. It is often stated or understood as "clear only if know" (or COIK).[17] The authority figure knows precisely and assumes everyone else does too. When a teacher, writer, or authority embodies this habit, they

---

15   Previous versions of HOWL are in: Asao B. Inoue, *Labor-Based Grading Contracts: Building Equity and Inclusion in the Compassionate Writing Classroom* (Fort Collins, CO: WAC Clearinghouse and University Press of Colorado, 2019), 27, 278–279, https://doi.org/10.37514/PER-B .2019.0216.0; Asao B. Inoue, "Classroom Writing Assessment as an Antiracist Practice: Confronting White Supremacy in the Judgments of Language," *Pedagogy* 19, no. 3, (October 2019): 373–404, https://doi.org/10.1215/15314200-7615366.

16   See, Tammie M. Kennedy, Joyce Irene Middleton, and Krista Ratcliffe, eds., *Rhetorics of Whiteness: Postracial Hauntings in Popular Culture, Social Media, and Education* (Carbondale, IL: Southern Illinois University Press, 2017), 4–7.

17   A COIK orientation often operates from ambiguous or floating key terms and ideas. For example, in the statement, "Americans are a *free* people," the term "free" floats. It can mean a number of things depending on who you are. COIK orientations leave key ideas or terms floating but assume a universal understanding of them. To read about "floating signifiers," see, Claude Lévi-Strauss, *Introduction to the Work of Marcel Mauss*, trans. Felicity Baker (London: Routledge and Kegan Paul, 1987), 63–64; "Floating Signifier," *Beautiful Trouble*, ed. Andrew Boyd and Dave Oswald Mitchell (OR Books, 2012; repr. https://beautifultrouble.org/theory /floating-signifier/).

often do not realize it, assuming that everyone has access to the same languages, concepts, practices, capacities, histories, and logics that they do. In this way, the classroom, or an ideal paper, or an expected language performance becomes an extension of the White body, its habits, and its languaging in such a way that it is hard to distinguish it as an orientation, body, or space in the classroom or other place. It's just, for instance, a standard that is both associated with but understood as separate from Whiteness and White bodies.[18]

- **Hyperindividualism**—This is a stance or judgement that primarily values self-determination and autonomy as most important or most valued. It often centers or assumes values of the self as an individual, self-reliance, self-sufficiency, and self-control, which tend to also support logics like "survival of the fitness," "free and open markets," and competition as proving grounds for discovering the best or what is most ideal. It can appeal to ideals of universal truths and knowledge that come from inside the individual. This personal insight is often understood as universal insight. The logic is that everyone is the same because we are all the same inside, while also holding on to the importance and primacy of the individual, even the individual as the exception. Individual rights and privacy are often most important and construct the common good or what is best in society or groups. Thus the best outcome of a class or an assignment or activity is something personal—a personal grade, a personal insight or learning, a better draft—but not a benefit to the community, group, or class as a whole (that is an indirect, secondary benefit). In this way, the point of society, school, the classroom and its activities is to serve the interests and growth of the individual, not the community.[19]
- **Stance of Neutrality, Objectivity, and Apoliticality**—This is an orientation that assumes or invokes a voice (and body), or its own discourse, as neutral and apolitical, as non-racial and non-gendered. This is often voiced in the style of a "god-trick," which is a universal vantage

---

18   I draw on Sara Ahmed, "A Phenomenology of Whiteness," *Feminist Theory* 8, no. 2, (2007): 149–168, https://doi.org/10.1177/1464700107078139; Robin DiAngelo, *White Fragility*.

19   For this habit, I draw on, Richard Brookhiser, "The Way of the WASP," in *Critical White Studies: Looking Behind the Mirror*, ed. Richard Delgado and Jean Stefancic (Philadelphia: Temple University Press, 1997), 16–23; Catherine Myser, "Differences from Somewhere: The Normativity of Whiteness in Bioethics in the United States," *The American Journal of Bioethics* 3, no. 2 (2003): 1–11, https://doi.org/10.1162/1526516603766436072; David McGill, and John K. Pearce, "British Families," in *Ethnicity and Family Therapy*, ed. Monica McGoldrick, Joe Giordano, and Nydia Garcia-Preto (New York: Guildford Press, 1982), 457–479; DiAngelo, *White Fragility*.

or viewpoint by which to know something else in a nonpolitical or purely objective way. It is a view that is outside the person speaking or expressing the ideas. Often, this stance also manifests as an urge toward universalism, or a one-size-fits-all mentality. Facts are just facts, not created or manufactured by people or processes or language. Contexts are deemphasized or ignored. Ideas, from this orientation, can be outside of the people who articulate them. A rubric or set of language expectations in a classroom, for example is assumed to be apolitical, outside of the gendered and racialized people who made it (and the racialized and classed groups and places those people come from).[20]

- **Individualized, Rational, Controlled Self**—This is a stance or orientation in which the person is conceived of as an individual who is primarily rational, self-conscious, self-controlled, and self-determined. One's own conscience guides the individual. Sight (ocularity) is the primary way to identify the truth or to understand something (i.e. seeing is proof; seeing is understanding; seeing is believing). This makes social and cultural factors into external constraints on the individual, which must always be ignored or overcome. Meaningful issues and questions always lie within the rational self. Individuals have problems, making solutions individually-based. Thus, both success and failure are individual in nature. In a classroom or other space, failure is individual and often seen as weakness or confirmation of inadequacy or a lack of control. Personal control of one's self, body, and voice are important because it shows that the individual is in control and rational. Often part of self-control is the ability to continually work and stay busy or be industrious and productive in approved (or predefined) ways within the system or classroom.[21]

- **Rule-Governed, Contractual Relationships**—This habit focuses on the individual in a contractual relationship with other individuals,

---

20 I draw on Toni Morrison, *Playing in the Dark: Whiteness and the Literary Imagination* (Cambridge, MA: Harvard University Press, 1992); bell hooks, "Representing Whiteness in the Black Imagination," in *Displacing Whiteness: Essays in Social and Cultural Criticism*, ed. Ruth Frankenberg (Durham, NC: Duke University Press, 1997), 338–346; Timothy Barnett, "Reading 'Whiteness' in English Studies," *College English* 63, no. 1 (2000): 9–37, https://doi.org /10.2307/379029; Marilyn Frye, "White Woman Feminist," in *Willful Virgin: Essays on Feminism 1976–1992* (Freedom, CA: The Crossing Press, 1992), 147–169; Donna Haraway, "Situated Knowledges: The Science Question in Feminism and the Privilege of Partial Perspective," *Feminist Studies* 14, no. 3 (Fall 1988): 575–599, https://doi.org/10.2307/3178066; Myser, "Differences from Somewhere."

21 I draw on Brookhiser, "The Way"; Barnett, "Reading 'Whiteness'"; Haraway, "Situated"; Myser, "Differences from Somewhere"; DiAngelo, *White Fragility*.

either formally or tacitly, that tends to be understood as benefiting the individuals in the contract, not the whole community or group. This habit can be seen in syllabi as one kind of assumed social and educational contract that is dictated by those in power (teachers and schools) for the assumed benefit of individual students. Additionally, a focus on or value in "informed consent" (often confirmed in writing) is important. Ideal relationships are understood to negotiate individual needs or individual rights, which are apolitical and universal. Meanwhile, socially-oriented values and questions are less important and often understood as inherently political (and therefore bad or less preferable). There is an importance attached to laws, rules, fairness as sameness and consistency, so fair classrooms and other spaces are understood to be ones that treat every individual exactly the same regardless of who they are, how they got there, where they came from, or what their individual circumstances are. Very little, if any, emphasis is given to interconnectedness with others, relatedness, or feelings in such classrooms or in other arrangements, activities, and relationships. Individuals keep difficulties and problems to themselves because the important thing is the contractual agreement made.[22]

- **Clarity, Order, and Control**—This habit focuses on reason, order, and control as guiding principles for understanding and judgement as well as for documents and instances of languaging. Thinking and anti-sensuality are primary and opposed to feelings and emotions. Logical insight, the rational, order, and objectivity are valued most and opposed to the subjective and emotional. Rigor, order, clarity, and consistency are all valued highly and tightly prescribed, often using a dominant, standardized English language that comes from a White, middle-to-upper-class group of people. Thinking, rationality, and knowledge are apolitical, unraced, and can be objectively displayed. Words, ideas, and language itself are disembodied, or extracted, from the people and their material and emotional contexts from which the language was created or exists. Language can be separated from those who offer it. There is limited value given to sensual experiences, considerations of the body, sensations, and feelings. A belief in scientific method, discovery, and knowledge is often primary, as is a reliance on deductive logics. Other logics that often distinguish this habit in

---

22   I draw on David Roediger, *The Wages of Whiteness: Race and the Making of the American Working Class*, rev. ed. (London: Verso, 1999); George Lipsitz, *The Possessive Investment in Whiteness: How White People Profit from Identity Politics* (Philadelphia: Temple University Press, 1998); Myser, "Differences from Somewhere"; Frye, "White Woman Feminist."

classrooms and other spaces are those that emphasize usefulness or unity and pragmatic outcomes, all of which are predefined for individuals by authorities, such as a teacher.[23]

---

23   I draw on hooks, "Representing Whiteness"; Brookhiser, "The Way"; Myser, "Differences from Somewhere"; Barnett, "Reading 'Whiteness.'"

CHAPTER 1.

LITERACY IS (NOT) LIBERATION

When I was seven years old, I won my school's reading contest by reading the most books in the second grade. I set goals each week, read every night after dinner until I went to bed. For each book, I wrote a one or two sentence summary on a special slip of paper that my mom and I would sign, proving I'd read each book. I'd return to class each day with several of these slips in hand, giving them to my teacher, Mrs. Whitmore, a tall, husky, White lady with a gruff voice that softened at the corners of some words, especially when she asked questions.

Every book I read gave me more confidence to read the next one, to choose harder and longer ones. Engaging so intensely on this reading contest was a way I could escape the poverty we lived in. It came at a time when I was beginning to understand who I was, what was missing in my life, and what was present. It was also a moment when I realized that I loved words. Learning so-called "Standard English," reading and writing it well, symbolized to me what it meant to be successful, to be a man, and to be free from the oppressive conditions around me.

I don't want you to get the wrong idea. My growing up had lots of love and happiness in it, but there was also other not so great stuff. And that stuff got mixed up with my coming to my own literacy. It got mixed up with my understanding of myself as a boy of color in schools and public spaces. You see, during my elementary years, we were very poor, lived in North Las Vegas (North LV) in government subsidized apartments on Statz Street. Too often, there was more month than money, more days left until the first than we had boxes of macaroni and cheese or Top Ramen in the cupboard. And forget meat or milk, those were luxuries, like little food vacations—only the rich could afford those things.

Too often, I did not get new clothes or shoes for school. One year, I had to wear the previous year's shoes. My shoes had big holes right through the bottoms of them. They were brown sneakers with three yellow zig zag lines on the sides. They were an off-brand, Trax. I could feel the ground when I walked, the hot Vegas asphalt nipping at the balls of my feet with each step. I won't say that I was blissfully unaware of our circumstances, that the love in our home made up for the lack of most everything else. That would be a lie. I knew I was poor. I could feel it in our circumstances and on the bottoms of my feet.

At the time, North LV was primarily a Black city, a poor ghetto. It has changed since because of population increases in Las Vegas during the 1980s and '90s, but in the '70s, it was considered a poor and run down city. Of course, now I see where this language comes from. It is racialized, or rather it is the way racism is voiced today. "Run down" cities are always pseudonyms for race, and serve as warnings to White folks and those who can heed the warning.

In the US, most people avoid speaking of race, or labeling people or ideas or language as racial, in polite company. The habits of the dominant group in the US today, their standards by which we all get judged in and out of school, dictate that race not be mentioned explicitly in conversations. The Whiteness hides. If you have to, you say it in hushed tones and whispers. But to say it out loud, explicitly, that would be rude, and even racist itself, or so goes the logic. But race is threaded into all of our material conditions. We don't have to talk about it for it to still be integral to all that we do and say.

Such terms as "run down" are facially non-racial terms for where Black or Latine people live. It's the same as saying, "the bad part of town." Why is that area less desirable, and to whom? Of whose desire are we speaking? During the 1970s and '80s, the intersections of race, economics, and class coalesced in North LV around a mostly Black racial formation. And part of what made that Black racial formation and the negative image of the city was the redlining practices of banks in the 1950s and '60s, which allowed banks to refuse loans in the area. Banks drew red lines around areas on maps where people of color lived, and called those areas decrepit or run down, which gave them reason not to loan money to people or build in those areas.[1]

This meant that over time, no new development, housing or commercial building occurred. This meant no jobs. No money circulating in that area. This meant that things got worn out. People had to figure out how to make a living or survive or escape the rundown-ness of things. Some chose drugs or gangs or prostitution, and some like me, chose reading. But all of these options were the ways of escape that were available to each of us. Language happened to be available to me more so than most of my Black friends and neighbors. And yet, I'm positive I was only one or two decisions away from prison, and not a professor of writing at a big university.

This racist history of a generation before me created the North LV I grew up in. It kept opportunity out and Black and Brown bodies in. It meant that if you wanted to work, you had to have a way to get out of North LV and to the place where the job was, either with a car, which meant lots of gas, or by bus, which

---

1   To read about some of the redlining practices in North Las Vegas, see Jenna Kohler, "The Other Vegas," *Las Vegas Sun*, May 15, 2008, https://lasvegassun.com/news/2008/may/15/other -las-vegas/; or to see interactive maps of the US that show the redlining practices in many locations, see "Mapping Inequality: Redlining in New Deal America," American Panorama, University of Richmond Digital Scholarship Lab, accessed February 25, 2021, https://dsl.richmond .edu/panorama/redlining/#loc=4/39.854/-101.679.

meant lots of extra travel time. Bottom line, the history of North LV made conditions that kept everyone poor with little ability to create equity in homes or wealth.

Consequently, it is no easy feat to leave Statz Street because you also have to get out of debt and accumulate some wealth. My mom did it by working three jobs and getting help from her sister's husband, my uncle Bill, a university professor in another state who married my mom's sister. He was a working-class White man from Iowa who became an internationally known microbiologist with hundreds of patents under his name, mostly for processes that made cheese. And even with his help, our leaving depended on my mom finding another roommate to live with us and share the rent. So while we were poor, we had some privilege, some help, some friends, and some way out. We had some chances to get out and up. We took them.

At the time on Statz, our poverty affected the way I heard words, too. This is the time I can remember my mom talking about "making ends meet," scraping by until the next payday. But what I heard was "making ends-*meat*." I thought the expression was one that used the metaphor of food, of preparing the ends of meat, the leftover parts, perhaps the grizzly sections that might get thrown away in good times, but one could eat them in lean times to get by for just a bit longer.

Today, I still visualize in my head making ends-meat, because making ends meet doesn't make any sense to me. It just sounds like circular logic. What ends meet and where? Why are they meeting? How is connecting two ends of something a metaphor for getting by in tough times when you don't have much food in the cupboard? How does that feed a hungry belly? The contexts for getting by in my life's formative years were driven by hunger for anything to eat as well as a hunger for words. But in those early years, food was always on my mind. We were so poor that we didn't have much of it, and I was always hungry. So it makes sense that I'd hear a food metaphor in these daily conversations around survival.

So that second grade reading contest was important to me, even though I didn't really understand why at the time. I'm not sure why I wanted to win so badly; maybe it was because of the poverty; maybe I wanted to have something that others didn't. Maybe I thought it was a way to get some favor from a teacher who seemed to have none for me. It was a time when I was just discovering my love for words and language. It was an escape.

Words seemed like something I could control. Maybe this contest cultivated my love for language; maybe that love was already there, inevitable. I don't know. What I do know is that I thought about that contest every day for most of my second grade year. I hate to think what would have happened had I lost. But I didn't. Losing at words would not be my destiny, not then nor later, at least not when it really counted.

I still remember the ceremony. An administrator, perhaps the vice principal, came into our class, called me up to the front of the room, and presented me with two trophies, one for the most books read in our class and one for the most in all of the second grade classes. I was very proud, but the whole affair was tainted. After I got the awards, I was escorted, as was the daily custom, back to my remedial reading classroom for reading lessons. I was a remedial reading student through most of my elementary and junior high years.

It didn't matter how many books I'd read or what reading contest I'd won. It didn't matter that I loved reading from that point on, that I spent much of my spare time reading at home. I always had a stack of books checked out from the library. It didn't matter that my brother and I wrote stories to each other on my mom's Montgomery Ward Signature typewriter, just for fun. It didn't matter that in the cafeteria and on the block no one would verbally spar with either of us. We were just too good at words, too good at put-downs, at cappin, at talkin bout "ya momma." We could quickly undo your logic, tangle and reshape your own words, and use them against you—and strangle you with them.

Words were weapons and medicine that made my life better, that made me a king outside of the classroom and protected me or soothed my wounds in quiet moments. And yet in the classroom, my grades, while not bad, were not great either. I often teetered on the brink of failure in those early years of elementary school. And to make matters worse, during this period and throughout the rest of my schooling, I was constantly confronted with my racial identity. I would learn later in college that English language literacy and racial identity are closely related, wedded, in the US.[2]

Much later in my life, in graduate school, I'd learn about educators and language scholars who talked about how we make meaning of the words and other symbols in our lives from the material of our lives, from what we already know, experience, and read. We understand, hear, and see what we are prepared to understand, hear, and see. We recognize the things we have names for.

We see a dog because we have a name for such a creature, and that name helps us make sense of how to relate to this creature. Is it a pet or a guard dog? We see round objects because we have a concept and name for such an occurrence, an

---

2   There are lots of resources one can read to understand the connections between race and English language literacy. See, for example, H. Samy Alim, John R. Rickford, and Arnetha F. Ball, *Raciolinguistics*; Vershawn A. Young, *Your Average Nigga: Performing Race, Literacy, and Masculinity* (Detroit: Wayne State University Press, 2007); Suhanthie Motha, *Race, Empire, and English Language Teaching: Creating Responsible and Ethical Anti-Racist Practice* (New York: Teachers College Press, 2014); Morris Young, *Minor Re/Visions: Asian American Literacy Narratives as a Rhetoric of Citizenship* (Carbondale: Southern Illinois University Press, 2004); Victor Villanueva, *Bootstraps: From An American Academic of Color* (Urbana: NCTE, 1993).

object without straight or flat sides, no angles. These words help us make sense of what is otherwise meaningless and reveal patterns in the chaos of life.

The words we have also are keys to our liberation from oppressive systems. And this is what I subconsciously grabbed onto as a young reader of English. There are many examples today of the liberatory value of literacy and of those who have proclaimed such ideas: Henry David Thoreau, Frederick Douglass, Malcolm X, Margaret Fuller, Malala Yousafzai, bell hooks, Gloria Anzaldúa, Maya Angelou. Another was a mid-twentieth century Brazilian educator named Paulo Freire, who described the process of acquiring written literacy as a liberatory process, one that gives people power over their lives, power over the conditions that oppress them. Literacy gives people control of their lives' conditions, in part because it allows us to name them, abstract them, restructure them. Freire explains the connection between the written word and the material world: "Reading the world precedes reading the word, and the subsequent reading of the word cannot dispense with continually reading the world. Language and reality are dynamically intertwined. The understanding attained by critical reading of a text implies perceiving the relationship between text and context."[3]

Key to Freire's ideas about literacy and its attainment is the term "critical" in "critical reading." He means something very particular. It's not a deposit or "banking model" of literacy where the teacher deposits learning, ideas, or words into the student's brain, then that student uses that understanding to decipher text. This would ignore the fact that we have histories with words, objects, places, people, and ideas. Words have relations to us. They affect us, our thinking, and our views of the world and those in it. And these relations and consequences are different depending on who you are and where and how you live. It assumes people don't have prior or ongoing relations to the world and words. In fact, it ignores these relations completely.

To Freire, critical reading, on the other hand, is a process of what he calls "problematizing" one's own material and existential situation.[4] If we are being critical in our reading practices, Freire says, it should lead to our asking questions about our reality and about how it makes us and we make it. Our reading of words leads to rereading the world, and our experience of the world should

---

3   Paulo Freire, "The Importance of the Act of Reading," trans. Loretta Slover, *The Journal of Education* 165, no. 1, (Winter 1983): 5–11, https://doi.org/10.1177/002205748316500103. To read more about Freire's position on literacy, see Paolo Freire and Donald P. Macedo, *Literacy: Reading the Word & the World* (South Hadley, MA: Bergin & Garvey Publishers, 1987).

4   In case it helps, "existential" simply refers to the nature of one's existence. If our material lives might be questioned by asking, "what makes up my existence," then to question our existential lives, we might ask, "how do my material conditions make up my existence."

help us read words. The kinds of questions Freire urges are ones that help us pose problems about our world and the degree to which we control it and it controls us.

Critical reading, then, is a practice of reading words and pausing to pose questions about our relation to our material situation, our reality in those words.[5] Freire implies that the words we use can tell us a lot about who we are and where we come from. Critical reading urges us to do more reading, find out more information about our world and thus ourselves.

My hearing "ends-meat" was about more than a boy being hungry all the time, hearing what he needed to hear in words. The words that were important to me at that moment of my life when I heard my mom talk about the rent and what was left in the cupboard were usually about basic needs: food, shelter. They were never abstract. There were no metaphorical ends of something that needed meeting. The end was always food, at least in my mind. And I can see now that my rendition of that euphemism was not a mistake. I made the meaning I could, and those words made me as much as I made them. It was me languaging through my material conditions. Freire helps me see that my literacy is both my liberation and my oppression and many other things.

~~~

We live on Statz in a small, two-bedroom, white brick apartment. My mom sits at our small kitchen table, a wobbly, spindle-legged thing with a plant at its center. She always loved plants. She's got a pen in her right hand, even though she is left-handed. Her older sister, my aunt, trained her to write with her right hand when she was little, telling her that people don't write with their left hands, not realizing that one can write with either hand. So my mom is ambidextrous.

I walk up to the table and crane up to see what she's writing. It's interesting to me. There are papers and envelopes in neat piles. Her checkbook lies open in front of her. She has a worried look on her face, like she's trying to put together a puzzle without some of the pieces. She cocks her head one way, then another, trying to find another perspective on this problem. She mouths something. She's talking to herself silently. I'm watching her and hungry since it's close to dinner time, but I'm curious when I see the pen and papers.

"What's that?" I point at her familiar green steno pad. The pad has a hard, cardboard back and front, with a wire spiral binding at the top of the pages, allowing it to open like a sandwich board. Mom always had a number of these all over the place. Open any drawer in the apartment, and there were likely several

---

5   To learn more about problematizing and Freire's dialogic teaching methods, see chapter 3 of Paulo Freire, *Pedagogy of the Oppressed*, 30th anniversary ed. (New York: Continuum, 2000).

of them in there. Even today she keeps stacks of them. My mom likes to work in steno pads, saving them as a way to remember things years later.

She told me once that she'll pull one out and reminisce. It's like a history of that year or that time of her life. She dates pages. When one is filled up, she writes the date on the cover. Each pad shows the trials, the worries, the things needing money, things paid for, stuff she was thinking about or working out at that time in her life. Her steno pads are part of her memory and her relations to the world.

"Just trying to pay bills," mom says. I look at her list in her steno pad and I admire her handwriting. My mom's handwriting is delicate, not precise, but her letters have an ornate look to them and are smooth and flowing. I've always loved her handwriting. It seemed to me as a seven year old boy that her hand-writing, those hands, could fix anything.

"What's that?" I point to the list she's making in the steno pad. I touch the green paper. I'm curious about the words and numbers. What do they mean? What do they do? The words and numbers seem arcane, magical even. They are conjuring something, I just know it. This is something only moms can do, I think.

"Trying to make ends-meat, sugar plum. We gotta make ends-meat." I'm immediately reminded of my belly. I want dinner, and I think somehow mom is making dinner there at the spindle-legged table with the plant on it, somehow, between her steno pad and check book, somehow the ends of meat are made.

CHAPTER 2.

THE YIN-YANG OF LITERACY

While I didn't grow up with it formally, the philosophy of Taoism offers me a way to understand my own literacy practices and some of Freire's ideas about critical reading. That is, several of Taoism's core principles describe my own language habits. I don't know how this is, but it is.

Taoism is an ancient Chinese philosophy that explains the order of the universe and everything in it, and it is often encapsulated in the Yin and Yang symbol. Yin and Yang are two entities, male and female energies, that are joined and interconnected. They are interdependent, or mutually dependent on one another, in order to exist. They make each other. Both are necessary for the other's existence. Night needs day and day night. But when does day become night? When is dawn or dusk day or night? The idea is that yin and yang need each other, define each other, thus their borders blur into each other.

Each has the essence of the other in them, hence the circles of the opposite color in both the yin and yang swirls.[1] We need our material world, our reality, to make meaning of words or the symbolic world, while simultaneously, we need words (the symbolic) to help us make sense of our material world. The two elements and forces coexist and flow back and forth between each other. In some sense, they are each other. In Buddhist traditions, one might say these two energies or realms of experience "inter-are."[2] They are interdependent. Reality is symbolic, and the symbolic is reality. In Christian traditions, a similar concept exists in the idea of consubstantiality.[3]

Cultural psychologists explain that Chinese Taoist dialectic is one that accepts a unity of opposites, accepts that contradictions or tensions in the world

---

1   To learn more about the roots of Taoism, Confucianism, and Buddhism, see Lao Tzu, *Tao Te Ching*, trans. David Hinton (Berkeley: Counterpoint, 2015); see also, Robert Wright, *Why Buddhism Is True: The Science and Philosophy of Meditation and Enlightenment* (New York: Simon and Schuster, 2017).

2   The Vietnamese Buddhist monk and peace activist, Thich Nhat Hanh explains interbeing elegantly in *Peace is Every Step: The Path of Mindfulness in Everyday Life* (New York: Bantam, 1991), 95–98.

3   In Christian theology, consubstantiality describes the relationship between God (the Father), Jesus Christ (the Son), and the Holy Spirit. They are of the same essence. See Michael Jinkins, *Invitation to Theology: A Guide to Study, Conversation & Practice* (Downers Grove, IL: InterVarsity Press, 2001), 117–118. There is also a decent Wikipedia page on the concept; see Wikipedia: The Free Encyclopedia, accessed February 20, 2021, s.v. "consubstantiality," https://en.wikipedia.org/wiki/Consubstantiality.

are inherent and are not really contradictions.[4] So when conflict arises, there is not an inherent need or urge to resolve it, as in Western and Greek traditions. This is the interdependent nature of paradoxical things. What appears as contradictory or in conflict in the world or among ideas and positions is simply the necessary unity of opposites, yin and yang coexisting, commingling.

In Western philosophy, the word "dialectic" comes from ancient Greek ideas about dialogue. To the Greeks, opposing ideas are tested together in order to come to the Truth (capital "T"), or a singular truth, which the ancient Greeks called *Episteme*.[5] In Western thinking, a single truth is the goal of a dialogue or dialectic, two or more opposing voices, ideas, or words that produce one conclusion about the question or issue at hand.

This is linear thinking and can be visualized as a straight line with hierarchical points or steps in it from an origin to an end point. Think of it as an outline with topics (e.g. I, II, III, IV) and subtopics (a, b, c, d) under each topic. It's what most people in the West consider "logical," but actually it's just one kind of logic or orientation to the world, one of many.[6] It's the logic of Plato and later Aristotle that prevailed and was passed on, but there's nothing inherently better or clearer about linear thinking than some other way of thinking or ordering ideas or the world. It's just the kind of thinking that gained dominance for a number of reasons, which is an entirely different book.[7]

---

4   Kaiping Peng, Julie Spencer-Rodgers, and Zhong Nian, "Naive Dialecticism and The Tao of Chinese Thought," in *Indigenous And Cultural Psychology: Understanding People In Context*, ed. Uichol Kim, Kuo-Shu Yang., and Kwang-Kuo Hwang (New York: Springer, 2006), 247–262. Peng and his colleagues also provide a good explanation of Chinese Taoist thought in the chapter.

5   Technically, during the 5th and 4th centuries BCE in the area of what is today called Greece, there was no nation-state or country called Greece. The area was a collection of city-states, each self-governed, often referred to as *Hellenes* after the 4th century. This is called the Hellenistic period. For simplicity's sake, I refer to such city-states as "Greece." Most of the ideas and art that I discuss are from the Hellenic city-state of Athens. To read a good history of ancient Athenian rhetoric, see chapters 1–5 of George Kennedy, *A New History of Classical Rhetoric* (Princeton: Princeton University Press, 1994); or see Richard A. Katula, "The Origins of Rhetoric: Literacy and Democracy in Ancient Greece," in *A Synoptic History of Classical Rhetoric*, 3rd ed., eds. James J. Murphy, Richard A. Katula, with Forbes I. Hill (Mahwah, NJ: Routledge, 2003), 3–19.

6   I should note that even the distinction of "West" and "East" as a cultural or spatial concept or reference is Western European, as it tends to assume a White, Western, European global center. Re-center the globe on the continent of North America, and Europe is now the East, while Asia is the West.

7   Besides ancient Greek (Hellenic) philosophy and thinking that gained dominance in the medieval era of Europe when monks and priests copied and harmonized their texts with Christian doctrine, one can look to the Enlightenment for ways that Western dialectic became dominant in language and thinking, most notably in science and philosophy. While each are quite

Many cite Aristotle's use of dialectic as one origin of Western European traditions of logic. He inherited his ideas from his teacher, Plato, who got his ideas from his teacher, Socrates.[8] Socratic dialogue, as illustrated in Plato's dialogues, is a linear argument that consists of a question followed by an answer that leads to another question and another answer. It's a back and forth that is often adversarial. The answerer isn't usually on the side of the question-asker, Socrates. And the dialogue ultimately leads to the Truth, *Episteme*. For the ancient Greeks, to argue meant you engaged in conflict, comparison, and resolution.

This same dialectic logic can be seen all over ancient Greek culture.[9] The Olympic games are one example, with lots of individual contests and few team activities. The way the city center, or *agora*, operated is another. The *agora* was where most civic and economic exchanges occurred, where one argued and haggled as a matter of course. *Agon* or conflict was how life was transacted in ancient Greece.

Thus, one's life and success in the civic or economic spheres were centered on conflict. If you were lucky or good enough, the conflict ended with your success and triumph over others. Conflict also defined the realm of home and family, or *oikos*. Many scholars of antiquity consider Homer's epic poem, *The Odyssey*, to be a kind of encyclopedia of ancient Greek culture. The telling of the poem was how knowledge and practices were passed down from one generation to another. It exemplified the culture and its ideas through a series of individual conquests and triumphs over a variety of obstacles and creatures, all so that Ulysses, the hero, could make it safely home to wife and hearth, yang returning to its yin.[10] But for the ancient Greeks, getting home, being safe and in one's place, was dependent on previous conflict and winning. The epic poem's central lesson could be: Life is a series of contests that prove oneself and one's virtue, or *arête*.

The material conditions that made ancient Greek life afforded a particular set of relations to words, or *logoi*, that we inherit today in dominant English

different, thinkers like Kant, Bacon, Descartes, Hume, Locke, Adam Smith, and many others worked from linear and binary dialectic habits of language that created hierarchies and categories of phenomena and ideas.

8   To read more about dialectic, see Aristotle, *Rhetoric*, trans. W. Rhys Roberts (New York: Modern Library, 1954); Aristotle, *Topics*, trans. W. A. Pickard-Cambridge (Internet Classics Archive, 2009), http://classics.mit.edu/Aristotle/topics.html; and for discussion of Aristotle's works, see chapter 4 of James A. Herrick, *The History and Theory of Rhetoric: An Introduction*, 5th ed. (London: Routledge, 2016).

9   Richard Nisbett, a cultural psychologist, discusses the themes of "personal freedom, individuality, and objective thought" in ancient Greek culture in *The Geography of Thought: How Asians and Westerners Think Differently . . . And Why* (New York: Simon and Schuster, 2004), 30.

10   To read about epic poetry as an encyclopedia of ancient Greek culture, see chapter 4 of Eric A. Havelock, *Preface to Plato* (Cambridge, MA: Belknap Press, 1963).

language practices because of their Western roots. The term *logos* actually means "word," "idea," and "reason" itself. Since ancient Greece was primarily an oral society, logos was mostly spoken, breathed between people in exchanges. It makes sense, then, that the term used for words would also be the one used for ideas and reason in these conditions. The way one might experience an argument would be from the mouth of another person in front of them, coming from inside them, perhaps understood as a part of their essence, their virtue. Logos was a part of a person. It's easy to see how a person's ideas spoken, coming out of their body, might seem essential to that person, an inherent part of them. And in these conditions, words, ideas, like people are distinct from one another.

It also isn't hard to see how a back and forth, or "dialectic," is at the heart of most language practices. Our ideas about dialectic make up much of our orientations to the world and language. But how might dialectic in our world share in both the natures of conflict and consubstantiality, logos and Taoism? As you may be able to hear in my cursory description of Chinese Taoist and ancient Greek dialectic, they are quite different orientations to languaging and the world.

Of course, no orientation is unified, and there are lots of differences and nuances expressed through the ages; even the idea of a Western vs Eastern dialectic orientation is artificial. But my point in this chapter is to reveal the broader outlines of each orientation that are often embodied in habits of language that create us, so I'll speak mostly in generalities, knowing that while they break down eventually, they are still helpful. In the process, I want to argue tacitly that Taoist and Western dialectics are a part of my literacy story.

TAOIST DIALECTIC LANGUAGING

Almost every semester in the writing courses I teach, which can range from first-year writing to graduate courses on rhetorical theory, I get a few students who are brave enough to ask me about my writing assignments. Their confusion is not in how I'm asking them to engage in the writing but in what I'm expecting from them as a product of that labor. They are used to teachers assigning categories of writing. This week, we are writing an essay that explores . . . Next week, we are writing a research paper on . . . The following week we are writing a journal entry on . . . These categories of writing, or genres, are assumed to have essential or inherent features in them that a student will practice doing when they write them. These features make the genres known to everyone. I do not make this assumption. I don't think in terms of essential or distinct categories of writing assignments. This isn't how I understand languaging.

Part of my students' confusion comes from how I assign things. I pay careful attention to the process of labor I want them to engage in. The instructions are written as step-by-step processes. They are more minimal in describing what that labor produces, since I don't know what it will produce exactly for every student. I don't find it particularly fair to assume that all students in my courses will want or be able to produce the same kind of writing, the same kind of draft, for instance. I don't know if I'd want to read the same kind of draft from every student.

I also don't think it is necessary to fit every differently shaped student literacy into the same square hole of the assignment. Instead, I want to open up the act of writing so that it simply becomes labor. I give them simple expectations that provide estimated time spent on each step in the process (in minutes) and the number of words written or read (depending on what they are doing). I'll also give them key things I want them to engage in, like questions to address or ideas to wrestle with as they write.

Recently a student asked me in class, "What's a 'narrative inquiry?' I looked it up on the Internet but couldn't find any description or example of one." I called our assignment a "narrative inquiry" because the central goal was to inquire about or investigate some narrative in popular culture. Now, my labor instructions were clear about what and how I wanted them to do the work, but because some of my students had expectations about genres in such a course, they were trying to nail down the assignment as a category of writing. They were looking for the kind of document, the category, to draft that they thought I was telling them to write; meanwhile I was more interested in how they labored toward whatever draft they produced. Their orientation to school work was not to think in terms of labor instructions but to think primarily in terms of the category of product expected of them. And so I often ask some version of, "what happens in our class when the expectations for our languaging are not about a product to submit but labors to do?"

In my instructions, I give loose guidelines for the product that the labor will produce, such as "a document of about 3,500 words that focuses on one question you have about a narrative found in popular culture that you find interesting. Your central question should investigate how this narrative is made, understood, or created in a U.S. context." Now, this is just the description. The majority of my instructions offer a step-by-step process to engage in.

My larger purpose in such writing labor is to have a dialogue with each student through my responses to their work about what they've created and how it exercises the goals and competencies we are shooting for. Both writer (student) and readers (teacher and peers) are vital in assessing whatever they produce because we must dialogue, have a give and take. The assessment they receive on their writing is going to be a dialogue. It's gonna require both of us, and their colleagues' responses too. We can only make sense of the writer's work when we understand how it is read by others and ourselves in this classroom context.

41

This approach to writing assignments I consider a Taoist dialectical approach to languaging and learning. I resist a number of assumptions about writing assignments and how they are assessed that are conventional in most classrooms, which are informed by Western dialectic traditions. I resist an essential and knowable (nameable) list of distinct categories of assignments, making the yin and yang of each laboring process that leads to a product possible. I resist a focus on products that are categorized as learning, which often ignores the processes, the laboring and diverse learning that emerges in classrooms organically. I resist the practice of the teacher evaluating alone, then dialoguing with the student after judgements are made, since I find the student and I must assess together from our own positions and habits of language. We must inter-judge. This last resistance of mine also rejects a strictly hierarchical arrangement in the judgement of language. Both yin and yang are needed in evaluating language. Why hobble ourselves, hopping on one leg of our dialectic, in the most important part of a class, assessment and feedback?

~~~

I find myself flying across the country often these days, giving lectures and workshops on antiracist writing assessment, talking about White language supremacy in schools and disciplines. When I'm on an airplane and I strike up a conversation with the person next to me, inevitably I'm asked, "So what do you do?" I don't like to say what I do precisely. In fact, I try to avoid this conversation. I know people will change when I tell them what I do, and in my view, not usually for the better.

But if I'm pressed I'll say something like, "I'm a professor and associate dean. I do research on writing assessment and racism." Often I get surprised looks after "professor and associate dean." I don't look like a professor, let alone a dean. I've been mistaken for an athletic coach, even an athlete, but never a professor. I know why. I'm a brown guy who looks considerably younger than he is, mostly because of the standards of youth and age that circulate in our culture. I'm only 5'7" but athletically built, having worked out in gyms for the last thirty years.

When you are steeped in a culture that uses Western dialectic orientations to language, it's easy to make these kinds of categorical judgements about people without seeing the flaws in such categorical logics. Many would call them harmless mistakes, others, unfair assumptions and prejudices. Maybe they are harmless, maybe not. How harmless are they if they are ubiquitous, happening all the time everywhere? How harmless are they if they affect other judgements and decisions that circulate around them, many of which matter more, like who gets a job or who seems dangerous in a routine traffic stop by a police officer?

These are not just categorical assumptions we make but ones that have inherent hierarchies of value attached to them. Who seems more trustworthy on a plane, the mysterious, short, brown, muscular guy with black hair next to you—is he Mexican, Cuban, maybe Puerto Rican?—or the taller, White guy with thinning sandy brown hair on the other side of the aisle—is he a banker or businessman? The associations that are tacitly linked to each of these categorical bodies are different and have consequences beyond innocent mistakes on a plane. What my Taoist dialectical orientation helps me see in these occurrences is that they are a product of language and logic systems that afford us these mistakes in judgement. It's not our assumptions that are the problem. It's our unchecked logic that creates such judgement problems.

~~~

In school, I never really understood the five paragraph theme. I mean, I knew we were asked to write it, but I had a hard time doing that. Its linear structure didn't feel right to me. It was hard to fit the discussion in my head into that linear structure, even when I was trying really hard to do it. Why? Well, things just didn't fit into topics or points so neatly for me. Discussing one idea always seemed like five or six things at once. The claim I might start with was not necessarily my thesis or central idea, but I wanted to start with it because it made sense to be in a different spot on a journey than where I would end up. And sometimes, it felt—and still does feel—more right to just cut to a new topic, a new scene. No transitions. They just slow things down, keep the reader from the joy of figuring out the connections.

I also feel that my readers need to know more, need to know about the things on the borders and edges of a topic, in order to know something as I do. I hope this means that they also need to do work. You cannot have meaning just handed to you. Reading and communicating are hard labors for everyone, readers and writers.

Say I was writing a paper in school about time and clocks. I might start thinking about the way we have a twenty-four-hour day, how clocks represent this in twelve-hour halves, and how this system comes from Egyptians' methods for counting daylight and night. This would lead me to consider the Babylonians' numbering system, which was sexagesimal, or based on units of 60. I'd realize quickly that I don't need that word, "sexagesimal," but I like saying it, so I keep it. It's a gift to my readers. This system is similar to Sumero-Akkadian systems that were based on sixes. Do the Babylonians or Sumerians have something to do with our idea of time and clocks? Did the Babylonians and Sumerians talk to each other? They lived near each other, right? Was there commerce among any of these ancient civilizations? If so, could that affect these systems, which are representational, like the alphabet and hieroglyphics? And what about H. G. Wells' famous novella, *The Time Machine*, published in 1895? It compares different civilizations. That story explores time travel. Morlocks and Eloi. Hierarchical societies in time. Bad people of the dark and caves. Good people of light and the surface. But are these their essences or just categorical appearances? Do Morlocks and Eloi sound racialized? Is that racializing a function of time, day and night, light and dark, Eloi and Morlock? Cultural anxieties? Racialized projections? Do the symbols in front of us that create time also create race?

And a clock itself is just a symbol made up of other symbols. This would then make me think of the way divisions of six numbers are all over the place today—they are symbolic to us in a number of ways. Units of twelve, a dozen eggs, twelve inches makes a foot. This could lead me to think about the influence that ancient Egyptians (and Babylonians) had on what we buy today in stores, like a dozen eggs, or what seems complete. There are many religious traditions and myths that identify twelve as a sacred and complete number. Can you imagine buying just one egg, or three, or seven in a store? If there were just piles of eggs in bins at the supermarket, how many would you take at a time? Why? There seems to be a connection, a logic or link that connects our sense of time to Sumero-Akkadian counting systems and how many eggs we buy at any time, which is about what symbolizes wholeness or completeness. Twelve hours in a day. Twelve eggs in a dozen. Twelve Hebrew tribes. Morlocks and Eloi. Yin and yang. Time and the spaces it makes. Race and the divisions it makes. Symbols and the meanings they make. Division and the conflict it makes. Wholeness and the unity of opposites.

This kind of non-linear, even associative, logic did not pay off well in school for me. But it felt natural. It makes sense. It's fun. Perhaps my own languaging came about because of the dialectic I had grown in my home with my twin brother, grown through our twin ways of languaging together.

WESTERN CATEGORIZING AND ESSENTIALIZING

What made my literacy road rockier was that I enjoyed, even reveled in, paradox and contradictions, at least in thinking and writing, even for school purposes. The point of the Western dialectic is not to embrace opposing arguments, not to provide ambiguity and paradox, not to consider how those other voices might be reasonable or probable. The goal in Western dialectic, when translated to written argumentation in classrooms today, has been to offer an unambiguous answer and defend that answer, to present a strong and unified position which allows the writer to win the argument.

But I've never really been that interested in winning arguments. I have always been more interested in playing with language, playing with people together, and participating in verbal exchanges. Competing and conflict ain't comfortable for me.

But in classroom writing, the point usually wasn't to hold opposing ideas next to each other, to juxtapose them and let them be, although that can happen. The point was to compare and evaluate, then decide which is stronger. The point was never NOT to win the argument. But I wonder: Why must we have winners and losers at all in such language games? Why must the goal in any persuasive moment be to win the discussion or argument? Why can't the goal be to explain and understand your ideas next to others? Why can't our goal be to dialogue, or protect and encourage, even aid the one with whom you are engaged?

Western notions of logic that are encased in standards of English writing in schools tend to ask students to counter or synthesize opposing ideas into a singular, unambiguous conclusion. This is the definition of clarity, order, control, and logical organization in most standards of written English, and it comes straight out of Aristotle. It's one of the most common habits of White language (HOWL) in English. And it works with an assumption that there is usually one best view, one winner. It says that focusing mostly on one position is a stronger, clearer way to understand things. What I'm describing are two habits of HOWL, a universalized and naturalized orientation to the world (habit one) that is combined with categorizing and essentializing. The categorizing is understood as clarity, order, and control in language practices (habit two).

Growing up with a twin brother by my side who was always ready to discuss and test ideas with me made me perhaps more willing to sit with ambiguity and see questions less like linear problems to solve than as a give and take, a back and forth, a dialogue. Compromising with him or understanding my brother was always more fulfilling than winning or chancing a loss. I often say I think in webs of ideas, but maybe it's just that I don't usually think linearly. I don't think in terms of wins and losses, of hierarchies, of steps or things like that. I can, of course, and I'm often asked to think in linear terms, but it has not been my first inclination. But even after I'd figured this out, I still couldn't shake the Taoist-like orientation in school.

In my senior year's advanced writing class, I had to write a paper about some issue or question I was interested in understanding better. I was in a new school, having just moved to Corvallis, Oregon, and living with my nana, who would die of cancer less than a year later. I wrote a paper about how science and the arts might not need to be in contradiction to conservative Christian values and beliefs encapsulated in the Bible. I essentially was arguing that maybe I could be both a Christian who believed in the infallible word of God in the Bible, believed that my nana had a soul and was going to heaven, as well as someone who accepted scientific explanations of the world like evolution and carbon dating that showed the planet to be much older than many in my church and family seemed to believe.

I asked: Why can't I accept the idea that we don't have any proof of something called the soul, that there is no way to know for sure? Why can't I believe that there is no good reason for my nana's chronic, debilitating pain from cancer and chemotherapy, that her life makes no sense, hurts all of us, and depreciates the image of God? Why can't I hold equally to the belief of a loving God who would not hurt his flock, who has some kind of plan that we don't know? And yet, by having no evidence of such a master plan, it is right to question the existence of such a plan, to question the grounds of my own faith and that of my nana's, even as I hold tightly to that faith because it was all I had at that time to give me comfort? Why can't faith not be enough and simultaneously more than we need?

I showed this paper to my uncle Bill, whom I admired. He was a microbiologist, a professor and scientist at Oregon State University, and a respected member of our church, the Church of Christ. He baptized me earlier that same year. I figured he would have a foot in each world as I thought he did. I wanted his feedback before I turned in the paper. I wanted that paper to be good, and I wanted the conversation with him because he was the only man in my life. The question was important to me, as was my nana.

We sat on his bed in his two-story house on Roosevelt Drive in Corvallis, and he told me that I couldn't have it both ways, that if I believed in God and the Bible, then I couldn't believe this other stuff. He was expressing his Aristotelian and Western orientation to the world that he wanted me to accept, but I struggled with the categories, the essentializing, the this-or-that-ness of his response. I struggled with his HOWLing at me. I wanted things to be this-and-that. He called me agnostic, said I should be careful. I'm dancing with blasphemy, or worse, apostasy.

I thought it ironic that he would be so closed off given that he was a scientist himself—wasn't his own research a paradox in this question about God's plan and everlasting souls? The experience made me deeply sad and unsettled inside. I was disappointed that I wasn't encouraged the way I envisioned his words to me would be. I thought my words were good. I thought he would be understanding or at least provide a way to inquire with me about the questions I was asking. I didn't really want his answers. I wanted to have the questions. But to him, he was saving my soul, saving me from a Godless life, or a life of equivocation. He was demonstrating his Christian love for me. This paper, to him, led to hellfire and damnation. There was only belief and faith or nonbelief and equivocation. These were distinct opposites in his life. They shared no borders.

I thought he'd say that this paper really opened his eyes, that I was smart, that I could be someone like him. But I couldn't be someone like him, a White scientist from the Midwest, a mostly yang. I wanted both yin and yang. I wanted both the sciences and the arts, and I wanted my faith. It turns out ultimately I couldn't have the latter, the faith, at least not like his. I didn't lose it, as the popular saying goes. I never actually possessed it, but I know exactly where it is, where people keep it, and how they nurture it and often overfeed it. But in my youth, I just wanted faith like his. It seemed like the right thing to believe because everyone around me seemed to believe in it. It was comforting in the way a child believes his dad or mom can do anything, knows everything, so they don't see the weaknesses, the contradictions, the paradoxes. It's fast thinking.

Maybe what saved me at this moment when I could have taken a dive into a darker place was the considerably warmer response my teacher gave me. His name was Mr. Baldwin, a kind, soft spoken, platinum blond haired White man of about forty or so with a dry mouth. I could hear his tongue smack dryly in between his words. I remember very little of that class except this paper and one comment he wrote on it.

Beyond the many scribbles and circles scratched on my draft that noted the errors, he wrote at the top of the first page: "Most students your age don't think this deeply about such topics." That comment sustained me into my senior year of college, when another middle aged White male English professor would affirm me as a writer. I like to think that Mr. Baldwin looked past most of my non-Western orientation to language and saw the thinking on its own terms. But I don't know. What I know is his comment and how I read it as affirming, next to the errors and the "B-" grade.

PLAYING D&D AS LOGOS-CONFLICT

Because we were twins, my brother and I shared everything. We were always by each other's side. My brother and I played lots of games together. In part, we did so because we were latchkey kids. My mom could not afford babysitters, so when she was at work and we were not at school, we were behind a locked door in our apartment or trailer. The games we gravitated to eventually were not board games. Our games were language and dialectic games.

I had one problem though. I hate conflict and competition. It's a disposition I still carry today. All through childhood, I tried very hard to avoid conflict and situations that required a winner and loser. I disliked most board games because of this. Monopoly, Risk, chess, checkers, Stratego, you name the board game, and I likely couldn't handle playing it. I just felt awful and uncomfortable while playing. I didn't mind losing, but I really disliked seeing others lose. The competition was like razor blades on my feet.

I felt uncomfortable for those around me when someone publicly lost at a game or was losing. Sure, I wanted to win, but I didn't want to win by having others loose. Perhaps a part of this disposition against direct conflict was the fact that much of the time, I was playing with my twin brother, and I really didn't like to see him lose. It felt like I was losing, and in a way I was. In Buddhist terms, winning and losing inter-are. They share in each other's essence. They require each other.

When I think about winning that second grade reading contest, I realize that most of my experience of it was not of competing against my colleagues in school, even though technically I was. Most days, there was no face-off with my competitors. The play of the game itself was reading after school. It was a daily practice of opening books and fingering lines of text, speaking words, of pushing myself to read more, to do something I was just finding out that I loved. So I don't consider that contest a competition in the same way that I grew to feel chess or Monopoly was. It was a daily practice more than a competition to win. I really just wanted to read. I don't have those trophies anymore, but I still have my reading practices, my words, the daily practice of conjuring words.

I realize that I was also younger then, just figuring out who I was, and it isn't like the reading contest was not uncomfortable at times. On Mondays, the teacher would color in the bar graphs on the back wall of the classroom. Each bar had a student's name next to it. The wall showed our relative progress at reading books. It compared each student's progress next to their peers. How many books did each student read? The graphs were meant to help us set goals, but what I felt was this burgeoning sense of dislike for competition through quantified comparisons that made hierarchies, that is, a winner and levels of losers.

So when Dungeons and Dragons (D&D) came along, I jumped at it. I was fanatical about the game. My brother and I played that game just about every day from the sixth grade until we graduated from high school, then into college. If we weren't playing it, we were thinking about it, reading up on it, creating adventures and characters. We still play today.

In D&D, there is no winning, not in the traditional, board game sense. There is just never-ending play. A game or campaign never has to end. There's always another quest, another problem to solve, another land to explore. There is conflict, but that conflict is with creatures and people that are not real. They are make-believe, just words with relations to people who only exist in our minds. Playing was living and breathing a fantasy. Playing D&D did not feel like a conflict where someone in the room had to win and another lose. We were not pitted against each other. One of us was the Dungeon Master (DM) creating the adventure for the player, and the other was the player, the one who went on the adventure.

Playing, then, was a collaboration. It felt like acting and telling a story all at once, which is why it is called a "role playing game." Each session was a story in which neither of us knew what the next stage or step was going to be because that was determined by both of us together in concert and organically. For instance, Tad created a situation as the DM, and I as the player reacted to it in whatever ways I saw fit within the confines of my character, the context, and my present purposes, then he reacted, then I did. And the story continued in unexpected ways.

The characters and contexts continually changed. Most adventures were journeys, quests, and long strings of actions and reactions. The point of the game—and the fun of it—was the process, the journey, not an endpoint, not competition, not some signal that someone "won" at some point. D&D is a game that resists conventional winning and losing. It even resists thinking of the game as achieving a single goal or outcome, like scoring the most points, winning against other players. Instead, for us, it was about the ever-unfolding story we told and acted out together. And since everyone loves stories, everyone wins, especially since everyone has a hand in making the story.

The game should have been called Dialectic and Dragons. To play means a back and forth between the DM and players, players and NPCs (or nonplayer characters that the DM controls). D&D is a game made entirely of language. While it is only ostensibly about fighting and conflict, really it is about wording, creating, and collaboratively telling a story that always has a next chapter. And so, it is also about an endless cycle of ups and downs, of new contexts, and change, of endless creating with words.

This game nurtured my language dispositions, but more importantly, it offered a way for me to do Freireian critical practice as play. We were creating worlds and characters that required us not just to understand or invent such things but to question them, create opposing ideas, characters, motivations, and worldviews—and all through words written and spoken, all through interactions that required a yin and yang, a this-and-that-ness of play.

In a way, to engage seriously in the play of D&D, as we did, we had to engage in Freirian critical reading, pose questions about paradoxical word-worlds and word-characters. And the game was better when all sides were compelling, when choices and decisions were difficult to make because it was not a question of right or wrong, good or evil, but a question that presented one paradox after another. It was two boys of color storying themselves into existence.

I'm reminded of one refrain in Thomas King's autobiographical book on stories, a refrain that he repeats in each chapter: "The truth about stories is that that's all we are."[11]

~~~

"Okay, what are you gonna do?" Tad asks me. We're sitting cross-legged on the floor in our bedroom in the trailer, Dungeons and Dragons books arranged neatly around us, the *Dungeon Master's Guide*, *Player's Handbook*, *Monster*

---

11   King, *Truth*.

Manual, Deities and Demigods, the good one, the first edition with Cthulhu and Melnibonean Mythoi in it.

My brother has a DM's screen up to hide his notes and maps. It's late on a Friday night, our prime time for playing D&D. We've been playing for hours already. There's a pad of graph paper between us. We're using it to sketch out complicated arrangements: who is where, what rooms look like, etc.

"How many orcs jumped out in front of me? Where are they exactly?" I ask, scanning my character sheet, which has my magic user's stats, abilities, equipment, and spells written on it. His name is Schmindrake. He is my favorite character and will continue to be as I grow older, enter high school, college, and later. In fact, I'll end up keeping this character sheet, recopy it a few times, for another thirty-five years in real life, and slowly let the character retire.

Schmindrake the character will eventually become an Arch-Mage, a very high level magic user, and he will define me as a D&D player. I'll get to know him, flesh out his personality, use him as an archetype for other characters, a test case for ideas. He will come to voice many different things in my life, frustrations, joys, pains.

I'll think of him as my alter-ego of sorts, the mage who could do just about anything. The words that make him make me in the process, words I have made. And so, I have been Schmindrake, yet he isn't real. Through him, I will save cities, conquer empires, and build my own floating castle in the clouds. I will travel to different planes of existence. I'll go to Hell, the Astral and Ethereal planes, searching, usually finding. Schmindrake will save me as a boy from the cruelty of neighbors and teachers, from the racism around me. In critical moments when I needed an escape, Schmindrake's magic was real to me. He took me away to other lands where I was the hero.

I see now that being a professor in real life is very much like being an arch-mage in D&D. Both have their books and incantations, their spells and words that do things in the world. Both are magic users. Both must study. Both conjure things, one with the arcana of fantasy, the other with words, theories, and ideas. It's clear I have always been on the mage-professor path, even as a boy.

Sitting on the floor in our room, I have the *Player's Handbook* open to the page where the second level spell, "Web," is described. My character recently acquired the spell, and I'm excited to use it.

"There are just two orcs. Here's what it looks like." My brother draws the dungeon hallway on the graph paper. He draws the alcove where the orcs originally jumped me and puts little "O"s where they are and an "M" where my character is. "They are about ten feet apart, here and here." He points at the "Os." "And you are here, about ten feet from them." We had just rolled initiative, and I had the higher roll, so I get to go first.

"I'm going to cast my web spell at their legs and feet, anchoring the web to the floor right there and there. My range is two, so I can reach them."

"Saving throw?" he asks, his eyes stay looking down at his notes.

"Negate or half strength, depending on circumstances."

"They have room to jump out of the way, so if they make their saving throws, it would negate the web. Is that what you want to do?" Tad asks.

"Yes, I want to question them. I know Orcish." I make a web shooting sound and a motion with my hands, like I'm casting a spell. My brother rolls the twenty sided die twice. He makes a note on his paper, looks back at a page in the *Monster Manual*.

"Okay, you speak your incantation, and as you do this, you can see the orcs get nervous. You know they don't like magic. They seem scared now."

"You are mine, bitches!" I say, as my brother talks.

"The spell is verbal, material, and symbolic, so your web springs forth from your hands in a shimmering silver light as you speak. It comes through your hand gestures and sticks to one of the orc's feet, catching him in the gooey threads. He's stuck. He can't do anything."

"What about the other one?"

"The other one jumps free. He's now here." Tad erases one of the "O"s on the graph paper and puts it in a new spot near the middle of the dungeon hallway twenty feet from the webbed orc and in front of my character.

"Is it my turn still?"

"Yes, the orc used his action to jump out of the way. He had to re-adjust himself, but he will get to attack this round after you." Tad takes a sip of his iced tea. "What are you gonna do? You can see he's about to make a run for it."

"You mean like retreat?"

"Yes, he looks scared of your magic." Tad makes a scared face, imitating the orc's reaction.

"'You cannot escape, orc!' I'll say to him, and I'll hit him with my magic missile." I point on the graph paper at the free orc in the hallway. "I only need one of em to get the info." I make a laser sound. Magic Missile is my favorite spell. It doesn't miss. There's no saving throw. The only downside is that it doesn't do a lot of damage, but I don't need a lot in this case.

"You sure you want to do that? He looks scared, like if you did nothing, he'd run. Also, you may need that spell later." My brother is reminding me slyly that I have options, that it's not necessary to kill everything. I pause in my excitement at killing the evil orcs who just tried to ambush me. It's an ethical paradox for a fourteen-year-old boy. Do you kill the orc who is about to retreat, or do you let him run and live his life, perhaps to do more bad things or change his ways?

"These mother fuckers just ambushed me! They were gonna kill me. They were likely part of the orc clan that slaughtered the villagers. Don't I have to kill him? I mean, they did hire me to take care of this problem."

"But what does 'taking care of this problem' mean? Kill everyone?"

"Scorched Earth, man!" I yell. We both chuckle.

"Remember, you don't know if these orcs are the same orcs that attacked the village. For all you know, these orcs are just protecting their underground lair. This is an abandoned temple. Besides, Lord Vain never said you had to kill them all, just that he wanted to be free of the orc problem. Orcs are not that smart, nor brave. The villagers are mostly lawful good."

"Hmm. Right. What do I really know here? I'd probably do the same thing if I were these guys. I am good, but I'm chaotic good, so I don't have to always abide by the laws."

"You are more about good with personal freedom."

"Whatever gets the job done. Ends over means, man."

"Yes, but what means really help you get to your ends here? Your end could be to scare them off, or to kill them all, or something else. Keep in mind, you are fifth level. If you shoot magic missiles at him, he's likely dead. Just saying. And of course, you'll only have one more magic missile spell today. Might need it later."

"Well, he could run off and tell his buddies that I'm coming, and that wouldn't accomplish the mission. There could be a hundred of them."

"Actually," Tad looks at the *Monster Manual*, fingers the page, "between 30 and 300."

"So a lot more than I can handle at once," I smile at my brother. He raises his eyebrows and gives a look like, who knows? "Do I know how many orcs the villagers saw? Did they tell me?"

"Roll your intelligence." I roll the twenty-sided die.

"Sixteen after my bonus."

"Okay, you recall that Lord Vain said there was a *legion* of them."

"Legion? How many is a fuckin' legion?"

"In the ancient Roman army, that shit was thousands." I look at him with a flat, close-lipped smile and a raised eyebrow as if to say, how the hell do you know that? My brother knows I'm wondering that. "I looked it up, dude. DM-prep."

"So there's like thousands?"

"Not likely, given that you know they don't have clans much bigger than a few hundred. You think he meant that there were a lot of them, more than he could count."

"Okay, that settles it. While I hate to kill a dude running away, I'mma have to do that in this case. Ma job is to protect the village. This is the safest choice."

"You can see the orc is already turning to run away. 'Aaaaahhhh,' he's screaming in terror of the magic he just saw. If there is anyone around, they'll hear him screaming."

"I fire my magic missiles." I wave my hands in mock spell-casting and make more laser sounds. "Shut yo ass!" I say as if I'm speaking to the orc.

"They automatically hit. Roll damage." I roll a four-sided die twice.

"That's three, seven, plus two—nine points, baby!" I'm excited. I know orcs do not usually have that many hit points.

"He turns to run away screaming, 'aaaah, no, no!' The blue magic missiles tear into his flesh, one in his back, one right at the base of his spine and head. His orc flesh peels and burns away." Tad makes an explosion sound. "The orc cries out in pain. 'Aaaargh!' You can see his eyes are wide with fright as he dies. The orc crumples to the floor, dead. His corpse is smoking. The other orc drops his rusty sword and cowers. You can see he's scared shitless. He's stuck in the web up to his waist."

"I turn to him and strike a wizard pose, like I'm gonna cast something at him."

"He whimpers. 'Oooh, please, please,' he says, 'don't kill with your powerful magic! You great wizard.' He's speaking Orcish. He bows his head." I can tell Tad is trying to make the orc sympathetic, more interesting than what the *Monster Manual* describes him as. He may be an evil orc, but he ain't just that. Tad's roll playing the orc. I want to go along with it. It's more fun.

"I ask him in Orcish, 'Where can I find your clansmen who attacked the villagers?'" I wiggle my finger as if I'm going to cast another spell. "I will spare your life, orc, if you tell me the truth—and I'll know if you're lying," I say in an authoritative voice. Another finger wiggle.

"You can see that he pisses himself. 'But Wizard Lord,' he says, 'Spilge Bottom bound to orcish ways.' He pleads with you, 'Please do not kill poor Spilge Bottom. I have sworn my bones to clan of Flesh Eaters. For generations Lord Vain's family slaughter us. We fight back. We survive. This is our way,' the orc tells you." Tad is doing his best orc imitation.

"Well, does he seem like he is lying? Can I tell?"

"Roll your wisdom." I roll the twenty-sided die.

"Fourteen."

"You think, he's too scared to lie to you and too dumb."

"I say, 'Well, Spilge Bottom, you have chosen the wrong side; therefore, I have no choice.' I raise my staff in a menacing way, and see if this convinces him to tell me what I want." Tad thinks for a second or two.

"Okay, roll charisma." I roll a twenty-sided on the hard back of the *Player's Handbook*. The die makes the familiar sound, a thick crackle.

"Eighteen with my bonus, good?"

"Spilge Bottom says, 'Ol' Spilgey tell you all. It not Spilgey fault. Spilgey forced to take bone-oath in clan. Spilgey just want to live.'"

"Okaaay," I say, squinting my eye at him. Finger wiggle.

"Spilgey have new master, Master Wizard Lord. Please, please, Master, please, Ol' Spilgey realize me no match for Master Wizard Lord. Ol' Spilgey promise to do all Master ask. Spilgey tell you all.'" A chaotic good magic user taking on a lawful evil orc as a henchman, I think, it is odd, but those are our games, odd in their deviations from the rules, like real life, I think. Rules are artificial, just made on top of life. Besides, I feel I'm starting to like Ol' Spilgey. Maybe I can change him, help him. He'll bring spice to the campaign. The game is always better when I feel like we are breaking old rules and making new ones.

"Okay, Spilgey, you are gonna have to do what I say and change your ways. Got it? I'll take care of you."

"Oh yes, Master Wizard Lord, Ol' Spilgey change good, change every which way."

"Well, Spilgey, let's get to the bottom of things. Sounds like we got work to do."

THE PARADOXICAL NATURE OF TWIN LANGUAGE

My brother, Tadayoshi (or Tad), and I are identical twins. Growing up, most people could not tell us apart. Shortly after we were born, my mom had to return us to the hospital, have our feet dipped in ink and printed again, to find out who was who. She couldn't tell the difference. When we were toddlers, Tad and I had our own "twin language." That's what my mom called it. We spoke it to each other only. No one could understand it but us. It was fun to be a mystery to those around us. Perhaps we understood intuitively how powerful and magical words are. They create us. And so, you don't give them to just anyone. And many of us practice giving them to ourselves first.

Growing up, we talked the same, liked the same things, and were always together, usually playing D&D. Even today, most of these things have not changed. We loved each other, always have, and yet wanted to be different from one another. I wanted to be my own person, to be recognized by others as such, yet also deeply appreciated my twinness and the fact that no one could tell us apart. We liked the same movies but sometimes for different reasons. We both loved the films *Dragonslayer*, *Conan the Barbarian*, and *Excalibur*. They were fantasy adventures like those we enacted in our D&D language games. Tad liked the films for the dragon, Conan, and King Arthur. I liked Urlich, the wizard (played by Mako), and Merlin, all mages.

Tad was always there for me, always supportive, always had my back, always. He has understood me. I can trust him with anything. To family and friends, we were "the boys," and Asao and Tad, the individuals. In fact, most of our lives, my brother and I have joked that the other is the "yin to his yang," meaning that we made each other whole when we needed to. Together we have been complete.

But being a twin also created material conditions that produced a natural unity of opposites for me. We were the same to others, yet different to ourselves. We were the same to ourselves, making each other whole, yet different in some likes and dislikes. My brother did not pick up reading nearly as quickly as I did, for instance. He also is not much of a planner, is much more impulsive, and listens to his intuition to make most decisions. I like to plan, then deviate from it, but I want the plan. I've never really considered my intuition in most decisions, big or small. I have leaned on my wife, Kelly, for that.

We know these differences, yet feel and see many other similarities. So we were independent and strong willed but also needed each other, wanted each other in our lives. Sometimes my brother took the lead in social situations, at other times I did. The context and people determined when we would adjust our roles, so we were both leaders and followers. We shared a bedroom and bed for most of our growing up, well into junior high school years, when we got bunk beds, a bed that is two beds yet one bed. Through these material conditions as a twin, I was primed to accept more freely ambiguity and paradox, primed to resist categories and the essential characteristics that often went with those categories. Perhaps many twins feel this way.

Of course, I didn't understand any of this growing up. I was not raised in a culturally Japanese household, and my family did not practice Taoism, Shintoism, or Buddhism. And yet, our material conditions encouraged an orientation to the world and language that agrees with East Asian dialectic. In my preteen years, I experimented with various religions: Catholic, Baptist, Lutheran, the Church of Latter Day Saints, among others. I read other faith's literatures, even read the *Book of Mormon*. I went to their churches. Nothing about this seemed odd to me. Mom was okay with my experimenting.

As we've grown older, my brother and I, unbeknownst to the other, acquired Buddhist practices in our work and lives. Tad even got a degree in religious studies, went to Wesley Theological Seminary as a grad student (not a seminarian). Today, my brother is a diet coach and nutritionist, and he conducts his business with a strikingly similar philosophy as I do my teaching. His focus is on enjoying the journey of the diet or context prep (for athletes), not an outcome like some ideal weight or trophy.

Believing and not believing. Being this and that religion. Looking back now, it all fits the orientation to ideas and language that I see in my story. I didn't see why I couldn't have all of those religions, or all the good parts as I saw them at the time, while acknowledging the bad parts too. Richard Nisbett, a distinguished professor at the University of Michigan, offers another important element of Taoist dialectic that coincides with this impulse of mine:

> The Chinese dialectic instead uses contradiction to under-
> stand relations among objects or events, to transcend or inte-
> grate apparent oppositions, or even to embrace clashing but
> instructive viewpoints. In the Chinese intellectual tradition
> there is no necessary incompatibility between the belief that
> A is the case and the belief that not-A is the case. On the con-
> trary, in the spirit of the Tao (道) or yin-yang principle, A can
> actually imply that not-A is also the case, or at any rate soon
> will be the case. ("物極必反") Dialectical thought (Chinese
> version) is in some ways the opposite of logical thought. It
> seeks not to decontextualize but to see things in their appro-
> priate contexts: Events do not occur in isolation from other
> events, but are always embedded in a meaningful whole in
> which the elements are constantly changing and rearranging
> themselves. To think about an object or event in isolation and
> apply abstract rules to it (as in Western intellectual tradition)
> is to invite extreme and mistaken conclusions. It is the Middle
> Way that is the goal of reasoning.[12]

Nisbett explains the way context and the embeddedness of ideas and words in the world help make meaning for Chinese Taoist dialectic orientations. Con-tradictory traits or essences are allowable, even inevitable, in the world. Chinese dialectic presumes that you cannot separate abstract ideas, like "cow," from the cow you know (or don't know) in real life, or the cow in the context by which you know cows, or will know them, or the way others know them. This is similar to Freire's ideas about posing problems in his critical reading practice. The ques-tioning Freire asks of us helps us keep the ideas and words in front of us con-textualized, embedded in our unique histories, in our own material conditions. It helps us experience and feel the this-and-that-ness of our words and world.

In my early years growing up, I struggled with language in school work, yet I was deft at it on the block and in D&D sessions. I hated reading in school. It was the symbol of me as a remedial failure. At home with my brother, I loved reading and language, had a science fiction and fantasy book club membership. Language was the power I had. I was a mage, a spell caster.

---

12   Richard Nisbett, *Geography*, 27.

I had a White mom, but no one saw me as White. I was Brown. It all made sense if you knew my life, knew the story of my mom and dad. I was Japanese, but everyone saw me as a Mexican. I was a contradiction, a paradox. I was a member of the Church of Christ, actually enjoyed the sermons on Sunday, the hymns. I enjoyed the language of church, yet I struggled to buy into the doctrine, the extreme conservatism, the gender hierarchy that relegated all women to subordinate roles. Meanwhile in my real life, women were the most important people, doing everything. They were the leaders.

I also found beauty and elegance in the idea of grace while I resisted church doctrine and practices. Today, I still have fond feelings when I hear the sad hopeful sounds of the hymn, "Amazing Grace." It is my nana's voice, her sentiment to me as she held me in her warmth and rocked me in her green chair, singing me into being. It was reassuring to a poor kid in the ghetto to listen to hope in a song. Life may be shitty here, but not for long. I'll be bright and clean and, yes, angelic and White.

I lived with these contradictions as the landscape on which I cultivated my dispositions toward language and my love of language. Unfortunately, doing so didn't solve all the problems in my life, especially not the racism. Racism was connected to my own embodied languaging. And I did not control much of it. How does a twelve year old come to terms with such things? How does he acquire the language needed to understand and thrive as a languageling in a White world filled with White words?

CHAPTER 3.

RACIALIZING LANGUAGE AND STANDARDS

How could I have had so much trouble in school with language if I had so many language outlets at home? Couldn't a mage like me cast his spells in the classroom as well? What was happening? And what exactly does race—and its ugly offspring, racism—have to do with my literacy journey? The answers can be found outside of me and my habits of language. Yet paradoxically, those systems and structures are a part of me, and you.

Understanding the connection between language and groups of people helps with understanding the connection between race and literacy, between the standards typically imposed on everyone and White racial groups' control of those standards. We want to believe that social constructions like race do not have anything to do with language, that racism is just bad behaviors and not deeply ingrained in all standards of communication, that clear and compelling communication has only to do with using a neutral, apolitical set of language practices, but these beliefs are not true. If, as Freire says, reading the word and the world are simultaneous and "dynamically intertwined" practices, then language comes from communities of people who use language in their own contexts and for their own purposes.

Language standards do not come from grammar books or textbooks, nor from experts, tests, or standards. Textbooks and grammar books are really descriptions of language practices dressed up as prescriptions. That is, they're one group's language practices offered as universal English language rules. Language comes from people and their material conditions. English varies widely from place to place and group to group because language lives among people who live different realities. Their particular needs for the words they use in the ways they use them are responses to their environments. While race is not biological, it is a lived experience, a social, cultural, gendered, and economic aspect of our lives. Race is a set of structures that make up our lives and the histories we come from.

While we can say that universal standards are here to help people, to create safe industry working environments, or to help students become better communicators, that is not all that standards do, and they may not even do this much for everyone all the time. Take traffic and road laws. In a practical way, these are standards, too, standards for driving harmoniously and safely together in an area. We take for granted that each state and city has its own laws for driving. There are a variety of reasons for this difference, and we all accept this.

In Washington, where I previously lived, typical speed limits for urban interstates and similar roads were 60 mph, while in Arizona, where I live now, they're 65 mph. In Georgia, Mississippi, and Michigan, it's 70 mph. In South Dakota, it's 80 mph.[1] The point isn't just that different states have different standards but that safe driving standards can be dramatically different a few miles away in another state. This should call into question the standard itself as inherently correct and universal. How was it determined, and who determined it? What does this standard produce in the environments it operates? Does going 80 mph become safer once you cross the border from Iowa to South Dakota, where the difference in speed limits is 15 mph?

Standards are decisions made by people for particular reasons, but they are not universal, nor are they infallible. This goes for language standards too. They may very well be capricious and cause some people undue harm. Thus, it's reasonable to think that language standards are not infallible rules for clear or effective language practices. They are just the rules we have inherited today, made by people who had the power to do so yesterday.

We might say that language *norms* bubble up from a community of language users and tend to be *descriptive*. Norms show us what we have done or do with language already. Language *standards*, however, are decisions imposed onto a community of users and so are *prescriptive* in nature. They describe what we should do according to some group of people who made the standard.

Norms are what happen in communities, while standards are agreements by a group of people for what should happen. But did everyone affected by the standards get a chance to make those standards? When we say standards of language help us communicate effectively and accurately, it's not completely true, but not entirely false either. When we say this, we are choosing to see only one side of what standards are and do. We accept the yang without the yin.

In schools and other places, then, language standards are created to make judgements and rank students. This condition mostly punishes, and teaches little. Teaching and learning are supposed to happen before one tests for adherence to a standard. Schools usually impose external standards of English out of necessity. They cannot use the local norms unless the local people write the rules, but usually that is not what happens. Schools use externally created textbooks, guides, and curricula, often created by language experts who come from some

---

1   To see all the state speed limits for highways, see the Insurance Institute for Highway Safety (IIHS) website at https://www.iihs.org/topics/speed/speed-limit-laws. More information about the IIHS, a nonprofit organization focused on scientific research about vehicular crashes and educational efforts to reduce such crashes, can be found at https://www.iihs.org/about-us.

other place. And because the assumption must be that the local students will not share these same English language norms with the experts, schools impose standards and test for them.

In casual conversation, the distinction between standards and norms often doesn't matter. We know what we mean. Parents aren't going to grade their children's language use (at least most do not). But we don't get this message from schools, jobs, or even the dictionary. Here's what Merriam-Webster's Dictionary offers as the definition of "Standard English":

> the English that with respect to spelling, grammar, pronunciation, and vocabulary is substantially uniform though not devoid of regional differences, that is well established by usage in the formal and informal speech and writing of the educated, and that is widely recognized as acceptable wherever English is spoken and understood.[2]

So, according to Merriam-Webster, Standard English is regional, well established by formal and informal usage of educated people, and widely recognized as acceptable. I don't want to argue about whether this definition is true for most people. I think this is surely a way to understand how most people understand Standardized English. The problem isn't with its "truthiness," or whether this feels right to many people. The problem is with its accuracy as a definition for something we all use and are used by in our world.[3]

If there are regional differences in English, whose regional language users decide what is established usage and therefore *the standard* of English for all? What does "educated" mean here? Is it just those formally educated in colleges? What's the rationale for that? Can a person have read a lot of books and be "educated" even if they never attend any college? Does that person get to help decide language usage?

---

2   *Merriam-Webster's Dictionary*, accessed November 18, 2019, s.v. "Standard English," https://www.merriam-webster.com/dictionary/Standard%20English.

3   The word "truthiness" is a good example of the invention of a language norm for a particular purpose, political satire. It was coined on October 17, 2005, by Stephen Colbert on the opening episode of his show *The Colbert Report* on the Comedy Central channel. The word was meant to satirize the way politicians and others in the Bush Administration neglected facts and evidence in favor of their "gut" or their feelings about things. For a definition and discussion of the word, see, Sean Alfano, "The Truth of Truthiness," CBS News television broadcast, December 12, 2006, https://www.cbsnews.com/news/the-truth-of-truthiness/; "'Truthiness': Can Something 'Seem,' Without Being, True?" *Words at Play* (blog), *Merriam-Webster's Dictionary*, April 2020, https://www.merriam-webster.com/words-at-play/truthiness-meaning-word-origin; Wikipedia: The Free Encyclopedia, accessed January 17, 2020, s.v. "truthiness," https://en.wikipedia.org/wiki/Truthiness.

Kenneth Burke, a renowned and well-published rhetorician (that is, a theorist of rhetoric and language), never got a college degree, yet he is considered one of the most important and influential theorists of language in Western traditions.[4] Why does someone like him get to make language standards? Why not my best friend who never went to college but has read continuously for over thirty years? The point is, this definition is not terribly useful in deciding what standards of language are, where they come from, or what to do with them. It ignores completely the politics of language and standards—that is, who has made them and who benefits most from such making.

The sociolinguist Rosina Lippi-Green agrees with my criticisms of Merriam-Webster's definition. She says that the above definition assumes that the educated elite decide on standards and that those decisions are primarily based on written English, not spoken or both.[5] This is because academics and the educated elite tend to work with the written word exclusively, so they think about language as mostly written. This is to say, the written word is important to the material conditions of academics and the educated elite. Professors, teachers, and editors typically relate to language as text, as written, but this is not the typical way everyone else relates to language. Most others use and think about language as spoken, perhaps like those ancient Greeks and their logoi. Now, if you have a hearing impairment, you might think of language as embodied, or coming from hand movements, and facial expressions, not printed or auditory words.

No one relation to language (e.g. text-based, speech-based, or embodied) is better than others. They are just different ways people tend to think about and experience language. You can imagine that if you are not accustomed to organizing your ideas in paragraphs and text—not accustomed to seeing your ideas and being able to move them around on a page or screen—you might have trouble meeting a standard for communicating that asks you to organize your ideas in particular ways in textual form. You might not know when it is conventional to make a paragraph break or think in terms of linear or topical organizational patterns. These kinds of habits of language come out of a text-based relation to language, from seeing it done in text, from thinking about ideas as textual artifacts, sentences, paragraphs, sections.

---

4   Among his many publications, Kenneth Burke wrote numerous essays, academic articles, poems, fiction, and twenty-five books of rhetorical theory. He was awarded the 1981 National Medal for Literature. For a full list of his publications, see https://kbjournal.org/content/works-kenneth-burke, a list kept by the academic journal created for the study of his work, *The Journal of the Kenneth Burke Society*.

5   Rosina Lippi-Green, *English With An Accent: Language, Ideology, and Discrimination in the United States*, 2nd ed. (London: Routledge, 2012), 57.

When I was writing my doctoral dissertation, a very intensive process, one that usually consumes the person, as it did me, I typically awoke at 5:00 a.m., started writing at 5:30, continued most of the day, even eating at my desk, and stopped at around 9:00 p.m. I kept this schedule for at least a good six months. By my account, I clocked in at least 3,000 hours of writing toward my dissertation. This is likely an underestimation, given that I'm not accounting for the three to four months before and after this intense period of writing.

Now, I needed to finish the Ph.D., get a job, and stop taking loans to feed my family. Because of these writing conditions, my relation to language was not only constant and intense, but ubiquitous. All I did was fuck around with words. I thought about words, read them, studied theories about words, and wrote them. I even dreamed in words. In fact, I wrote an important chapter almost entirely in my dreams. I'm not kidding. I dreamed (or is it dreamt?) the text, paragraphs moving, words being typed then deleted. It became so constant that I kept a pad of paper and pen on my nightstand so that if I awoke in the middle of the night, I could write down my dreams.

My relation to words and language was thoroughly textual, so much so that even in my dreams I saw text, imagined ideas and manipulated them as textual artifacts. I realize that my relation to language during the writing of my dissertation is a privileged relation. That is, while my family and I were technically poor (my TA salary was only something like $14,000 a year), I still had the ability to spend just about every waking hour writing. That's a privileged relationship to language! Not everyone gets to have this kind of language norm. Do you think it is wise to use my relations to language, my language norms, as the standard for judging all language? Of course not. But unacknowledged privileged norms aren't the only problem with Merriam-Webster's definition and how we often think about standards.

The Merriam-Webster definition also assumes more agreement than has ever been established about things like "uniform" usage and grammar rules. Take the example of the plural pronoun, they/them/their. It is a surprisingly political and ethical problem of language, and has been for a long time, but it may seem quite simple.

At least as far back as the 1800s, there has been a popular standard for written English that says you don't use they/them/their as a singular pronoun reference. You use either he/him/his or one (if you're British), if you are referring to a generic, genderless person in writing. Today, many also use she/her/hers, but this is a recent phenomenon. In common, daily exchanges among many English speakers, the pronoun they/them/their has been used as a singular pronoun for a long time, and this is now acceptable in written usage.

It's the pronoun I use. This is language disagreement, a contradiction between language norms and expressed language standards. But really, it's just a difference in language norms between groups, those who make the standards and those who do not.

When someone in a car swerves into your lane and cuts you off on a busy street, you might say, "Hey, they cut me off!" perhaps with an expletive included. Or you might use the pronoun when you don't mean a gendered subject, just anyone, such as: "I get annoyed at the one person who is always running late. They hold up everyone in the meeting." The plural pronoun works in these cases, but apparently it isn't correct writing, or so says this long standing rule.

Paul Brians, former professor of English at Washington State University, gives this explanation for why the use of "they" should be avoided in many cases: "In many written sentences the use of singular 'their' and 'they' creates an irritating clash even when it passes unnoticed in speech. It is wise to shun this popular pattern in formal writing."[6] It may be wise, if you care much about holding on to traditions of a particular language group, but this reason tells us more about the language tastes of White, middle-class, academic readers like Brians than anything else. I hear no clash when someone uses "they" in their writing. But Brians' explanation hints at why such norms are so durable. How do we change a clashing word practice if we don't make it clash, at least for a time, until no one hears the clash anymore?

Now, to be fair, readers are not going to Brians' book or website on common errors in English to learn about nuances in language norms. They want quick answers to their error questions. But these quick answers are fast thinking. And the real clashes are those between a local language norm and other groups' norms assumed to be a universal standard. The bottom line is: We shouldn't confuse language norms with standards. Norms do not cause White language supremacy, universal standards do.

What I hope you can see is that how we use language is a product of the communities we are a part of. Yet paradoxically, individuals in a community help make the language of that community. This means that language and people form a dialectical relationship, a back and forth in both directions. That is, the language that makes me is itself made both from the communities I am from and by my own language choices.

---

6   Paul Brians, "They/Their (Singular)," The Web Site of Professor Paul Brians, accessed February 26, 2021, https://brians.wsu.edu/2016/05/25/they-their-singular/. This website offers a version of Paul Brians, *Common Errors In English Usage*, 3rd. ed. (Portland, OR: William, James & Company, 2013).

WE ARE WHAT WE DO IN THE PLACES WE ARE AT WITH THE PEOPLE THERE

Where and when you live, as well as who came before you in the places you live, will determine a lot of your material conditions for acquiring language. This is why we have so many different versions of English in the US. It's a big place with lots of different living conditions and people. In some parts of the country, people refer to a group of others as "you," while in much of the Southern part of the US, it's "y'all." Meanwhile in Pittsburgh, folks say "you ones" or "yinz." In the St. Louis area, people often pronounce the "r" sound in the back of their throat, swallowing the sound a bit, and include it in some words that people in other areas of the US do not, such as "wash" (warsh).

Black English is perhaps the most obvious example of a fully functioning and widely used English that has different words, rules, and pronunciations from standardized Englishes. Most, however, judge this difference as deficit or substandard, but not being of a standard doesn't make something substandard, even if the politics of language make it subordinate to that standard. It is not hard to see how any standard for English will be closely connected to the group of people who came up with that standard. It comes from their unique material conditions. Those conditions are a product of the places in which that group lived, the people they talked to, the things they needed to use the language for, etc. In other words, your languaging—the way you know, use, and embody language—has relations to (is a function of) where and how you live (and have lived), who you know (and have known), and how you responded uniquely to all those material conditions.

A simple way to say this is: We are what we do in the places we are at with the people there.

What I mean is that language is something we do all the time, and the places we do that languaging affect us, define us, and make us, just as we affect, define, and make language in particular places. It's a kind of chicken-and-egg dialectic, in that language creates people as people create language. And we operate from this understanding intuitively. For instance, places in the United States, like "urban areas" and "suburban areas," have been racialized in the course of U.S. history.[7] That is, particular bodies are associated with particular places.

Do you think mostly of White people mulling around an "urban" area or street? When someone says "urban youth," what is the image in your head? When I say "banker" or "stockbroker" or "lawyer," you likely think of a White

---

7   Insight into the racializing of space in the West and in the US can be found in Charles Mills, *The Racial Contract* (Ithaca: Cornell University Press, 1997), 41–53; Craig L. Wilkins, *The Aesthetics of Equity: Notes on Race, Space, Architecture, and Music* (Minneapolis: University of Minnesota Press, 2007), 3–61.

man, even though there are women, Black, Asian, and Latine bankers, stock brokers, and lawyers. I'm not asking you who you think is a possible or ideal banker or lawyer. I'm asking, who is the image that pops into your head when the word is spoken or presented to you. That tells you something of the racial and gendered associations—biases—with places and professions that circulate in our culture, often unconsciously. These biases are implicit biases, operating as fast thinking much of the time, and they inform our languaging.

Part of what creates these racial biases are the histories of the kinds of people not only who have been such people but who have inhabited places where such people frequent, like banks, stock exchanges, and attorneys' offices. These are White male dominated places. So all language practices are racialized because language comes from racialized people in particular racialized places. This is to say, race has come to be attached to or associated with particular places, the people who circulate in those places, and by default, the languages those people use together in those places.

The same kinds of racialized biases have affected schools and literacy class-rooms too. The fact that I had no teachers of color in all of my public schooling is important, no matter what the politics or language practices of any of my teachers were. This racial pattern of teachers in Nevada and Oregon is a product of the biases in our educational systems and the racialized places that funnel particular kinds of people into professions like teaching.

Racial segregation is another way to understand why race and language go hand in hand. Historically in our society, racial groups have been segregated, sometimes by laws and social norms that demand such separation (despite it being unfair and wrong), sometimes by geography or topography, and some-times by those in positions of power and decision-making ability. One way to see such disparate conditions between, say, White and Black people in the US is to compare the conditions in which each group tends to live. The U.S. Department of Health and Human Services offers stark statistics.

In 2017 on every metric measured, Blacks fall behind Whites. Of those 25 years and older, 86 percent of non-Hispanic Blacks earned a high school diploma, while 93 percent of non-Hispanic Whites did. Twenty-one percent of Blacks got a bachelor's degree or higher, while 36 percent of Whites earned such degrees. Eight percent of Blacks earned graduate degrees, while 14 percent of Whites did. The median household income for Blacks was $40,165 compared to $65,845 for Whites. And poverty levels? Twenty-three percent of Blacks lived in poverty, while 9.6 percent of Whites did. And what of unemployment? Among Blacks, 9.5 percent were unemployed, compared to only 4.2 percent of Whites.[8]

---

8   Office of Minority Health Resource Center, "Profile: Black/African Americans," U.S.

I could continue with insurance coverage, health and death rates, obesity rates, diabetes rates, etc. But the point is, these statistics point to very different conditions for Blacks and Whites. We could look at Asian groups, Indigenous groups, Latine groups, and we'd find similar patterns. Different conditions mean that the groups live differently, meaning they are segregated in a number of ways, not just by location.

We know that we are a racially segregated country,[9] but we do nothing about it. Or maybe it is that we don't know what to really do about it except set up hierarchies and blame individuals for the failures in their lives that are mostly a result of the conditions in which they live. This place is better than that one. The English in this place, of these people, is better or more professional than the English over there, of those people. So the typical solutions are to encourage Blacks or Latine or poor people to use the language of the people in so-called better places, White middle- and upper-class places. The problem is that the racial hierarchies in such distinctions are not questioned. And it ain't that easy to get to those other places, if you didn't start there.

This doesn't mean, however, that if you're Black, you use a Black English or African American Vernacular English (AAVE), or if you are White you inherently use a more standardized English. No. There are exceptions even to the patterns, such as the groups of poor, rural Whites in areas of the US who use various non-standardized Englishes. Or myself, who lived in predominantly Black and poor areas of North LV and spoke Black and White Englishes as a child. The point is that these language patterns are strong because we live in a segregated society. Race has been a characteristic of all communities. It is in the segregation, in the different places and conditions people live, that creates different needs for language.

Because it has been a White, male, middle- and upper-class group of language users who have made our language rules and standards, those language standards are connected closely to the material conditions of that group. This is why I often refer to such English standards as *White middle class racial habits of language*, or HOWL.[10] There's no inherent biology to any language habits. Race

---

Department of Health and Human Services, last modified August 22, 2019, https://www.minorityhealth.hhs.gov/omh/browse.aspx?lvl=3&lvlid=61.

9   To see just how segregated the United States still is by city and state, see Aaron Williams and Armand Emamdjomeh, "America is more diverse than ever—but still segregated," *Washington Post*, updated May 10, 2018, https://www.washingtonpost.com/graphics/2018/national/segregation-us-cities/. Using U.S. Census Bureau data from as far back as 1990, the article includes an interactive, searchable map of the United States.

10   I offer six habits of White language and judgement in chapter 0, of which I'm referring here.

and language are not biological. They are social, structural, and experiential, just as the economics of groups are. But because accepted language habits—the standards—come out of a White racial group in history, *that group's* unique material conditions are assumed to be everyone's material conditions.

This dynamic is the same reason I use the term "Black English." It's an English created and practiced historically by Black racial groups, even if today non-Black people use the language also. The racialized terms I use to identify White or Black English simply keep the racial histories and the power dynamics attached to those versions of the languages. Hiding or ignoring the racial references of our language practices and preferences means we can lose track of the racial injustices—the White supremacist outcomes—that too often follow.

In 1974, my mom moved my brother and me to Las Vegas, Nevada, from Dallas, Oregon. We hadn't grown at all in a calendar year, not an inch, and the doctor told my mom that it was the ryegrass in the Willamette Valley. Someone told me once that the valley has the highest concentration of grass seed pollen anywhere. It's where most of the grass seed is grown in the world. It's an industry that began in the early 1920s by a guy named Forest Jenks.[11] By the early 1970s when I was living there, it was a thriving and dominant industry. It still is today. If it hadn't been for Jenks and the ryegrass industry, I would not have come to my languaging in the conditions I did. I would not have gone to North LV to escape the ryegrass allergies. I would not be me in the way I am today.

In the Willamette Valley, there are grass fields everywhere. My brother and I were highly allergic to the pollen. We'd wake up each morning with our eyes swollen shut with a thick crust encasing our long, black eyelashes. The minute the door opened, we'd get strong hay fever reactions. Sneezing. Itchy eyes. Asthma. All of it. The doctor felt that our bodies were trying to fight the allergies so hard that we couldn't grow. My mom, ever-brave, always thinking of our best interests, decided to leave her home and family in Oregon and move to Las Vegas, a dry, desert climate. She had a cousin whose husband was in the Air Force, and they lived with their four young daughters in family housing on Nellis Air Force Base. We moved in with them for a short time, maybe three months.

While staying with my mom's cousin, Maisie, we started going to the nearby J. E. Manch Elementary school. We didn't stay the whole year, and over the next 16 months, we'd move three times, attend three different schools. The next one would be Oran K. Gragson Elementary, then Fay Herron Elementary, which I attended during my second and third grade years. All of these schools are in

---

11   Katy Giombolini, "Grass Seed Industry," The Oregon Encyclopedia, March 17, 2018, https://oregonencyclopedia.org/articles/grass_seed_industry/#.XkwQIpNKiWY.

North LV, the poorest part of town. We moved because we had to. Rents go up. Jobs get lost. But my mom was persistent. She was like water, always flowing where the resistance was the least, where we could pool, save, and build a bit for the next move.

There isn't a lot I recall until Fay Herron, but there are a few things, vivid things. At Manch, I remember the classroom, the coloring of pictures, the playing of red rover and duck-duck-goose out in a bright lawn. I remember trying to learn letters and words, or recognize them. I remember being baffled and never talking. I remember my teacher, a White lady who was distant. The only memory of her that I have is one of her standing over my desk as I stared at a sheet of paper with bold, black letters on it. I looked up. She looked down. She seemed really tall and had a disappointed look on her face, as if to tell me, "You can do better. C'mon." My recollection is that I floated through the school, almost like a ghost, as if no one could see me. I had no exchanges with others I can recall.

Similarly, at Oran K. Gragson, I remember the classroom and drawing silhouettes of our heads on cardboard, the rows of desks, and the sterile neatness of the classroom. I remember the rows of seats and spartan blankness of the room. One morning on our walk to school across a big park, my brother found a cigarette pack with a silver dollar in it. We felt rich in that moment. On that day, the sound of the ice cream truck would not be a melancholy thing, a sound of yearning and ache only. It would signal a sweet taste of something soon, of desire fulfilled, a rare thing for us in those days.

I remember forgetting my new Raggedy Andy doll at school, a soft doll I loved, given to me by my nana who was still in Oregon and whom I missed greatly. I returned to school a few hours later to find the doll had been stolen. No one knew where it had gone. More floating. No interactions with anyone at school.

Some of my strongest memories of this time are deep, meaningful, and precious to me. I remember sunny, warm Saturdays when my mom would clean our small two-bedroom apartment, humming to Neil Diamond. To this day, I get a warm feeling in my belly when I hear "September Morn," "Cracklin' Rose," or "Song Sung Blue." In my mind, they are bright orange and yellow Saturdays, with the sun dancing on my skin and the smell of Pledge furniture polish in the air.

My mom had a metal stand with several shelves on it that she kept in a prominent spot in the living room. It was maybe five feet tall and had ferns and green plants all over it. I remember climbing it. I didn't weigh enough to tip it over. I didn't think much of it then, but now it is a beautiful memory of green and iron and my mom and the smell of metal and potting soil. I remember a Christmas with Six Million Dollar Man action figures and Maskatron, his enemy. It was a time right before I would understand how poor we were, how dire our situation was, how Brown I am. I was blissfully innocent. My world at Oran K. Gragson was one circumscribed by my mom and my brother, Neil Diamond, Pledge, and warm, sunny Saturdays.

There were few language lessons during this period of my life that I recall. I just remember always feeling that I had no words. I was silent in school. My mom didn't have much time between her two or three jobs (depending on the time of year) to sit and read to me or help me read. So language and books didn't figure in my earliest memories of school or home. What figured most prominently was how loved I felt, how secure I felt, how joyful my life seemed, at least in retrospect. Part of this was me being too young to understand our circumstances, and part was that I'm sure mom sheltered me from the realities of our conditions.

At Fay Herron, my memories are clearer and more frequent, but still I was not a talker in school, not yet. I entered midway through first grade, but it is the second and third grades I recall most. I remember my mom going to a parent teacher meeting about me, about my lagging behind everyone in reading and language skills. I remember her being insistent about something, even upset in that dark room.

At that time, I still took allergy medicine. It made me drowsy. I was a small, slight child of less than 50 pounds. The medicine likely affected my abilities to focus and stay awake in school. I remember being startled awake, confused, disoriented by a water gun shot at my face. I had fallen asleep in class. I awoke to find the entire class standing around my desk laughing at me and Mrs. Whitmore's White face grinning from ear to ear, water gun still pointed at me. Perhaps it was things like this that made me hold on to that reading contest. I could beat them all, get them all back, by being the best at reading. There were not a lot of good reasons to communicate, to use language, in this period in my life, except at home. Language was a private, family affair and very different from the conditions of school.

Even at seven or eight years old at Fay Herron, I recognized the racializing of people and places, who was where. At school, language was a White woman writing words on the chalkboard. It was books I could not understand, words I didn't know, and commands I wasn't fully sure how to follow. It was a White place filled with kids like me, Brown and Black who usually spoke English differently than expected by the White teacher. School was where you were wrong about language, a place of silence and White noise.

At home in my poor, Black neighborhood, language was my twin brother, my mom, our love and closeness. It was a next door neighbor, Lester, a Black friend who had a younger sister. The two of them were always outside ready to play. It was my other Black neighbor, a tall, well-built man who would bring out his bongo drums every weekend and play them. We'd sit and listen to him play, and talk, ask questions about where the drums came from and what song he was playing.

Language was also the Black couple in the first apartment on the other side of Lester's who didn't have any children, or if they did, I never saw them. But they would smile and say hi and talk to Lester's parents, sometimes ask us how our day was. At home, language was everywhere, and no one judged you harshly for it. This place, the place of home and the block, was a freer, more natural place of language. We exchanged it without consequences.

Our language was economical too. I remember, even at seven or eight, when grown-ups and teachers were not around, we used curse words. It was just normal. We talked with our bodies, and if you were a boy, you grabbed your crotch a lot. It was like an exclamation mark, although now I realize it was also how we were working out our masculinity.

~~~

"Hey, whatchoo do?" Lester asks me as I come out of the front door to our apartment.

"Notin'—you?" I give my head a slight nod upward at him.

"We goin' the Circle-K. Gettin' some candy, dude." He extends the vowel in "dude" just a half beat longer. He grabs his crotch, and cracks a slight smile, like he's gotten away with something.

"I ain't got no money." I extend the "o" sound in "money" back at him. I'm emphasizing it. The morning sun cracks through the big tree in the courtyard behind Lester. It's the tree we play in. The raggedy rope we swing from dangles in the sun from a thick branch. The light is bright and yellow, like butter.

"Shi—I found some food stamps, dude. You can use em fo' candy!" He says the last sentence almost like a question, as if he just discovered this fact, raising the pitch of his words in the middle of the sentence.

"You sharin' ma-fucka?" I give him a flat smile and grab my crotch. I lean slightly back and raise my eyebrows.

"Stch, I gi' you some." The sound that starts his sentence is a sucking sound from the sides of his cheeks, which means, "Please, homie. I gotch you."

"Ahight, let's go!"

Even today when I read those sentences out loud, I get a warm and comforting feeling in my body. The sentences sound soft and right in my mouth. It's like putting on an old sweater you've hung up in the back of the closet decades ago and now discover it. Does it still fit? Will it be snug in the wrong places? You put it on, and the contours and form of it still hug ya right, soft and comfortable. And the way it feels on your shoulders, arms, and back is like your nana's arms

71

around you. I wanta go back to my nana's hugs, back to that soft-in-the-mouth sweater, but of course, I cannot.

ENGLISH STYLE GUIDES THAT DETERMINE STANDARDS

Now, I see that the language of school, the one so initially off-putting to me, was dictated by another world, another place and a different people—that is, White places and White people, all of whom I simply had little experience with up to that point, except for my mom. Historically and still today, White men control the standards of English taught in schools and judged to be "correct" or "professional." Consider grammar textbooks and writing style guides. These are the kinds of things that often caused me the most trouble.

Look for an English style guide not written by a White man or woman from a middle- or upper-class economic background. It will be almost impossible to find. Doing a quick Amazon search for the top college English style guides sold today gives these results:

1. *The Elements of Style*, 4th edition by William Strunk and E.B. White
2. *Dreyer's English: An Utterly Correct Guide to Clarity and Style* by Benjamin Dreyer
3. *Um . . . : Slips, Stumbles, and Verbal Blunders, and What They Mean* by Michael Erard
4. *Other-Wordly: Words Both Strange and Lovely from Around the World* by Yee-Lum Mak and illustrated by Kelsey Garrity-Riley (not a grammar book)
5. *The Only Grammar Book You'll Ever Need: A One-Stop Source for Every Writing Assignment* by Susan Thurman[12]

Of the six authors (and one illustrator) represented in Amazon's most purchased English style guides, four are White males, one White female, and one Asian female. And really, number four, by Yee-Lum Mak (the Asian female author), is not an English style guide or grammar book. It's a book that offers interesting words and their definitions from all over the world. Thus, most of the writers of the top four English grammar books and style guides sold on Amazon are White males. These authors come from the typical places that have historically made rules and judgements about English language standards and practices in the U.S., namely elite families and schools on the East Coast.

---

12 The Amazon page is titled "Amazon Best Sellers" and states it is "updated hourly." You can find this page at https://www.amazon.com/Best-Sellers-Books-Grammar-Reference/zgbs/books/11981.

The number one book above is the oldest, most influential, and arguably the archetype for all style guides after it. It still influences classrooms, teachers, students, and literacy standards today. It was first published by William Strunk in 1920, then expanded and republished with E. B. White in 1959. William Strunk was born in Cincinnati. His father was a teacher and lawyer. Strunk got his Ph.D. at Cornell, then taught there for 46 years, where E. B. White met him as his student.

White may be the one person you recognize in the above list of authors. He was born in Mount Vernon, New York, to upper-class parents. His father was the president of a piano firm, and his mother was the daughter of the famous American painter, William Hart. After graduating from Cornell University, White wrote *Stuart Little, Charlotte's Web*, and was a writer for *The New Yorker* for almost six decades. He is considered by many to be the father of the modern "essay," the kind most college students have to write.

I remember reading some of White's essays in my first-year writing class in college. His essays are personal, ruminating pieces that inductively move from his experiences in the world to reflecting on them and coming to ideas that sound universal. Taken by themselves, they often suggest that truth about our existence can be understood almost universally from within. That is, his essays imply that truths can be found by thinking objectively and carefully about our experiences.

White's essays are a demonstration of three habits of White language, which makes them literally habits of *White's* language (HOWL). The three most conspicuous to me are "hyperindividualism," or an over-reliance on the individual as most important in understanding and making knowledge or truths; a naturalized orientation to the world that assumes everyone has a similar orientation and access to ideas and things, which is often discussed today as unacknowledged White privilege; and a stance of supposed neutrality, objectivity, and apoliticality, which suggests that an individual can see things, judge them from a neutral, unbiased position, one unencumbered by one's position or politics in the world. These qualities have come to be understood by many as markers of an appealing, authoritative writing style and surely were a big part of what made White's writing so popular.[13]

On Goodreads.com, *The Elements of Style* has more reviews than any other grammar or style guide I can find, way more.[14] As of this writing, it has been reviewed or rated 78,590 times, with an average rating of 4.15 (out of five). It receives on average an additional hundred ratings each month. Nearly half of all the ratings (46 percent) give it five stars. As a way to compare those ratings, the

---

13   I discuss the six habits of White language and judgement in chapter 0.

14   To see the list of English style guides that have been rated on Goodreads.com, see https://www.goodreads.com/shelf/show/style-guide.

next closest style guide of English in terms of numbers of ratings is Steven Pinker's *The Sense of Style: The Thinking Person's Guide to Writing in the 21st Century*. Pinker's book has an average rating of 4.06 by 7,092 readers.

By these measures, Strunk and White's guide is by far the most influential English style guide in the last 100 years. But Pinker, a White, middle-class academic, is not that dissimilar to Strunk or White. Pinker is a Harvard cognitive psychologist and linguist, who was born in Montreal, Canada, and received his PhD. at Harvard. His father was a lawyer and mother was a vice-principal of a high school, while his grandparents owned a small, Montreal necktie factory.

The others on the above list are much newer, with less known publicly about them. Benjamin Dreyer's book was published in January 2019. Dreyer is a White, middle or upper class American writer who lives in New York and attended Northwestern University. He is the Vice-President, Executive Managing Editor and Copy Chief at the publisher Random House. His book received an average Goodreads rating of 4.36 from 6,130 raters.[15]

The number three book was published in 2007. Its author, Michael Erard, is a White, middle-class American journalist and writer who earned his master's degree in Linguistics and a Ph.D. in English from the University of Texas at Austin and lives in Portland, Maine. The final book in the Amazon list was published in 2003 and again in 2012. Susan Thurman is a White English teacher at Henderson Community College in Henderson, Kentucky. While it is less clear of the backgrounds of Erard and Thurman, from their college pedigrees, where they live and work, and what they do now, the habits of English language that they embody and promote match closely those of White, male, middle- or upper-class English language users of elite families of the East Coast.

This isn't to say that what these guides offer isn't good, helpful, or interesting if read in careful ways. There is no evil conspiracy here. My point is that the language practices that get published and taught in schools, that readers find worth buying, that publishers—which, by the way are mostly located in New York City—find worth publishing, reproduce a monolingual, middle-to-upper-class, White racial set of language habits. This is a White supremacist outcome achieved by people who are not White supremacists, but surely are White. This pattern exclusively places a White racial set of English language habits as the standard by which everyone is measured. This standard is used to determine who gets scholarships, jobs, and other opportunities in society, including who gets published more often. It has a lot of consequences.

~~~

---

15   You can find the ratings for Dreyer's book at https://www.goodreads.com/book/show/400 63024-dreyer-s-english?ac=1&from_search=true&qid=LqsS8dTIOv&rank=1.

I'm nineteen. I've returned home from my training in the Oregon Army National Guard. I trained at Fort Dix, New Jersey, then Fort Leonard Wood, Missouri. I'm a Technical Drafting Specialist, 81-Bravo. I left in September and returned in March of the following year. I tried to begin classes during that spring quarter at Oregon State University, but I couldn't do it. It was all too much. I withdrew from all of my courses. I spent the summer and fall thinking I was not going back to college. I had washed out.

I think: I'll work. I can do that. I was an exterminator and a vacuum salesman, the door-to-door kind. In the fall, I settled on a job I liked. I'm working at a bookstore in the Clackamas Town Center Mall. I receive shipments of books, then unpack and load the books onto carts in the back supply room. The front sales folks, all twenty-something White women and one White man (the manager), take the carts and shelve the books. I rarely go out on the floor. It is just me back there for four or six hours at a stretch with a radio and boxes and boxes of books.

The best part of the job is that I can "check out" any of the books we have on the shelves for free, read them, and return them. I just have to be careful not to damage them. That is the rule. I read mostly physics books, the ones for popular consumption. The theories about life, the quantum world, and the stars are interesting to me. I feel smart. I like Carl Sagan's *Cosmos*. I read John Gribbin's *In Search of Schrodinger's Cat: Quantum Physics and Reality*, then Stephen Hawking's *A Brief History of Time*. Hawking's book has just come out. It is a treat to read it so soon. It feels extravagant. Only people who could afford to buy a book new, the hardback kind, get to read books as soon as they come out. I satisfy my hunger for words silently in the back supply room of a bookstore in the mall.

At this time, I'm living with my mom and stepdad in Oregon City, Oregon, near Portland, in a spare room. I decide I should give college one more try. I can't live with my mom forever. And my job just doesn't pay enough to do anything else. I attend Clackamas Community College. I'm in my first-year writing course, the second time around. The teacher is a White lady who never seems to come from behind the desk in the front of the room. She's always seated at that desk. I don't even know if she's thin, tall, or short because she never stands up, never isn't seated at that desk.

This is around the time that the Exxon Valdez oil tanker hits an iceberg and spills almost 11 million gallons of crude oil in Prince William Sound, Alaska. The reports and news about it and the alleged drunk captain are everywhere. Turns out: No drunk captain. It is Exxon's fault. The company knew about the faulty equipment meant to detect such icebergs and a lack of communication among ships that had long since stopped running in that area. I am trying to write about this story for the class. I have no way to do it. I just feel the injustice and shame and failure of it all, the damage to the coastline and its ecologies. I turn in something incomplete. It seems all I could do. I accept my failure at school writing, again. The Valdez seems really important, worth writing about, so I hold on to that. It's my failed writing of an ecological failure.

I am in that writing class. We're reading from Strunk and White's *The Elements of Style*. This appears to be her teaching method: Someone reads out loud. We all follow along. We then do some writing. That's it. It isn't something I find engaging. I'm sitting alone at my table, one with two chairs. It's meant for two people. One chair is empty.

Page seven of Strunk and White, item six: "Do not break sentences in two."[16] Perfect, I think to myself. I have this problem. This is what I need. It has something to do with what my teachers keep telling me. All those red marks on my papers. What's it called? That thing on my papers? Comma-splices, maybe? No, that's ma problem too, but it ain't that. I start to feel myself moving back into the language of Statz, even if much of it is gone, meshed into my White English.[17] This meshed English is a surer way I can think through things, get stuff straight in my head, and feel like I'm in control. Fragments! Thas it. You break something in two and ya got two fragments of it.

The text says, "Do not use periods for commas." Okay, so when I can use commas? Now I'm not sure if I'm using periods right, either. I'm feeling more confused. How this explanation help anyone? This tells me the rule, but not in a way I understan. I tell myself to think like a White kid. Things start to get shakier for me. When the hell I use commas and periods? I can feel the anxiety rise in me. This school-shit feels so arcane, I think. Yeah, *arcane*, that's the word, like in D&D. This is motha fuckin' Black magic. Hexes! The editors offer two examples. Perfect! Examples should help.

The first example: "I met them on a Cunard liner many years ago. Coming home from Liverpool to New York." What the fu—. Jeez. "Cunard," what the hell is that?

Wait, I can figure this out. Liverpool, that's where the Beatles came from. So that's England, and New York is America, so Cunard must go with "liner"— what the fuck is a liner? Like a pencil line? That's stupid. Stop being stupid, I tell myself. Think White. Think right. It's gotta be a plane or a boat or something

---

16   All quotes in this section come from William Strunk Jr. and E. B. White, *The Elements of Style*, 3rd ed. (New York: Macmillan, 1979), 7.

17   To read about code-meshing, see Vershawn A. Young, *Your Average Nigga*; Vershawn A. Young and Aja Y. Martinez, *Code-Meshing As World English: Pedagogy, Policy, Performance* (Urbana, IL: National Council of Teachers of English, 2011); Vershawn A. Young, "Should Writers Use They Own English?" *Iowa Journal of Cultural Studies*, 12.1 (2010), pp. 110–118, https://doi.org/10.17077/2168-569X.1095.

like that, something people are on. Why would something like that be called a liner? More frustration, mostly from translating my mind's language into White language. It's like putting on and taking off clothes you didn't fully know how to wear yet. On and off, on, off.

How these sentences wrong exactly? Wait, maybe this an example of how to put the period in correctly? I breathe heavily on my book. Slow down, I tell myself. I try to blink the anxiety away.

The second example: "He was an interesting talker. A man who had traveled all over the world and lived in half a dozen countries."

More travel sentences. What's that about? Who the fuck travels and meets talkers? Wait, the rule is not to bust a sentence in two. So maybe these examples of the problem. But they sound right. I mean, I can read em and I understand exactly what they mean. Don't errors cause readers to not understand shit? The periods must not belong there. But why? There is a pause where the period is in each one. That's right, right? Fuck.

The internal pressure grows in me. The right White language is elusive. I'm trying hard. I can hear the other students read past this part. They are moving on without me, as usual. I'm stuck in this one rule, stuck at the periods. Commas. Pauses. Breaking things. Cunards and liners. Travel. Anger and confusion rises up in me. I grit my teeth. Breathe through it all.

I realize I've not heard the following explanation when it was read. I was too busy figuring out what kind of examples we were reading. The explanation is: "In both these examples, the first period should be replaced by a comma and the following word begun with a small letter." Strunk and White continue, "It is permissible to make an emphatic word or expression serve the purpose of a sentence. . . . The writer must, however, be certain that the emphasis is warranted, lest his clipped sentence seem merely a blunder in syntax or in punctuation."

Wait, I think, so not a rule? Or I should know when to break this rule that ain't no rule? These examples, why are they not examples of emphasis? What's "warranted" mean? Crap. I'm losing more control of my language, of language. But the examples still seem okay. I need different examples. Maybe then, I understand. Double-crap. That second sentence in the first example, it emphasizes when he met em, right? So there's a period, right? No? Ya met em on a fuckin' liner on yo way to New York, right? I've never been to either of these places, man. Is that important? Arrhhh. The second example emphasize the interesting thing about talker-dude. He everywhere in the world. Still, these seem okay to me. Breathe. Calm down, man.

I look one last time at the page. Both of these examples still feel right to me sitting in that class at a two-person table alone. But the book, its White authors, one who is named literally "White," seems to be talking to someone else, not me, not the Brown kid from North LV. Apparently, I ain't never gonna escape that place. It's like these authors are talking to someone who already fuckin' knows this answer. The class moves on. I finish the course barely getting a B grade, or maybe it was a C, mostly for trying hard, and feeling lucky to survive.

THE WHITE HABITS OF STRUNK AND WHITE

In my English classes in school, I got language norms as standards, especially through grammar books and style guides. These books are how my teachers and professors got their language norms as standards. It's typically how we all get them or know where exactly we can find them. This may be why so many people feel they are not good writers or communicators. The formal systems that help us shape our language practices work from a flawed assumption: There is one standard for good writing, and you can find this standard in grammar books and style guides or in your teacher.

The flaw in this systemic assumption is that it quietly reproduces White language supremacy, all in the name of teaching people how to communicate well. Let's return to Strunk and White's *The Elements of Style*. The rules for good and clear writing in this book are presented as universal ones, even though they come exclusively from Strunk and White's own monolingual, White, upper-class, masculine language group. They enact an orientation to language that universalizes their language conditions. That is, they take their own language norms as universal language standards. Strunk and White HOWL like no one can.

The authors offer a rule that demands the singular pronoun he/him/his be used exclusively. They tell us to avoid the pronoun they/them/theirs in cases where gender is not important, otherwise your prose may sound "general and diffuse." They open this entry with an explanation of the written norm, which is stated as a standard:

> **They.** Not to be used when the antecedent is a distributive expression such as *each, each one, everybody, every one, many a man*. Use the singular pronoun.
>
> Every one of us knows   Every one of us knows
> they are fallible.   he is fallible.[18]

They offer two example sentences to illustrate. The one on the left shows an allegedly incorrect use of the plural pronoun, while the right is the correct use. The confusion here is of the same nature as Merriam-Webster's confusion

---

18   Strunk Jr. and White, *Elements*, 60.

between norms and standards. Part of the problem is that both examples are grammatically accurate and communicative, but this is only part of the underlying issue.

Accepting the grammatical correctness of the right example does not make the left example grammatically incorrect, nor any less communicative. The norm governing the right side example as correct is one that says that the singular noun "every one" agrees with its antecedent, "he," which is supposed to be another singular noun. But there is nothing inherently grammatically or communicatively better or clearer about this norm of agreement by number. This is why it has been common for many to use a sentence like the one on the left side.

There is always more than one way to do anything, but Strunk and White see only their way. Seeing two norms that are different doesn't have to mean that one must be right and one wrong. If norms are meant to help us understand an expression or idea—that is, communicate with each other—then the real test is: Do you understand both of these sentences? Is there unnecessary ambiguity? If not, what is the *real* problem with "they" in the left example? What is really going on? It is just something Strunk and White and people like them do not do in language.

Strunk and White assume a naturalized and universal orientation to the language. It's how you can think your norm is everyone's standard. To accomplish this, there is a slight-of-hand maneuver done. They disregard everyone else's contexts, purposes, material conditions, and language customs. But their left example sentence works just fine. There is no missed communication, no confusion about meaning. To my ear, it is no more "general" or "diffuse" than the right example.

In fact, the left is more accurate than the right. By definition, "every one" includes men, women, and non-binary individuals, so it is difficult for me as a contemporary reader to not hear the exclusionary nature of the singular pronoun, he, in the second example. And the fact that in other cases "he" is used as a masculine gendered pronoun makes this use potentially ambiguous. This makes the second weaker for me, unnecessarily exclusive, or to use their term, "diffuse."

The authors make the argument that the singular masculine pronoun, "he," "has lost all suggestion of maleness in these circumstances."[19] They offer no evidence of this, only their word. They assume that how they hear the pronoun is the way everyone hears it, or maybe everyone who knows better. As gentlemanly as they may be, their word is not sufficient for such an argument, especially since so many people do not agree. Why do all those other ears not count in this instance? Besides, why have a gendered pronoun if we are going to disregard

---

19   Strunk Jr. and White, 61.

the gendered-ness of it? Another rule that is not really a rule, and someone like White or Strunk has to tell the rest of us when to break it.

To counter such concerns, Strunk and White make the argument that using the feminine pronoun she/her/hers is ridiculous and will not be very effective writing: "No need fear to use *he* if common sense supports it. The furor recently raised about *he* would be more impressive if there were a handy substitute for the word. Unfortunately, there isn't—or, at least, no one has come up with one yet. If you think *she* is a handy substitute for *he*, try it and see what happens."[20]

The misogyny in this passage is blatant by today's standards, and it's casually justified by the authors in elitist terms through their habits of language. They HOWLing. They appeal to "common sense," which for them is dominated by a monolingual, White, male-centered, educated world, the one they come from and exist in. This is how most appeals to common sense work. They assume authority to dictate a common logic or a central, common view on the subject, despite there not being one. It's their feelings about language stated as fact, their ideas of clarity, order, and control that are universalized. Common sense, then, is the "truthiness" of things. The language norm is a standard because, well, it feels right in *their* guts.

Much like Paul Brians' sense that the use of the singular "they" can "clash" in a reader's ear,[21] Strunk and White also assume that their ears are the same as mine, that we all hear these words in the same way, or should. To be fair, I hear Brians offering more room to hear the use of the pronoun differently. But Strunk and White confuse their own language norm with an illusionary standard for all. They justify this use from their own sensibilities, ones they've cultivated in their social and material conditions, which are assumed to be accessible to everyone.

They also discount quickly "the furor" of concerns about gender inclusive language practices by saying that these concerns are not a problem, because, well, there is no better solution out there (from their view, of course). A problem without a solution does not make the problem not a problem. Not having a "handy substitute" is not an argument for falling back on flawed practices. Their book is all about making such language practices common, so why not offer a few here? Why not offer some handy substitutes?

In fact, there is at least one handy substitute right in front of them, the pronoun they/them/theirs. Why not use this, especially since so many others around them clearly are already doing so? If they weren't, the authors wouldn't need to make this admonition. Furthermore, if a woman or someone else feels excluded or hurt by my use of language, do I not have an ethical obligation to

---

20   Strunk Jr. and White, 61.
21   Paul Brians, "They/Their."

listen and change my practices? Is it not insensitive and callous to brush these concerns aside with a few words?

Strunk and White cannot see their own perspective on language as a perspective. They see it as the rule. Their view seems universal and natural to them, but it is a god trick played not simply on their readers but themselves. In their world, Strunk and White are never ignored. They have always made the rules from their common sense, from their norms of behaviors. Those rules have always benefited them and people just like them. Their truthiness can be stated as fact, and few resist it. They've likely not been confronted by others with contradictory language norms. They are used to ignoring the perspectives of others and demanding that others see things their way. Their world has rewarded them for HOWLing, which has made language standards.

As referenced in chapter 0's discussion of the first and most common White habit of language and judgement, Strunk and White embody Sara Ahmed's idea of Whiteness as a universalized orientation to the world, as a kind of habitual way or seeing and experiencing the world that is taken as reachable to all. They think and speak—make decisions—as if most everyone else thinks like them, sees things as they do—or can do so. Ahmed says that "we inherit the reachability of some objects, those that are 'given' to us, or at least made available to us, within the 'what' that is around."[22] Common sense is what is reachable here, at least for Strunk and White. It's their common sense in their textual world to not include women and non-binary individuals in this way. Doing so is unreachable for them.

This White habit of language is also a version of what Ruth Frankenberg reveals in her studies of White women and their own complex and contradictory ways of understanding racism and their own Whiteness. Her study reveals how difficult it is for White women to recognize racist ideas and White supremacist orientations to the world, even when the person has expressed antiracist views. She quotes one of her participants in the study as saying, "Whiteness: a privilege enjoyed but not acknowledged, a reality lived in but unknown."[23] I cannot think of a better way to identify the stance that Strunk and White take.

If you think I'm being too hard on Strunk and White, then consider their last sentence above about substituting "she" for "he." It is a snarky, "I dare you,"

---

22   Ahmed, "Phenomenology," 154. For an older but still significant discussion of Whiteness, see James Baldwin, "On Being White . . . And Other Lies," *Essence,* April 1984, repr., Antiracism Digital Library, accessed January 15, 2020, https://sacred.omeka.net/items/show/238.

23   Ruth Frankenberg, "Growing up White: Feminism, Racism and the Social Geography of Childhood," *Feminist Review,* no. 45, (Autumn 1993): 51, https://doi.org/10.2307/1395347. To see further evidence of the way White people have a hard time seeing the racism in their own attitudes and words, see, Eduardo Bonilla-Silva, *Racism Without Racists.*

statement. It's what a bully would say. They are intentionally flexing their authoritative muscles, their power. If we accept that they have come to this language norm like everyone else, through the communities they practiced language in, then we must accept that there is no inherently correct English norm—no universal standard—since lots of contradictory norms are developed in communities for the same linguistic and rhetorical purposes. This then means that Strunk and White's parting shot illustrates just how well they understand the politics of language.

I'm not the only one who finds Strunk and White and the English language style guide tradition to be White supremacist. Laura Lisabeth, a Lecturer at State University of New York at Stony Brook, argues that the tradition of style guides in the U.S. was a part of a larger White supremacist project in which particular habits of language have been promoted and protected. She explains that style guides and etiquette handbooks started to become popular just after the Civil War and have continued through the twentieth century. All conceived of the English language as White property. Lisabeth connects Strunk and White to the more recent style guide by Benjamin Dreyer (mentioned previously). She explains: "Like E. B. White before him, Dreyer promotes a historically classed, racialized and gendered code, that of the privileged White man alert to dispossession, who patrols the boundaries of a White system of knowledge production."[24]

You might feel that you can discount Strunk and White as two archaic authors of yore, ones we all can safely ignore today. But Strunk and White's guide is still the most popular one around. They are not ignored. According to the Open Syllabus Project's website, which gathers millions of syllabi from a range of college courses from across the country, Strunk and White's text is the most common textbook assigned of any kind of textbook—that's all courses, all disciplines.

As of this writing, it has 15,533 appearances in over seven million syllabi.[25] The next closest competitor of style guides is *On Writing Well: An Informal Guide to Writing Nonfiction*, by William K. Zinsser, with 2,925 appearances.[26] It's not even close. So Strunk and White's book is important because it embodies the structures that make standards of English in all kinds of classrooms and editorial offices. In many instances, it is the structure. The book, if read in the critical way

---

24   Laura Lisabeth, "White Fears of Dispossession: Dreyer's English, The Elements of Style, and the Racial Mapping of English Discourse," *Radical Teacher* 115, (2019): 22–23, https://doi .org/10.5195/rt.2019.673. For another critique of Strunk and White, see chapter 2 of Stanley Fish, *How to Write A Sentence and How to Read One* (New York: Harper, 2011).

25   See "Most Frequently Assigned Titles," Open Syllabus Project, accessed March 27, 2021, https://opensyllabus.org/.

26   Diana Hacker's *A Writer's Reference* (St. Martin's/Bedford, 1989) is the referenced in 14,931 syllabi on the same website; however, Hacker's book is a grammar and writing reference book, not a style guide.

I have in this chapter, shows us the politics of language and its judgement that influence millions of people. It suggests why I, an avid reader from an early age, still had trouble with such standards in my college writing courses.

Also according to the Open Syllabus Project website as of this writing, considering all texts assigned in college syllabi, the first author of color doesn't show up until the 17th spot; that's Martin Luther King Jr.'s "Letter From the Birmingham Jail." But the list goes on with exclusively White authors of textbooks for math, anatomy, more grammar books, and history. The next author of color appears at number 40, Chinua Achebe. Paulo Freire shows up at 49. All three of the authors of color in the top 50 textbooks of syllabi are dead men. No women of color. No Asians of any kind. No Mexican. No Muslim. Just a sea of White authors. This is White language supremacy.

We don't escape our language history nor the past's White supremacist structures simply because we think we know better today or even because we haven't used Strunk and White to write in school. My point is, even if you haven't used the book, even if you didn't know about it, you have been judged by its standard. You are a product of Strunk and White's language habits as standards whether you know it or not.

Now today, the use of the plural pronoun "they" is mostly acceptable in writing.[27] No one bats their eye at its use. But don't let this inclusive change fool you. This practice isn't new to English; even Paul Brians acknowledges this, yet it's been debated for some time. The practice goes back at least to the 1500s CE. There are instances of singular-pronoun-they usage in Shakespeare, the Bible, among other English literature.[28] And Strunk and White ain't complaining about Shakespeare.[29] Why has it taken over 500 years to change the practice? Politics. No group willingly gives up power.

---

27   To read a good article on "they" pronoun use as inclusive practice, see "Does Traditional Grammar Matter When it Comes to Singular 'They' and 'Themself'?" Thesaurus.com, accessed March 1, 2021, https://www.thesaurus.com/e/grammar/they-is-a-singular-pronoun/.

28   Wikipedia actually has a good page with several references to English uses of they as a singular pronoun. See Wikipedia: The Free Encyclopedia, accessed March 1, 2021, s.v. "third-person pronoun," https://en.wikipedia.org/wiki/Gender_neutrality_in_languages_with _gendered_third-person_pronouns.

29   For example, in *The Comedy of Errors*, act IV, scene iii, Antipholus of Syracuse says, "There's not a man I meet but doth salute me / As if I were their well-acquainted friend;" and the eighteen stanza of his poem, "The Rape of Lucrece" contains "Now leaden slumber with life's strength doth fight; / And every one to rest themselves betake, / Save thieves, and cares, and troubled minds, that wake." There is a good argument for the grammatical correctness of the singular pronoun "they" at Geoffrey K. Pullum, "Shakespeare Used *They* with Singular Antecedents So There," *Language Log* (blog), January 5, 2016, http://itre.cis.upenn.edu/~myl/languagelog /archives/002748.html.

And in fact, the word didn't start as an English word. The pronoun "they" actually was not a part of Old or Middle English. Those languages did not have a third-person pronoun. Apparently back in the day, it was not a practice to reference a third person who was not named. Eventually, speakers found a need for this and began borrowing, among many other words, a third-person pronoun from a nearby source, Scandinavian.[30]

Scholars have found a use of the word "they" in a homiletic poem from 1175 CE called *Ormulum* by a Scandinavian guy named Orm.[31] This language borrowing came about likely because of several intersecting factors: geography, migration patterns of Scandinavian peoples, and likely the intermingling and marriages of Scandinavians with the Angles, Jutes, and Saxons inhabiting the British Isles at the time.

I offer this because it makes my point that language travels with people. In those travels, it changes, picks up other words and ways with existing words from various material conditions, all of which are uneven or inconsistent over large expanses of geographic space and time. Language is antsy, dynamic, and always in the act of becoming something new. Language standards, then, are seemingly antithetical to language norms. Standards are treated as static. Norms are understood to change.

Even Strunk and White acknowledge this and suggest that they are not guarding gates. They argue that good style in writing is individualistic and often breaks well established rules as well as works clearly inside of them. In their final pages of their last chapter, "An Approach to Style," they explain,

> The language is perpetually in flux: it is a living stream, shifting, changing, receiving new strength from a thousand tributaries, losing old forms in the backwaters of time. To suggest that a young writer not swim in the main stream [sic] of this turbulence would be foolish indeed, and such is not the intent of these cautionary remarks. The intent is to suggest that in choosing between the formal and informal, the regular and the heretical, the beginner err on the side of conservatism, on the side of established usage. No idiom is taboo, no accent forbidden; there is simply a better chance of doing well if

---

30 To read about some of these language adoptions from Scandanavian to Old English, see David Crystal, *The Stories of English* (London: Allen Lane/Penguin Group, 2004), 73–76.

31 To read more about the English borrowing of "they" from Scandanavian, see Philip Durkin, "Middle English—An Overview," *OED Blog*, August 16, 2012, https://public.oed.com/blog /middle-english-an-overview/; OED.com., s.v. "they," updated September 2013, www.oed.com /view/Entry/200700.

the writer holds a steady course, enters the stream of English quietly, and does not thrash about.[32]

Is this bad advice to a young writer? Is it wrong to say that English is like a living stream, constantly in flux? Of course not. This is, to my view and many others who study language, accurate. It's what the story of Orm illustrates. And yet, there is no better recipe for maintaining control of the standard that their language group set up than to ask new writers to err on the side of conservatism, err towards the *status quo*, to wade into the waters of the English language cautiously.

I say, splash around. Get drenched. Find out how far you can take your language, especially when you are learning it in school. Where is it safer to do so?

What Strunk and White might have included in their advice to younger writers is that these observations about English are paradoxical. They might have mentioned that such observations and advice reveal the politics of English and how it is judged in the world, that to err on the side of conservatism means to accept their authority and their language group's ways with words over perhaps your own. It means it can take 500 years to stop being exclusionary in pronoun practice. To shift or change the river of English in some way is to buck a power relationship with a dominant group of English users.

I don't think we should overly blame Strunk and White for contributing so greatly to White language supremacy. They too are fighting the stream of their lives with the English language they know. They are not evil racists. It's just that the current they swim in has always been in their favor, always taken them exactly where they wanted to go. So their advice makes perfect sense to them, and they've not had to think of anyone else's experience but their own. It's hard to hear language we are not used to hearing as anything but incomprehensible babble, or general and diffuse.

I do believe they are trying to help people be better communicators, but their ideas stated the way they are means they remain the experts. It means that if we use their book as a standard, we privilege the same privileged group's language that we always have and disadvantage everyone else's ways with words. It means that those not from material conditions that lead to using an East Coast, middle-to-upper-class, monolingual, IV (or Ivy) League English will be harmed, will not be heard as communicative, or smart, or coherent, or clear. They won't get the higher grades in school or the jobs in life. This also means you won't find a style guide from a Black author, or a Latine one, or an Asian or Indigenous author.[33]

---

32   Stunk Jr. and White, 84.

33   Recently while visiting Indiana University, a participant in a faculty workshop I was leading gave me a reference to a grammar book written by an indigenous author of the Opaskwayak

THE TACIT LANGUAGE WAR

In my view, the systems in which we teach and judge English language amount to a tacit language war, one that most of us have already conceded because we've put up our hands and accepted the sole authority of people like Strunk and White, often out of necessity. I'm guilty of this in my life. My edition of Strunk and White comes from my college days. I, too, used it. It was my style guide bible for a time.

Is this language war a race war, or a class war, or a gender war played on the battlefield of language? Perhaps, but more likely, grammar and style guides taken as standards are just one battlefront in a larger war for White racial supremacy, one that arguably started in the late nineteenth and early twentieth centuries with treatises and arguments for eugenics and White world supremacy written by people like Francis Galton, Karl Pearson, Lothrop Stoddard, and Hans Gunther.

Their arguments and logics are the same because their HOWLing ends up producing in history the same results, White supremacy. All the while, no one today is consciously fighting language race battles, so the race war goes on. People get hurt. We, people of color, blame ourselves for being lazy, or stupid, or slow, or just not having "what it takes" to make it, to succeed.

Keep in mind: There are no bad people fighting good people in this war. We all think we are fighting on the good side, and from one view, we are, even those who, like Strunk and White, argue for clear and unambiguous universal standards of English. There is room for Strunk and White as a particular norm, but not as the standard of all good writing.

The actual war is against larger systems, structures, histories of norms taken as standards. It's a political war, a war of power. And again, this isn't an explicit war like Neo-Nazi or White Nationalist groups proclaim. This war is a tacit one, one that goes by other purposes and names, like a concern over the illiteracy of our youth or a push for standards in English language use, or anxieties about how our kids don't read enough good literature anymore, or how our nurses and other professionals need "good communication skills."

Cree Nation in Canada. Greg Younging, *Elements of Indigenous Style: A Guide for Writing By and About Indigenous Peoples* (Alberta, Canada: Brush Education, 2018). Younging was the managing editor at Theytus books, Assistant Director of Research for the Canadian government's Truth and Reconciliation Commission (TRC) of Canada, and Professor and Coordinator of the Indigenous Studies Program at the Irving K. Barber School of Arts and Sciences at the University of British Columbia, Okanagan. He died in 2019. The style guide offers several principles for publishing as or about Indigenous peoples but is non-directive in what it offers writers. And perhaps this is the kind of style guide that is preferable to the more directive, "how-to," kind that seem steeped in their Whiteness, which tend to assume the author's orientation to language is the best way to use language. This is not Younging's orientation in his noteworthy style guide.

One way to measure how this battle is fought is to consider who is enlisted in the fight and what are their dispositions in language. Who are the examples of good style and writing that are used in classrooms and style guides? Of the identifiable examples of external authors used by Strunk and White in their book, I count sixteen. Of those sixteen examples of good writing, fifteen are White men, one is a White woman, six are from the UK, and five are from the Northeast US.[34]

Because authors who HOWL are used most of the time as examples of good writing, White language supremacy is maintained in this mostly invisible way. Usually this is done with no reference to race or to how historically those habits and features in the examples are associated with White racial formations in the US or Western English language traditions. No alternatives are offered, even as abstract ideas of language as a living stream with thousands of tributaries feeding it are given. Apparently, the tributaries only come from one direction, one kind of White place.

In that same final chapter cited previously, Strunk and White offer a comparison of two passages about "languor" from two very different White writers, Faulkner and Hemingway, two tributaries. They are demonstrating style as an individualistic feature of writing. They note that style can look and sound like a wide range of things. They say, "style not only reveals the spirit of the man but reveals his identity, as surely as would his fingerprints." They explain that both authors use "ordinary" words and constructions that are not "eccentric." I'll put aside whether I or other contemporary readers would find such phrases like "supremely gutful lassitude of convalescence" or "mendicant" to be ordinary or not eccentric. Instead, listen to the way they explain these styles of writing: "Anyone acquainted with Faulkner or Hemingway will have recognized them in these passages and perceived which was which. How different are their languors!"[35]

Apparently, Strunk and White are speaking to a certain class of people, a certain group who have had material conditions in their lives that have granted them an "acquaint[ance] with Faulkner or Hemingway." Is that too presumptuous? What if someone has not read Faulkner or Hemingway? What if they cannot recognize the differences? What if they don't see or hear differences in the two passages? It's quite possible.

---

34 The identifiable authors and pages where I found them in Strunk Jr. and White's *Elements* are Jean Stafford (21), Herbert Spencer (23), George Orwell (23), E. M. Forester (26), the Bible (26 and 59), William Wordsworth (37), John Keats (37), W. Somerset Maugham (60–1), Thomas Paine (67), Thomas Wolfe (67), William Faulkner (68), Ernest Hemingway (68), Walt Whitman (69), Robert Frost (69), William Allingham (73), and Wolcott Gibbs (83).

35 Strunk Jr. and White, 68.

From my experience, there ain't no Faulkner or Hemingway in the trailer park or in the ghetto.[36] This short explanation of the two quotations is all they offer. They move on, expecting that we, their readers, can follow their view, their reach of things. Again, they mistake their own sensibilities cultivated in their reading and conditions for larger, abstract rules about language and style in English that anyone can see and hear. They assume that a good writer will be able to recognize the differences in these two White male authors.

Strunk and White cannot notice that all of their book's examples are White men (except one, a White woman). I suppose it makes sense that they'd not see why there is a need for a gender inclusive third person pronoun. Their use of "he," as in their explanation of style, is really referring to men, like Faulkner, Hemingway, Strunk, and White. It's about *their* identity as White men, their habits of language. It's about *their White spirits*. And so when men like these get together and create a style guide like this one, this kind of obvious example is agreed upon. It's obvious and natural to them. And if you haven't read Faulkner or Hemingway, well, shame on you. You should.

And if you think that today there are more contemporary style guides that avoid most of these problems of unexamined Whiteness, uncritical elitism, and unconscious misogyny, you'd be wrong. They all follow a similar template. Why? No one escapes history or its influences on us. We don't leave our language habits, ideas about language, or notions of who can make the rules behind just because we openly claim to have a more egalitarian and fair society. The structures, the systems, already in place make us. The pull of people like Strunk and White is strong in the living stream of language, especially when too many people tread into the current carefully and their first impulse is not to make waves, especially when too many think we are just talking about how to be clear communicators, especially when we ignore the racial and gendered politics of language and its historical impulse to maintain White language supremacy.

~~~

I'm sitting at my desk in the third grade, Mr. Hicks' class. We are taking a vocabulary test. A list of words is introduced on Monday. The practice test is on Wednesday, and the real one is on Friday. This is not a time that I enjoy. I have not done well on these spelling tests. I sit with my head down and look at the strip of paper that is four and a quarter inches wide, with twenty numbered lines on it running down the page, and a line at the top with "name" next to it. It's

---

36   I take this expression from a colleague of mine in graduate school at Washington State University, Dometa Weigand (now Dometa Brothers), who, when asked by a professor, "Have you no Latin?" replied, "There ain't no Latin in the trailer park."

the spelling test sheet. Every week, we do this dance. Usually, I might get one or two of the words spelled right on Wednesday, and I often double that number correct on Friday, but that's only four or six out of twenty words. I want so badly to break the halfway mark, get ten words right. That's still an F though.

I'm failing this part of the class. I know it. I see it. I don't know what to do. I do what Mr. Hicks tells us all to do. I write each word ten or twenty times. I read them over and over each day. Those things don't seem to help. The spellings seem to slip out of my mind as I try hard to hold on to the order of the letters. When I try to phonetically sound out words, I don't have better luck. I must be pronouncing them wrong.

I give up somewhere in the middle of the year, not with the trying but with the expectation of anything else but failure. I say, I'm not a good speller. Words are for speaking, hearing, and feeling. I don't pass one spelling test that year, and I am trying hard. It's on my mind a lot. It's why I can still remember the spelling tests. Still, despite all this, I love words.

This is early on the road, the academic road lined with my failure at words, a road that would get straighter and flatter later, but not for a while. At this point, it's got lots of rocks, branches, and twisted snags in it. It's not a road you can jog on easily. And in some places, you have to get down on all fours and crawl with blood on your hands and knees, pull sticks and twigs out of your hair, or pluck gravel out of the palms of your hands. Everyone around you tells you it's worth it, and you believe them—rather, you have to believe them, otherwise . . . You believe you can do it, make it farther, or further (whatever), down the road with a bit of your nana's amazing grace.

Things feel bleak that year, third grade. But as was the case in many points in my life, something wonderful happens. I find a smooth, level part in the road. At the time, I find a collection of books by Donald J. Sobol that I love, *Encyclopedia Brown*. They are books about a boy, Leroy Brown, so smart that they call him Encyclopedia Brown. His dad is the Idaville, Florida, Police Chief, and Encyclopedia Brown helps his dad solve crimes and mysteries. The books are written so that the reader can solve each mystery or crime along with Encyclopedia Brown. These are the first books I yearn for, savor as I read them.

The words seem much better than the spelling test words. They are more alive to me. They make me solve mysteries. I am the hero in these words. I am part of the telling of the story because I get to solve the mystery with Encyclopedia Brown. The words are incantatory, magical. I cannot wait each day to get back to the books. They make me feel like I felt as I read for the second grade reading contest, hungry for words, only this time I am not chasing a trophy, or first place, or validation from a teacher. I am chasing words themselves, words that make me something. I gobble them up each afternoon after school, reading out loud as I walk home away from school with its White rules for spelling and language, and judged numerically on thin, white sheets of paper.

But these words in these books are medicine for the cuts and scrapes caused by spelling tests at school and by teachers who misunderstand me. I swallow spoonfuls of vowels and consonants daily; soon it's ladles, then buckets. I start to feel better on the way home back to Statz. The cuts and bruises of the road begin to heal. I feel I can walk, continue along the road. I walk away from school, homeward, toward real language, soft sweater language, reading along the way about a smart kid, Encyclopedia Brown, who makes a difference in his town, a boy who can't be put down.

I think: Leroy Brown, you gotta be ghetto. You ain't White. Wit that name? C'mon. The cover and pictures make him look White. And I guess he talks that way in the book. Still in those moments walking home and reading, I want so badly to be a smart Brown kid, not a spelling flunky. I wanta be Leroy Brown. Somehow both Brown and White. That cat solves crimes. People like him. He got a dad, and nat dad listen to him. They partners. I know I can do that. It's just all this school shit, the language of school, White teachers and they White rules and White language that come from they White world. Imma play both parts. Imma be Brown and White. So I put the darker language of Statz in a closet in my mind and lock it. I tell myself: Imma –no—I'm *gonna* be Encyclopedia Brown. I'm gonna make a difference in my town. No one can put me down.

CHAPTER 4.

RACE-JUDGEMENTS AND THE TACIT LANGUAGE WAR

By the sixth grade, we were living in Pecos Trailer Park in Las Vegas. We'd moved out of the ghetto of North LV into a White working-class area. I'd come back from an afternoon of swimming. The park had a swimming pool, one I'd eventually be banned from swimming in by the White trailer park manager, who didn't like us, my brother and me, called us "wetbacks." At this moment, we were not banned.

It was a fun afternoon. I made a friend at the pool, Chris, a tall, thin, White kid with family from the Buffalo area. He was French Canadian, smart and very White. He couldn't even tan. Just got red. I liked him. He was the only kid in the park who could officially be friends with my brother and me. His dad was rarely around, worked a lot.

After the pool, I went home. I was in the bathroom changing, and as I slipped off my swimming trunks, I stood in front of the mirror looking at a sharp tan line on my waist and thighs. It went from dark brown to what looked like a pale white, the kind of white I saw in Chris' face and arms. In that moment, I wanted badly to be White, maybe French Canadian. I made a face in the mirror, one of disgust. I saw my skin. It looked like dirt. I rubbed and rubbed and rubbed, then got a washcloth and washed and washed, but the dark Brown would not lighten. The dirt would not go away.

~~~

In a very real sense, we are made up of the words we know, as much as those words are made by the material conditions we live in and through. As a boy, my relations to words, like everyone's, were cradled in my life-conditions, in my poverty, in my curiosity, in my love for my mom who I thought could do—and did—magic through steno pads, delicate scripts, and careful planning. And this is all to say that you cannot read a text without using the material reality of your existence to make sense of it as it makes sense of you.

Thus, when we have the ability to understand, manipulate, and question words, we read our world differently, perhaps better, because then the practice of literacy offers critical distance from our world as much as a way to make meaning out of it. In Freire's view, critical literacy produces questions the answers to which are about us, our material world, and the words that help us make sense of all three things. This arguably leads to liberation, if liberation means a critical view of ourselves, our world, and the words that mediate it all.

But wait. It's not that simple, is it? Literacy may be the key to liberation, but not all literacies liberate. Who controls literacy and its standards? Where do those things come from? Am I just trading one ideological shackle for another? Am I just choosing my oppressor by choosing the language I use or by accepting the language presented to me? Maybe there are no third-party oppressors. Maybe I am oppressing myself? Maybe literacy is just another way of saying I have been colonized.

Many people use critical notions of literacy and language against all of us for their own purposes. Consider Lee Atwater's language policy, one later called "the Southern strategy," a way of invoking race but never mentioning it because it had become taboo by the 1970s. It is racial language without using racial language, and it's still used today for a wide range of discussions and decisions. Atwater was a Republican political strategist and advisor to Ronald Reagan and George H. W. Bush. In a 1981 interview, he explains this language strategy (warning: he uses the N-word):

> You start out in 1954 by saying, "Nigger, nigger, nigger."
> By 1968 you can't say "nigger"—that hurts you. Backfires.
> So you say stuff like forced busing, state's rights and all
> that stuff. You're getting so abstract. Now you're talking
> about cutting taxes, and all these things . . . you're talking
> about are totally economic things and a byproduct of them
> is Blacks get hurt worse than Whites. And subconsciously
> maybe that is part of it. . . . But I'm saying that if it is get-
> ting that abstract, and that coded, that we are doing away
> with the racial problem one way or the other. You follow
> me—because obviously sitting around saying, "We want to
> cut taxes," "we want to cut this," is much more abstract than
> even the busing thing, and a hell of a lot more abstract than
> "Nigger, nigger."[1]

The Southern strategy for politics was really a language strategy that maintained White supremacy. Its method was to get rid of explicitly racist language but keep racist outcomes. It avoided explicitly racializing the policies being promoted and ignored or denied their racist consequences. It's also a White

---

1   The Atwater interview is available in Rick Perlstein, "Exclusive: Lee Atwater's Infamous 1981 Interview on the Southern Strategy," *The Nation*, November 13, 2012, https://www.the nation.com/article/archive/exclusive-lee-atwaters-infamous-1981-interview-southern-strategy/. A version can also be found in DiAngelo, *White Fragility*, 33.

language supremacy strategy that HOWLs at its audience. The language stays abstract and nonracial by being unconcerned with the racialized and other political consequences of the things referenced, even though the consequences are quite racial in reality.

The Southern language strategy understood that hearing or reading a text and judging it to be a clear expression is not a neutral act. It is not an apolitical judgement. It is an exercise of a person's biases and politics—that is, an exercise of your own personal relations to power and language. Your ability to understand an instance of language as clear or persuasive—as meaningful in a certain way—is connected to where you have been, with whom you have communed, what languages you have used, and what languages were sung to you in the cradle of your mother's arms as an infant. And as long as your audience doesn't know this, you can manipulate them, get them to agree to things that they wouldn't otherwise agree to, things they may even disagree with if stated another way, things that may even work toward their own oppression.

The Southern language strategy worked from the critical assumption that language can mean different things to different people because we all have different relations to language and material conditions that create those relations and because these differences are patterned and somewhat predictable. It encourages the listener or audience to engage in fast thinking, namely the availability heuristic: I don't see cutting taxes as a racial issue or having any racist consequences, so it isn't.[2] If I see it this way, others can (or should) too. This is an unseen, universal, orientation to the world wedded to another, hyperindividualism. The Southern language strategy used fast thinking and HOWL to promote racist government policies, policies that seemed to be about other things, such as cutting taxes, fairness, a war on drugs and gangs, family values, or good schools.

This kind of language strategy can easily oppress or liberate. It is a White strategy for language mostly because it has been used to promote White supremacy. It is a primary strategy in the tacit language war. But anyone can use the practice to their advantage, convince people to agree on something that ends up having racist and White supremacist outcomes, yet never mention race.

Politicians are not the only ones who consider the ambiguity of language and meaning. We are always wondering if others are saying one thing but meaning other things, or if others hear something else in our words. This language

---

2   As I discuss in the Appendix essay to this book, the availability heuristic is a thinking process that our brains use to make fast judgements from information we have most readily available to us at the moment. It inadvertently tricks us into assuming that the available information an individual has is enough to make a decision at hand. It's fast thinking as described in Kahneman, *Thinking*, 80–81.

paradox is also what makes things like literature and poetry wonderful, interesting, and surprising. We don't escape the slipperiness of language and race by denying its ambiguity; we help ourselves and others by understanding it better.

LANGUAGING AS RACE-JUDGEMENTS

It's hard to explain to some, especially to White people who usually have never experienced racial ambiguity in social settings, just how difficult it can be, how unsettling it is, for others to constantly misunderstand you, to mistake you for Mexican, for example, when you are not, then act in racist ways on that mistaken judgement. Additionally, being perceived as racially ambiguous as I have been complicates one's English language learning because racial and gender markers often help people understand each other. We judge each other's words through a variety of bodily and other cues as well as what we see on the page or hear in a voice. This is why things like comedy, sarcasm, and satire are so difficult to recognize in a text. They are a lot easier to get in person when you have more cues to go on than bare words.

The term "race-judgements" makes explicit the association between our notions about race and our judgements of others' ideas and words that get wedded together, often unknowingly. That is, what I'm trying to identify are the ways that our own understandings of race are always already interlaced with our words, language practices, and judgements. Everyone has these biases, and we use them all the time. And if you think you don't have ideas about race, or particular races, or you think you don't use those ideas to make judgements, then you haven't systematically examined your own ideas or the ways you make judgements.

Just because you don't immediately recognize racial, gender, or other biases in your judgements doesn't mean you don't have those biases. It just means you don't recognize them. They are not immediately apparent. And we are not often in the habit of examining what we do not immediately see, feel, or hear. It's like looking for something lost and unknown to you in a room filled with things, except that you don't realize that you've lost that thing. You aren't looking for the thing you don't know you've lost in a room filled with things that seem not lost.

If you still don't believe that you have implicit racial biases, or you want to find out how strong your own biases are, you can test yourself online. Project Implicit, a nonprofit organization that started in 1998 and moved to online testing in 2011, offers free implicit bias tests on a range of social dimensions, one being race. The organization was founded by three scientists, Anthony Greenwald (University of Washington), Mahzarin Banaji (Harvard University), and Brian Nosek (University of Virginia).[3] To date, they've tested millions of people's biases and found that everyone has them to some degree. No one gets to escape racial implicit bias.[4] We all have racial biases, and we use them because making judgements and decisions is a cognitive act that requires biases of all kinds. That is, to judge means to apply biases to a question or problem in order to come to some decision.

Even the idea that you don't think race affects how you judge language or people is an understanding about race that you use, but that claim doesn't hold up to the copious research that Banaji, Greenwald, and Nosek of Project Implicit, among others, have pioneered. Of course, race is only one social dimension that informs our judgements and language practices. There are many others, gender, sexual orientation, class, economic standing, religious status, to name a few common ones. I focus on race because that dimension has played a key role in my own literacy experiences—it has been most salient to me—and it is historically linked to literacy in the US. Furthermore, race's significance to language and its judgement goes mostly unnoticed by most people. And it does much harm. Just like the Southern language strategy, we should pay attention to our implicit racial biases. If we don't, we may be languaging in racist ways and perhaps contributing to our own oppression in the process.

Cheryl I. Harris, the Rosalinde and Arthur Gilbert Foundation Chair in Civil Rights and Civil Liberties at UCLA School of Law, has shown how U.S. law has historically understood Whiteness as property and acted on this premise in the courts.[5] This has direct bearing on literacy in the US as White property in the various court decisions about separate but equal accommodations and school segregation. When the very institutions that are charged with educating everyone conspire to preserve Whiteness as property with the institutions that are meant to safeguard everyone's liberties (the judicial system), it is very difficult for anyone to see what is happening. It is difficult to see that underneath what we are learning is enslaving us with new kinds of chains—chains of words welded by our race-judgements. It's internal colonization.

In *Literacy and Racial Justice: The Politics of Learning After Brown v. Board of Education*, Catherine Prendergast argues convincingly that historically in the US the courts have worked from a fundamental premise that "literacy is first

---

3   To take any of Project Implicit's tests of implicit bias, go to https://implicit.harvard.edu/implicit/. The website offers several implicit association tests (IAT) beyond the Race IAT, including tests that deal with age, gender, disability, and more.

4   See Appendix A or page 47 of Mahzarin R. Banaji and Anthony G. Greenwald, *Blind Spot*.

5   Cheryl I. Harris, "Whiteness as Property," *Harvard Law Review* 106, no. 8 (1993): 1707–1791, https://doi.org/10.2307/1341787.

and foremost White property."[6] She looks closely at the logics and consequences of Brown v. Board (1954), Washington v. Davis (1976), and The Regents of the University of California v. Bakke (1978), all of which demonstrate what Prendergast calls "the economy of literacy as a White property," or a dynamic rooted in figurative or literal "White flight" in places, like schools, where people of color begin to accumulate. She explains the dynamic: "Literacy standards are perceived to be falling or in peril of falling" when too many people of color, often African American and Latine, are included or present in the place in question, be it a school, police department, community, etc.[7] These racist biases of our past have submerged in many ways and become implicit biases today.

Now, I do not mean to suggest that we are all racist or prejudiced because we notice or use ideas about race in the judgements we make about people's language. I mean that, whether we recognize it or not, our ideas about race travel with our language and the judgements we make in language because that's how language and judgements are built. Judgement can only be built with biases. Judgement is the application of biases to something else, like a decision to cross the street or the many micro-decisions about what this text is saying as you read these words.

To see a stop sign at an intersection and recognize it as red in color is a judgement. You've applied one bias about what your brain decodes as the color red to what you see when you look at the sign. To further interpret the red stop sign as a signal to apply your brakes and stop at the intersection is another judgement based on your previous judgement about what you've understood to be the red sign.

Some biases are benign like identifying the color red. Some are poisonous, such as those about inherent attributes of African Americans or Asians because of how they use English. Some are somewhere in between, depending on the context. Biases are necessary and inherent, but they can also be harmful to us if we don't realize exactly the nature of our particular biases. If we don't understand them, then we don't get to choose them. We just inherit them uncritically, and they end up controlling us because they seem natural and absolute.

This gives us less power as languagelings and perpetuates lots of unfairness and, well, White language supremacy. While I didn't have the words for it at the time, I felt this problem of implicit racial bias all around me growing up because of how so many people confused me for someone else. My perceived racial ambiguity to others gave me some insight into what later would be termed racial implicit bias.

---

6   Catherine Prendergast, *Literacy and Racial Justice: the Politics of Learning after Brown v. Board of Education* (Urbana: Southern Illinois University Press, 2003), 167.

7   Prendergast, 41.

Growing up on Statz Street, I was seen as not White and not Black. My brother and I were the only Brown kids in a neighborhood of almost all African American families. We used the Black English[8] of our neighborhood and friends, but not in school. And because I was not seen as Black or White, I often felt misunderstood since the discussions and representations of race in North LV and most of the US were Black and White. Framing race in this way left people like me out. People would often ask me, "Where are you from?" or "What is your background?" I could tell by the look on their faces they were confused by me. Even after I would say, "I'm Japanese American," they'd say, "Hmm, you don't look Japanese," skipping the American part—that was obvious. Or they'd say, "wow, you have good English." They expected me to have some kind of accent. They assumed my English would be "broken."

I didn't look American, but I sounded like it. What is a Japanese boy supposed to look and sound like? What is an American supposed to look and sound like, for that matter? We know the answers, but we can't say them in public. Which is another way to say that we know our racial biases, the image and sounds of an "American" that pops into your head when you hear the word, and we hope that one day that image and those sounds will change, be broader, more racially ambiguous, more open to regional dialects, more gender fluid perhaps. But what exactly are we doing about changing that image or those sounds?

I don't mean what do you change in our head or heart. I mean, what are you *doing* to create those changes? What language structures are you changing? Changing language structures in schools and society starts with understanding our biases, questioning our judgements of language and people as race-judgements, not to beat ourselves up or blame people, but to do better tomorrow, to take responsibility, to recognize that implicit biases are working. Ultimately, it's a systemic answer to racism, at least to the race-judgements we all make with language.

---

8   This version of English has been called "Ebonics," but that has become a negative term today. It is also called African American English, or African American Vernacular English. I use both African American English and Black English to refer generally to the version of English that is associated with African Americans in the US today. A lot of research validates Black English as a rule-bound, complex language. To read more, see Geneva Smitherman, *Talkin and Testifyin*; Geneva Smitherman, *Word from the Mother: Language and African Americans* (New York: Routledge, 2006); John Russell Rickford and Russell John Rickford, *Spoken Soul: The Story of Black English* (New York: John Wiley and Sons, 2000); John R. Rickford, "Geographical Diversity, Residential Segregation, and The Vitality of African American Vernacular English in Its Speakers," *Transforming Anthropology* 18, no. 1 (April 2010): 28–34, https://doi.org/10.1111/j.1548-7466.2010.01067.x.

RACE-JUDGEMENTS EVERYWHERE

I'm a teenager, a senior in high school in Corvallis, Oregon. I'm with my girl-friend, who is White (Irish mostly), born and raised in Oregon. We are shopping at a local clothing store. I have a question. We both walk up to the register where the attendant is waiting. The attendant, who is a White woman and appears to be in her late 20s or early 30s, addresses my girlfriend, "how can I help you?" I ask my question. The attendant answers but looks at my girlfriend, as if she had asked the question. The attendant glances at me a few times during the exchange, as if she could be nervous. She never speaks directly to me. I'm used to this in groups, people talking away from me yet to me. It doesn't seem unusual, even if it annoys me.

Around the same time in my life, I'm in a department store, one of the big ones. There are only White patrons in this store. It's Oregon, so this is normal, but obvious to me. I'm just browsing, killing time. I can swear a man is follow-ing me. I go down one aisle. A few seconds later, he turns into the same aisle. He is older, White, and dressed in business casual. I leave that aisle and turn down another a few aisles away. A few seconds later, he's there again. This occurs several more times, but he never approaches me. He's always just looking in the same aisle. This is not the first time this has happened to me, the feeling that others are watching me shop, wondering why am I there, what am I up to, fol-lowing just a few paces behind. I think that maybe I'm just being paranoid. But I can hear the words of the trailer park manager of my youth echo in my head, "you are a troublemaker," "go back to where you came from, Spic." I leave the store feeling guilty for something, but I don't know what.

I'm in college at Oregon State University in the same town. I am a senior, an English major. I recently found my calling, language and rhetoric. My class, an advanced writing course, is having a discussion about language and identity. Who belongs in the club and who doesn't. How do we decide? In the class discussion, I say it's often hard to separate our language practices from who we are, from our identities. Today, I'd qualify this. We are fragmented, have many identities, some social, some personal or understood by ourselves alone. I'd also say we focus on particular social dimensions in order to purposefully make our-selves. I'd say that race, language, and judgement are symbiotic. We don't just make judgements with language. We make language with judgements. And we are made by judgements and language.

Erik, a friend I admire because he is a year farther along than me in grad school, is sitting next to me in the class. Erik always has something smart to say. He seems to have read everything. He is a new grad student that year, got his B.A. at Berkeley, where his dad, the corporate lawyer, and his grandpa did. He was a legacy. Erik is White from a Norweigian background, took private guitar lessons as a teenager. He is firmly middle class, likely higher, always casual about his money and spending, or the vacations in Norway to see his mother's family. I admire this about him, his ease with everything, how he wears his privilege with such unassuming grace.

In the conversation, Erik says to me, "I consider you like any other normal person here. I don't think of you as Brown or Asian." He means I belong in the club, the English language club. He means I fit in. The comment feels like other things White people have said to me, like "your English is really good," or "why are you here?" I feel my friend's unexamined biases in his words, biases he's never had to question because his life, his material conditions, up to that point have not presented him with such contradictions. I know he has good intentions. He's not a bad guy, quite the opposite. And yet, his words feel like a hard, stinging pat on the back, one that thumps you and jolts your body forward. Race travels with our words, with us. For some, the connection is more salient.

I think: if I'm *like normal*, then I'm not normal, right? The comment makes me feel abnormal. It makes me feel my Brownness while denying my own feelings about such matters. Always the Brown spot in the educational bowl of milk. I smile, knowing he is meaning to be complementary, but the pat-wound stings. I have no words after that.

That spring, between graduating in the winter quarter and starting in the same department as a grad student and new teaching assistant (TA), I am working at a coffee shop. I'm a barista. I love the job. It's a good local company. They treat their employees well. We get vacation, summer BBQs, good hours, and a 401k. It's where I learn what good coffee is. I'm working a rare afternoon and evening shift. I usually work the early morning shift.

I can see the sun going down through the front windows. Shadows on tables are getting longer, as I recognize another new grad student walking in. She's a few years older than me, Cecilia. She's White, and conducts herself in a way that assumes a lot of things. I think of the Simon and Garfunkel song when I say her name in my head. She has much White skin privilege. I don't think she knows it. I read her as arrogant. I don't know her that well, but I had a few classes with her the previous year. She is a good student, but not as good as she thinks she is. She works hard though, has a child, is a single-parent. She feels her class and gender mostly. Those dimensions seem most salient for her. We both finished the B.A. at the same time.

I'm at the front counter. It's just her and me. We say hi to each other, and she asks, "did you get one?" She's meaning did I get a TA spot, would I be teaching First-Year Writing in the fall while also taking grad courses. It takes me a second to realize what she's asking about. I get excited.

"Yeah, I got one." I smile, thinking she'll say she did too. I received my letter that same week. In my naivete at that moment, I assume every grad student got a TA position, but no. Not every grad student gets one. They are a recruitment tool and a way to support some grad students in their education. Each TA position is coveted because it pays for your tuition, gives you a monthly stipend, and offers valuable teaching experience. "Did you get one," I ask.

"No," her face turns on that word. "*You* got one?" she asks, cocking her head back a bit, scrunching her nose as she says "you." She is clearly shocked. "Why would they give *you* a position?" Again, she emphasizes "you." It is a mystery to her. Somehow the TA position is not in her grasp. It is not as close to her as she assumes it is. At this moment, I doubt myself. Did I get a TA spot because I'm a minority? Am I a token?

"I don't know," I say, and turn to my work, feigning business, as the stings of her "yous" are still in the air between us.

I'm now in a Ph.D. program in Rhetoric and Composition at Washington State University in Pullman, a college town on the East side of the state right on the border of Idaho. I have to take a second language for the degree. It's a requirement. So I choose French. I took two years in junior high, three in high school, and two more as an undergrad at OSU. While it's been years since I thought about it, I've been studying and brushing up on my French for the last six or seven months. The test is a translation test. I submit something from my field originally written in French to the French professor in charge of the proficiency exams. He chooses a section from that piece for me to translate in his office, then determines if I pass.

I come into his office. I meet the French professor. I'm a little nervous. This is high stakes. He's an older, tall, greying, White man with big rough hands, like he's known work in his life, but a long time ago. He has lots of Japanese paraphernalia on his walls, kimonos, paintings, pictures, little things in frames. He's been to Japan every year for many years. He tells me this. I'm really nervous now. If I don't pass the test, I cannot get my Ph.D. He holds the keys to that gate. Why is there so much Japanese in this French professor's office? Shouldn't it be pictures of Paris or Nice?

He recognizes my name as Japanese. He talks and talks about Japan, how much he loves it and the people. This is not helping me, I think. Get out of your own skin for a minute, man. I feel like we've been talking for twenty minutes about a place I've never been. He asks me if I know Japanese. Is that required here? I'm getting more nervous and intimidated. I wonder, does he ask this shit of every grad student who comes in to take a French translation exam? I feel like I'm supposed to cradle his White ego, make him feel like he's okay because he loves Japan so much, like I'm a tool for his validation. I give short answers to his questions.

I take the test. He looks at my translation of the section and tells me, "well, this could be right, but I don't really understand the rhetorical theory. So I'm not sure if it passes. You'll have to take it again." Fuck, I think. I gotta bear *this* again? No benefit of the doubt here, White, Japanophile French professor? It feels like another hard slap on the back by someone who thinks they are doing me a favor.

Years later, I live in Fresno. I'm a professor at Fresno State. My wife and I just bought a house. It needs a permit for an addition to the garage, my office. I go into the permitting office downtown with my contractor. He is Mexican, has dark skin and a thick Spanish accent. We apply for the permit, and the White man behind the desk says, "it will be about two weeks." He's firm about this. I'm upset because we planned on starting the addition that week. I go home, tell my wife, Kelly, who is White from a middle class family in Oregon. Her grandma on her dad's side is Welsh, one of the original settlers of Monmouth, Oregon, where her mom and dad still live.

We met at OSU, where her father and grandmother had graduated. Her grandma was a professor at Western Oregon State College (now Western Oregon University), up the road from OSU in Monmouth. Their family several generations back was one of the original families who donated land from their land claims so that Monmouth College, a normal school, could be established, which is now WOU. That same day, Kelly goes into the same Fresno office, talks to the same White guy in her Whitely Oregon standard English inherited from her family in Oregon, and leaves with the permits to begin work immediately. No problem.

There are a lot of ways to explain my experiences. Maybe that store attendant just liked my girlfriend, maybe business casual guy was just shopping, maybe my college friend was really being nice, maybe Cecilia was just upset at herself, maybe Japanophile French professor was trying to soothe my nerves or make a connection with me, maybe something happened in the Fresno City office in the two hours between my visit and Kelly's that opened up a spot for a new permit? Maybe I'm just too sensitive about this stuff.

What makes race-judgements so tricky to see or understand, however, is how all people of color experience them in our daily lives, how often they happen, how they can seem so normal, natural, harmless to White people, how they seem like other things. And how quick many White people want to downplay them, or brush them aside, tell us that we are too sensitive, that we are seeing race in everything when it ain't there.

It is very difficult for any of us to separate our own words, or those of others, from the feelings that travel with them, feelings that may have started somewhere else, somewhere earlier in a government subsidized apartment building on Statz, or in a third grade classroom filled with unknowable words, or in a department store, or in the questions of others about where you are from, or why you are there in that place. Our feelings that we carry like luggage through countless airports halo onto our judgements about people and language around us. We keep opening our luggage unknowingly, letting its contents spill out, but we don't notice. My language is me and how I know much of myself. It's also you and how you know yourself. It's how I tell me to others. It is how others make sense of me, even if I think it is the wrong sense to make, yet it is also their sense they make to get them through their airports.

This isn't, however, just a matter of knowing our own biases. There are larger structures operating beyond individuals. Most of the time in the U.S., Brown equals not American, and that equals not worth responding to, not the correct person to address, even when I have asked the question. Brown means I'm a possible thief, even though I've never stolen anything from any store in my life. But I look like I have. Brown means I'm not supposed to take a teaching position from a White woman. I'm not supposed to teach English to college students in Oregon. Brown means I don't get the benefit of the doubt, my words are suspect despite my Japaneseness.

Brown means I must wait. White people have to go first. White people get the benefit of the doubt. They get the permits to start work immediately. Brown folks get our benefits in two weeks. And Asians, well, we are the good ones, the "model minority," the model that artificially makes other people of color look like slackers, even though this hides a lot of problems—and it ain't true.[9] Hang us on a wall or use us as exotic stories to tell others, but that's it. We are supposed to validate White peoples' sense that they are not prejudiced or racist. My yellow parts can cover enough of my Brown parts, assuming that I sound White, so that I'm *like normal*, and I can punch a White man's ticket to ride the antiracist bus. I get to be in the club, but I don't get to determine my membership. White people do. My membership ain't a real membership. It's not based on merit or

---

9   Studies have shown that Asian Americans with similar educational levels as White Americans have higher rates of unemployment. See Marlene Kim, *Unfairly Disadvantaged? Asian Americans and Unemployment During and After the Great Recession (2007–10)* (Washington, DC: Economic Policy Institute, 2012), https://www.epi.org/publication/ib323-asian-american -unemployment/. Furthermore, the category of "Asian" or "Asian American" is quite complex and diverse, not simply in the cultural and linguistic backgrounds that this term references, but the vastly different living conditions and lives that are typical in such various groups. For instance, in the US, those of Indian descent have an average household income of $101,591, while those from Bangladesh earn an average of $51,331. Asian American poverty rates (13.8%) are higher than that of White Americans (10.9%), with Hmong (37.8%) and Cambodian (29.3%) the highest in poverty. For more on these economic nuances, see Sammi Chen, "Racial Wealth Snapshot: Asian Americans," *Prosperity Now Blog*, May 10, 2018, https://prosperitynow .org/blog/racial-wealth-snapshot-asian-americans.

my inherent worth. It's contingent on the gracious attitudes of White people around me.

These race-judgements are difficult for anyone to admit, because they feel damning. We are supposed to be better than this. Still, the image and sounds of an "American" in most people's minds is clear. A bias for a White man as an American is, of course, not something you admit to if you don't want to be called racist in today's society. So we say an American can look like anyone, sound like anyone, but our race-judgements betray this wishful thinking. We say that we do not see race. We are beyond it. We're post-racial. We say it is just the rules. Permits take two weeks. Most Asians have accents. We say there was probable cause to think he was going to steal something. We say we didn't mean to . . . fill in the blank. Halos over all our words.

Perhaps this is because the racial biases in the standardized Englishes of civil society have not changed over the last two hundred or so years. Structures are durable. Maybe it's because our relations to people and languages that are different from the White, middle class standard have not changed. Maybe those who make the rules haven't changed. Maybe the training in language and our attitudes about language haven't changed. Maybe the same White, middle- and upper-class, monolingual, masculine habits of English continue to be the only standard against which everyone is judged. Maybe all we've done is stopped talking about the differences. Maybe we talk about our similarities as if that negates differences. Maybe we all use the Southern language strategy in our daily lives, talking about racialized things without mentioning race. Maybe we just stopped admitting that we see and hear differences, allowing our biases to run implicitly wild.

The absence of racial talk in society has meant we have not critically read our own words, and the relations they create with our world and others. Our inattention to race-judgements in our English languages has been a recipe not just for the denial but the reproduction of racial problems. How do we get to hard solutions about racism and White supremacy if we have no language for them, if we have no questions about them that we all can discuss? Yet sometimes, I admit, language is too magical to talk about. It has too much historical power. We don't always know how to proceed, how to untangle or unbend tangled and bent words. But we have to.

In Mrs. Whitmore's second grade class, the same class that I had won the reading contest, one of my Black classmates called me, "honky." We were casual friends, or friends at school. I don't recall his name, but I don't think we were arguing or fighting either.

The word was so loud that Mrs. Whitmore heard it about twenty feet away, or maybe she was listening for it. I don't remember our exchange. I just remember standing in front of Mrs. Whitmore next to my friend, feeling guilty, the class behind us supposedly working. This White teacher looked down at us with stern eyes, wagging a finger in one hand, the knuckles of her other on the corner of her desk. "Do you know what that word means?" her eyes darting between him and me. Her silence and waiting for an answer hurt. I mean, my skin burned.

I didn't expect such harshness from her. Her words had hard intonations, "what that word means." The T's and D's had something extra in them, like stones. I felt assaulted, hit by little word hammers in the face. I thought she might actually physically hurt me. I didn't really know how she wanted us to answer her question, even though I'd heard that world a lot around school and on Statz. It wasn't usually thrown at me, so I was shocked because it just seemed like we were talking, nothing to get upset about. But she was clearly upset.

"Honky is a mean word. Can you think of another word just as mean?"

Mrs. Whitmore looked right at my friend. He lowered his head and brushed his hand along a table near him that had art supplies and stacks of construction paper on it. Another long, burning pause. More stones and hammers. I just stood there, silent. I knew the word she was wanting us to imagine in our heads. The word was too magical, too powerful, too heavy. I could not say it.

I wish that I could say that I was righteously mad at her, asking us to conjure that word in our heads, as if a word for a word was the appropriate response here, but I wasn't that keen. I wish I could say that I understood how unfair and badly she handled this incident, but I didn't know. I wish I could have just thought: "Go ahead, say it, say the fucking word! You want to square things? As if that word will square it. So square it, angry White lady! Show us how wrong we are!" But I was frightened and confused. I was seven. I was not that righteous. I was silent.

What was equally confusing and disorienting to me in all this was that I knew that the word honkey was really about her, not me. I'm not a honky. I'm Asian, and to some Mexican, but Brown for sure—that was in my head. Maybe that's why I didn't take offense to the word. I knew this, and even if my friend didn't, he knew I was Brown. No one mistook me for White.

Now, I see unexamined implicit racial biases circulating in that moment in all three of us. The bias of race as only a binary. I had to fit into that binary somewhere. The bias of being outside of race, of thinking that others' ideas of who I am did not matter or were wrong. I stood aloof, outside of the word honky, even though my mom is White. The bias of assuming everyone must be treated exactly the same. It is a language stance of false neutrality, one that ignores history and context in the name of fairness. You cannot ignore so many structures that make you.

All words are not created equal. The two words in question were not equal in power. And yet, the one with the most power got to act on her biases, act as if they cause the same damage, act on her halo of feelings.

RACE-MIXING AND LANGUAGING

When race is a mixture, or when we mix up race, mistake it, race-judgements also get mixed and mixed up. My mixed race background has often created problems for most people around me, particularly when they first meet me. My father is Japanese from Hawai'i, two generations removed from immigration to Hawai'i. This makes him Sansei, and my brother and me, Yonsei. Everyone on my dad's side is Japanese from Japan. My mom is a mixture of a number of ethnic heritages: English and maybe Scottish, likely Irish, and either Greek or Italian. But much of that history is fuzzy. Her family migrated a generation before from Oklahoma and Arkansas to California and finally settled in Oregon.

I never really knew my dad. By the time I started school, my parents had long since divorced, and my mom was a single parent living far away from her family in Oregon. Our dad didn't pay any child support until I was deep into high school, but my mom was ingenious, smart, and hard working. She worked two, sometimes three jobs, all low-paying, most menial. During my time on Statz Street, I didn't feel rejected and shunned by my friends and neighbors. I just felt different, but not in a bad way. I wasn't ostracized, or put down. It was school that gave me most of my trouble.

Once we reached junior high school, we had moved to a primarily White, working class trailer park on a different side of town, near a working class Latine neighborhood. No one in Pecos Trailer Park wanted us there from the first day. There were petitions to get us kicked out and lots of complaints about us, the two Brown kids. When my mom signed the lease originally, my brother and I were not with her—she looked White—so when we showed up, everyone freaked out. My mom had to call an attorney to threaten the park to leave us alone. You can't kick people out because they are Brown. That's essentially what the attorney had to say.

The Vegas sun darkened my skin considerably, so much so that I was usually mistaken as Mexican, called "wetback" and "beaner" every day by those neighbors and others at school. I can remember the awful, guilty feeling in my skin that I'd feel in every room I entered, every social situation. I could see their stares of disgust or disdain when they looked at my brother and me. The racism and resentment toward us was explicit. I can remember the feeling of cold dismissal by the White working class parents of my friends living around us in the neighborhood. It was a cold stare from their porch, a slow turn away. No words. No smile. No "how are you." No "good day," just silence and stares. We'd gotten out of the ghetto, I'd thought, but had we gone up? It often didn't feel like it.

At park get-togethers, someone would inevitably ask me, "why are you here?" It wasn't an existential question, but one about "going back to where you came from." I was told that many times too. Once my brother and I crouched beneath our front window, hiding alone in our trailer, as a middle aged White man from down the street yelled at us from outside with his fist in the air. "Your days are numbered!" he said to us, with a crowd of White kids around him.

We couldn't figure out what the hell we'd done, but that guy was really mad, demanding that we come out and pay the piper. Keep in mind, I'm a child of 12 or 13, not an adult. He, the White man yelling at us, was the adult. Needless to say, I did not feel at home or welcome most of the time in that trailer park. It seemed pretty clear. No race mixing.

It wasn't just our neighbors that made such race-judgements. It was the park management too. My brother and I were often stopped while walking around the park by Fred, the park manager, who would ride around in a golf cart each day. He'd stop us, ask us in an accusatory way, "What are you doing? Someone was throwing rocks at a trailer down the street. Did you do that?" This was not a question he asked any of the other numerous kids in the park. Just my brother and me. I know this because I asked the other kids, and I knew Fred's grandkids, who also lived in the park. They told me in no uncertain terms that their grandfather, Fred, did not like us. He was looking for ways to get rid of the two beaners in the park.

Of course, we never did any of the stuff they accused us of. Mom was explicit about us always being "on our best behavior." The family had two strikes against us, one more and they could kick us out for real. That threat was in an official letter from the park management. Forget the fact that there was no reason for the two strikes in the first place. The lesson I learned was: Some folks only get one pitch at the plate. Others get more. Life is not generous or understanding when you are Brown.

My mom lived her life by this creed: You get one swing at the plate. Don't fuck it up. But Fred and the other White, working class adults in the park didn't care about any of this. Their racism was obvious, even to a child. They weren't trying to be fair. They were using their race-judgements to preserve the world they knew, only they called those judgements about behavior and wrong-doing. It was a kind of Southern language strategy, with actual racist language bursting out at times. They never would have said they were racist. But their world didn't have Brown kids playing with their kids in it, or dating their daughters. That was always off limits. Their world only understood Brown people as beaners and trouble makers who resided on the other side of the trailer park wall. No place for Japanese nuance. Go back to where you came from. We don't want you here. That was always their implication.

From my perspective, I hadn't done anything wrong. I was a good kid. My favorite hobby was reading and writing stories for god's sake. How was I so bad? We couldn't leave our trailer after school because my mom didn't get home from work until after 6 pm. How could I get into any trouble? I didn't even like doing any of the things that they accused me of constantly, throwing rocks at trailers, chalking up sidewalks and streets, vandalizing soda machines. I was not a risk taker. I wanted people to like me. There was too much at stake. Only one swing. I had to make every at-bat count.

None save Chris, my French Canadian friend, was ever allowed to socialize with us in public. That friend, whom my brother and I still know today, lived with this dad, who was a no-bullshit guy. He drove a truck and was gone a lot, so he had no time for trailer park politics. Outside of that one friend, we had to have the rest of our friends in secret. We, the Brown kids, were off limits. Chris did not fucking care about the others, and he didn't like the trailer park management either.

What may have helped at this moment, the transition from junior high to high school, was that I was starting to do well in school. The three of us took classes in school together, some honors classes. Chris was really smart, likely had a near photographic memory, spoke French, English, and some Islandic. He respected others who were smart. The other kids in the park didn't seem smart to him, or to me for that matter. They weren't in our classes in school, and they didn't do things we did, like read for fun.

There was likely a class thing going on too. Chris always had a thing about class, that is, him not being working class or lower class. He had lived in houses in nice neighborhoods before this. He could afford things like new clothes, albums, and video games. His jokes and digs made fun of the people around us in the park. How they talked, what they looked like, how they dressed. But this gave us, Chris and me, a common enemy, the racist, White working class people around us. We just had different reasons to hate them. Looking back now, all his comments and digs at Fred and his grandkids and the others in the park were likely his way of saying, I'm not like them. I'm not "White trash." I'm better. Chris was the one who introduced me to this racialized socio-economic term, White trash. It was his demon, likely one that followed him from his Buffalo roots.

So when at thirteen, the girl across the street and one trailer down from us had a crush on me, told me several times, I was conflicted. She wanted us to be boyfriend and girlfriend. She was persistent. I refused her many times. I kind of liked her, didn't mind hanging out with her, but her dad would throw rocks at me when I walked home from school past his trailer. Can you imagine that, a grown-ass man throwing rocks and racist insults at little boys walking home from school? "Go back to where you came from, you fucking beaner!" he would say. That is a direct quote. I would purposefully walk the long way around, taking a different street than my own, so that I could avoid walking in front of his trailer. That route took me past most of my friends' trailers. Their parents' mean stares and cold shoulders were better than dodging rocks and insults.

I'm positive my neighbor knew nothing of his daughter's feelings for me, but even then I wondered if she was trying to get back at her dad for some reason. She didn't seem to like him, and would tell me so. "My dad, oh, he's an asshole," she would say flippantly. Huh? That made no sense to me. Kids were supposed to love their parents. At least, you gotta dad, I thought to myself. That's a precious thing to throw away. While I agreed with her—her dad was an asshole—I surely would not tell that to anyone. On top of this confusion, I remember wondering why would she want to be my girlfriend? I'm trouble. Her dad hates me about as much as anyone can hate anyone, so I thought. But she clearly did not hate me, or did she? Maybe she just hated her dad more than she hated me? I could not tell.

In her trailer, we would play her Atari video games when her parents were away, Frogger, Asteroids, Space Invaders, Pitfall. It was fun and thrilling, yet scary at the same time. What if her dad or mom came back and caught me in their home? We were both taking risks, and maybe that was the excitement in it for us. And there was always this undercurrent of sexuality between us. Maybe it was her open nature, her willingness to just ask me to be her boyfriend out of the blue, I'm not sure. Maybe it was her constant flirting with me. She wanted to show me her body, and me to show her mine.

We never had sex or did anything like that. It felt too dangerous to me, but we were both just becoming teenagers, learning about ourselves and our sexualities. We did talk. And yet, as exciting as all this was, as much as I wanted it and didn't want it at the same time, as much as I hated her dad but enjoyed her company, I wanted to leave the trailer park, leave her and her racist dad behind. I wanted to walk down my own street without being accosted by adults and their words. I wanted to not be in the middle of a daughter's disagreements with her dad. I wanted to be more certain that when a girl said she liked me, she really did like me, and I wanted her dad to like me too. I didn't want to be the only Brown kid around, the outsider.

I have always had lots of reasons to leave the places I've lived, the first reason was poverty, after that, it was usually racism.

It didn't help matters that my physiognomy seemed to match my mistaken identity in the park. My Black hair, Brown eyes, dark skin, and short stature confirmed to everyone around me that I was Mexican. It has never mattered what my English sounded like, and it really doesn't. That's not a clear indicator of one's cultural or racial heritage. But it matters just enough to be ignored and not enough to make things fair. I've often been stopped in stores or on the street and had a question asked of me in Spanish. But I don't speak or read Spanish. I just look like I do. I get why the mistake happens. It's understandable. Race-judgements.

Because we avoid race talk so much in the U.S., our language is usually ill-equipped to articulate race and language together. We don't know how to understand the social phenomenon of race and of language as paradoxical, as both and, as both important and unimportant, as vital and something to put aside. We think that mentioning race is racist, that noticing it and talking about it is racist. We don't have ways to cleanly and compassionately talk about race as a way to make decisions that are not about being racist. Part of this problem is due to the fact that racism is an almost inevitable outcome of most language-judgements baked into our systems, society, and the ways we communicate.

We usually don't mean to be racist, but it happens as a matter of course. Mrs. Whitmore, my trailer park neighbors, Fred, my college friend Erik, Chris, even me, none of us meant to be racist most of the time, but we all worked from the same kinds of race-judgements. We were trying to be good, trying to do what we understood was good for each other and ourselves. Our conditions didn't quite allow this. Our intentions didn't matter. We are all, whether we admit it or not, fighting in the tacit language war.

The racist insults and aggressions toward my brother and me were so frequent that I cultivated a racist hatred for Mexicans myself that would take many years to shake. I couldn't see how such racism around me was not only infectious, like a virus, but pitted similarly oppressed groups and individuals against each other. I had more in common with the working poor Mexican kids in the nearby areas—just over the trailer park wall, in fact—than my working class, White neighbors. But the messages that surrounded me, many of which came from the books I was reading and the language practices that were reinforced in school, as well as others' misunderstandings of who I was, moved me to reject this kinship and seek White acceptance. Or rather, I sought acceptance by taking on White racial habits of language—by being literate in so called standard and conventional ways with words. I knew, even back then, that my languaging would not be enough. I was trying to jump to the winning side of the war, not realizing that winning ain't the point when you're in the middle of the war. It's making peace, and how you fight it, and how you stay alive, not just that you do.

The keys to the gates of success and acceptance were, I thought, in mastering standardized English, in being smart. In reality, this kind of impulse divided me from my brothers and sisters of color nearby and conquered us all, either by keeping us in poverty or colonizing our minds and tongues. It is hard to fight a revolution against an oppressor with their own gun, a gun that only shoots at you.[10]

This psychology is deceptive and enticing because there's some truth to it. There is an element of truth to the argument that someone like me would improve himself, could get up and out, if he learns to HOWL, if he learns a standardized English. I certainly have done this, but this ain't completely true. We can fool ourselves into believing that our best option is to learn standardized English, to be on the White winning side of the war. But that ain't fully true either. It ignores structures that need changing. It ignores the harm done to those who do not live in conditions that allow them to survive and thrive in school or other White places. It ignores the vast numbers of people who cannot jump sides in the war. And it ignores the fact that being a winner in an unfair and racist system means you lose the ethical fight for your own soul. You are a bad guy who won. I'd rather be a good guy losing than a bad guy winning.

This psychology of White acceptance through taking on habits of White language divides those of us who do not inhabit the world already using such an English. It creates tremendously difficult obstacles to success in school or elsewhere for those who do not fit into the stereotype of what an English speaker is supposed to look like, or who a "real American" speaking English is supposed to be. To see HOWL as the only way to conduct business, logic, school, learning, whatever, is misguided and promotes White language supremacy. This was easy for me to feel growing up, but not understand.

In my first semester as a Freshman in high school, I was determined to get all A's, to be smart, to study hard every day, so I did. I made lists of short, medium, and long term goals and connected them to my path, a narrative, to college. I was thinking about college, getting in, and getting out of this place. It's a pattern I'd keep for the rest of my life. Make goals. Always be looking for a way out of this place. That year, I wrote my goals out on paper, put them in my school binder to look at each day. I worked at school harder than I ever had before. It was all I thought about.

When report cards came out, I had achieved all A's and one B. I was taking mostly honors courses, French, Biology, Algebra. And the class I got a B in? English, not honors English, regular English. How is that possible? I was a voracious reader, loved writing, did it all the time at home. I studied every day for several hours. The only game I played was a reading and writing game, a language game, D&D. I had explicit goals about my grades and learning, read

---

10   I take inspiration for this analogy from my reading of Audre Lorde, "The Master's Tools Will Never Dismantle the Master's House," *Sister Outsider* (Berkeley, CA: Crossing Press, 1984; repr., *This Bridge Called My Back: Writings by Radical Women of Color*, 4th ed., ed. Cherríe Moraga and Gloria Anzaldúa (Albany, NY: State University of New York Press, 2015), 94–97).

them ritualistically to myself every morning. How could an English teacher give me a B in the only non-honors course I took? Now, I think, how could I have gotten anything else? English and the body go hand in hand. We don't just write or speak our languages. We embody them. English is racialized. Brown kids don't get A's in English.

I was coming to understand this insight, but I didn't have it yet. Instead, I took the B in English as a personal failure. Just one more pothole in the road, but I'm still on the road, at least. I must not have worked hard enough. I didn't put all the clues together. Our judgements of language are also about people, bodies, and places, which makes them also about misplaced or displaced people and bodies.

I could discern the broad brushstrokes, the racism, the unfairness, the mis-judgements, the pain, the anger, the disappointment, the yearning. I could feel the paradoxes in my situation, in my own languaging and how people judged me and my language, how they judged me out of place, but I couldn't see how it was all connected to bigger systems, like school and the English I loved playing with. I couldn't see that if we could just stop seeing the world of language as an unordered world in need of ordering, as tangled tongues in need of straighten-ing, then we might do better.[11] We might see or hear difference not as a threat but as an invitation.

But the system had another answer to fight this truth, an answer I accepted for a long time. The system got me to tell myself that my initial kind of English was not even a kind of English, but a deficit, a substandard, flawed English. I could shoot the gun back at the oppressive system, say in school by using my first English, the language of Statz, but I knew I'd get hit instead. I'd be the one hurt. I'd get bad grades. I'd stay remedial, a label that took up to ninth grade to shake. Like Chris and his needing to not be White working class, I too didn't want to be remedial, to be stupid, to be stuck in such places as I was for the rest of my life. I wanted to live in a house, not an apartment or a trailer. I wanted that home to be clean. I wanted to live without cockroaches. The English of books and school seemed to be the pathway to that better place.

But the main reasons for why this strategy seemed to work for me was not because I worked hard. It is because I have some racial privileges that my Black friends on Statz didn't have. Race ain't a toggle or an either-or thing, it's a sliding scale of color. The darker you are the worse off you are, the steeper the climb, the more obstacles there are in front of you on the road. Because I had an advantage over my Black peers in school, the advantage of Brown and not Black skin, the

---

11   I draw inspiration for the metaphor of tangled tongues from Gloria Anzaldúa, *Borderlands/ La Frontera: The New Mestiza*, 2nd ed. (San Francisco: Aunt Lute Books, 1999).

advantage of a White mom who spoke a dominant English, the advantage of model-minority Asian-ness, even if ambiguously and contingently Asian. My hard work in those remedial reading classes over time paid off because my racialized conditions allowed my work to pay off. Maybe not in A's, but in B's.

Don't get me wrong, a B ain't bad. In most cases, it's very good, but I now see that it exists in a linear judgement system, one that takes a multitude of Englishes and ranks them on one scale. That scale requires a single standard, and that standard has to come from somewhere, a place I was not from. Like the A or F, the B grade is a symbol of a flawed system for judging language. And I could feel even then that it meant I was "like" normal but not, like my White peers but not, like Chris who always got straight-As but not.

~~~

On the first day of my Freshman year in high school, the teacher, a kind White lady from Boston asked my brother and me to write something on the board. My teacher would say "bah" for bar, and "cah" for car. And yes, my brother and I were in all the same classes together that year. We walked up and wrote the answers on the board. Some students laughed. I don't know why they did. Maybe because we were twins. Maybe we looked funny to them. We were short and slight of build. Maybe they didn't know how to react to twins like us. The class was a mix of White, Black, and Latine students, but mostly White. It was an advanced course, so while we were freshmen, most in the class were juniors and seniors. The teacher interrupted their laughter.

"Don't laugh at em," she said with a half-smile in her Boston language. "They're likely smata than you ah." The reference was to our Asian-ness, our being only Freshman in a class taken mostly by juniors and seniors, our being small and young in an Algebra class meant for older students. She was assuming a lot. She didn't know us yet. She was trying to help though, but such help also hurts everyone. It's a mixed up and mixed race-judgement.

PASSING IN THE TACIT RACE WAR

I'm in Corvallis, Oregon in college with friends. It's the first days of spring and the sun is out. In Oregon, when the sun starts to come out and the grass dries up, and the air is warmer, everyone wants to go outside, to feel the sun's rays bathe them. It makes sense after so many months of clouds and drizzle. The sun makes you feel good. On this day, there are lots of students out in the MU lawn, on rooftops, in front yards sunbathing. They are all White kids. It is Oregon State University. It is not a place known for its color. No one notices this, but me.

I'm with a few friends (all White) who suggest we get some towels and blankets and find a warm sunny spot and take advantage of the sunny afternoon.

"You go ahead," I say. I'm not interested. In my head, I think that I prefer rainy days. I'm not melancholy. I just enjoy the smell of wet asphalt. A cloudy day gives me a comforting feeling like a cozy blanket. It offers a gentle mood to me. It clears my mind, lets me think. An overcast day feels like the world is slowing down and hugging me. I also like to feel water from the sky. I think how amazing it is that a drop of water can travel so far, from the Pacific Ocean up into the sky tens of thousands of feet, then back down to hit me on the forearm or tongue. Or maybe, I think, it is growing up in Las Vegas, too much sun and other things. I'm done with the sun and all that.

"Why? C'mon, we'll have fun. We're all going. It's so nice out," a friend says cheerfully. She's really excited about it. She's White, speaks Spanish, did a few semesters in a South American country. She always seemed extravagant and elegantly oblivious to her privilege.

"No, thanks. I have some homework to do inside. You have fun." I leave. They go to lie in the sun. And as I walk away, I know why I don't like sunbathing for sunbathing's sake. Browning for Brown skin's sake. It's the same reason I've been afraid to go to Mexico—still cannot go today. I have an irrational fear of not being let back into the U.S. once I cross the border. My home will be denied me because to others I don't seem to be from my home. They'll tell me I have to go back to wherever I came from.

After a few years in Oregon, my skin has begun to lighten up. I think that my wish is coming true. I look White. I'm passing. I am becoming Encyclopedia Brown. I have all these White friends. I don't want to look Brown. I want to look White. I think, if I get too much sun, I'll look dirty. I ain't dirty. Ironically, this too, the need to stay out of the sun, separates me from my White friends. No race mixing in a race-mixed world.

CHAPTER 5.

THE WHITE LANGUAGE SUPREMACY IN JUDGEMENTS OF INTELLIGENCE AND STANDARDS

In the last few chapters, I explained that we learn and use language from our material conditions that are patterned from groups of people, who are among other things raced, classed, and gendered in systemic and historical ways. Our different ways of using English come from the material of our lives, from how we work and play and with whom we do that work and play. These systems give us the materials to make the languages and judgements we do. Simultaneously as we work and play, we make these systems dialectically with language. Meanwhile, because the people who make and circulate in these systems are racialized, our language and judgements are made of race-judgements, most of which we have a hard time seeing as racialized because the standards of good English have always been presented to us as a single, apolitical standard and as objective, neutral, and universal.

An important part of these systems that I'm saying produce White language supremacy is tests and language standards. Tests and language standards have associated with them intelligence. Who is smart and how can we tell? This is because language has historically been a marker of intelligence, or a lack of it. And because we have whole industries and disciplines dedicated to testing intelligence and language use, testing and standards become a powerful way White language supremacy is maintained. And because we are all a part of such testing systems in schools and workplaces, we are implicated in these systems. The trouble is, as I'll discuss in this chapter, most of our ideas about intelligence and language, testing and standards, are flawed, and end up being racist.

JUDGEMENTS ABOUT LANGUAGE OFTEN CONFIRM OUR OWN BIASES

Both consciously and unconsciously, we judge people's intelligence by the way they talk or write. Lots of other judgements and decisions, big and small, flow from this one. But it should come as no surprise that those judgements are usually flawed and can easily be racist. The association between intelligence and language is so deeply a part of American ideas that it often goes unquestioned.

Former President George W. Bush was often ridiculed and satirized for his unconventional use of language and malapropisms in his public speaking, so much so that his verbal blunders were called, "Bushisms."[1] This contributed to many viewing President Bush as dumb or slow witted, but the linguist Mark Liberman of the University of Pennsylvania argues that Bush may not have actually made more language gaffs and errors than any other public figure.[2] There were just a lot of people looking for them in his words. So they found them. We all experience this same mind bug all the time. When something is on our minds, say White Ford trucks, we often cannot help but see White Ford trucks everywhere. This is a well understood phenomenon by a number of researchers in various fields.

Joseph M. Williams, a former professor of English Language and Literature at the University of Chicago explained how this reading phenomenon works. He called it, "the phenomenology of error."[3] Phenomenology is "the study of structures of consciousness as experienced from the first-person point of view."[4] It's the study of how we experience things, like error or Bushisms, from the point of view of the person experiencing those things.

Essentially, Williams says, if you read a text (or listen to a speech) looking for, even expecting to find, errors and problems with the language, you will. If you don't look for them, you will not find many. The key to seeing or hearing error in language, according to Williams, is in what a reader or listener expects beforehand or how they plan to read or listen. Error in language is a phenomenon that is a part of a reader's or listener's experience of language and what they are predisposed to see or hear. Error, then, is not simply an objective feature in a text or an instance of language. It's often an individualized experience.

In experimental psychology, there is a related phenomenon called "priming." It's when a word or idea is put in front of us, often unconsciously, and that word or idea affects what we see or do afterwards.[5] The initial word or idea primes the person to do or see something else. For example, doing a crossword puzzle with

---

1   A quick search on the Internet will reveal a lot of resources on Bushisms; see Jacob Weisberg, "The Complete Bushisms," *Slate*, March 20, 2009, http://www.slate.com/articles/news _and_politics/bushisms/2000/03/the_complete_bushisms.html; "The 'Misunderestimated' President?" BBC News, January 7, 2009, http://news.bbc.co.uk/2/hi/americas/7809160.stm.

2   Mark Liberman, "You say Nevada, I say Nevahda," *Language Log* (blog), January 3, 2004, http://itre.cis.upenn.edu/~myl/languagelog/archives/000292.html.

3   Joseph M. Williams, "The Phenomenology of Error," *College Composition and Communication* 32, no. 2, (May 1981): 152–168, https://doi.org/10.2307/356689.

4   David Woodruff Smith, "Phenomenology," The Stanford Encyclopedia of Philosophy Archive, ed. Edward N. Zalta, last updated December 16, 2013, https://plato.stanford.edu /archives/sum2018/entries/phenomenology/.

5   To learn about priming, see, Kahneman, *Thinking*, 52–58.

food names in it can predispose (or prime) you to see or generate food-related ideas or words later that day. It's the White Ford truck phenomenon.

It's reasonable then to see how our political culture in the U.S. during the early 2000s would prime some people in the media to hear errors and gaffs in President Bush's language. Or those who politically did not align with President Bush might have been looking and listening for gaffs and malapropisms in his words. These folks already viewed President Bush as a fool, so they heard his language as foolish and error-filled.

What I'm getting at is that error in language is more complex than it might seem. Errors and nonstandardized English language are associated with a lack of intelligence, but error is not an inherent or objective part of a text or speech. This makes it an unreliable and questionable marker of intelligence. It's more likely a marker of what the reader or listener is looking for, or primed to see or hear. It's a marker of a reader's biases.

In his academic article, Williams points this out to writing teachers, who often read student writing for errors, and read other texts differently. He's asking readers, particularly teachers, to recognize just how subjective and personal error in language is. That is, readers and audiences form error and things like Bush-isms through their experiences with the language, how they go into reading a text, and the biases they start with.

This suggests that writers and speakers have less control over error in their own language than we might initially think. To prove his argument, Williams shows how numerous grammar and style guides commit the very errors they ask their readers to avoid (one of those style guides is none other than Strunk and White's). No one seems to notice these errors in these authoritative books, until someone reads those texts looking for errors, which they will find, as Williams does.

But Williams cleverly goes one step further. He embeds about 100 errors in his article, and asks his readers at the end of the article, whether they noticed any of them and to write to the journal editor with their locations in the article. Of course, no one does. I searched through the next four years of the same journal's issues. No one wrote back. Likely, Williams' point was made. Professors do not read professional scholarship in academic journals, like Williams' article, look-ing for errors. So they didn't notice any. And that is his point and proof.

Thus, seeing Bushisms is not a good indicator of former President Bush's intel-ligence or anyone else's. He may not be smart, or he may be brilliant, but someone finding errors and malapropisms in his speech does not prove his lack of intel-ligence. Finding error is actually, according to Liberman and Williams, a better indicator of the finder's own politics or what that person was looking or listening for in the first place (how they were primed). This is not to say that one cannot judge President Bush to be a fool or dumb. You can. You just have to keep in mind that it is not an objective fact. Your judgement is a conclusion you are making from language markers that you see or hear because you are primed to see or hear them, then judge them as markers of foolishness or lack of intelligence.

Hearing accents in English is a similar phenomenon. Linguists have known for decades that accent in speech is more a product of the listener who hears an accent than the speaker speaking. In fact, accent is a relative term, one relative to the listener who hears an accent that others may not hear. We hear accents when we compare what we hear to what we consider accentless English. But there's no such thing as an accentless English. We all have accents to someone else's ear.[6] An accent is just a noticeable speech difference from what a listener expects to hear.

Accents like malapropisms are the evidence that many people use when making conclusions about people or their ideas, conclusions that often confirm our original biases about that person. Meanwhile, like errors, accents are more complicated than they appear. And too often we think too fast about them, engaging in mind bugs like the halo effect, and implicit racial, gender, or class biases that are closely linked to language. We mistake what seems available to us as all we need in order to make a decision about a person or their intelligence (the availability and the WYSIATI, or the "What You See Is All There Is" heuristics).

Regardless of the mind bug, the connection in people's minds between language and intelligence is strong. We look for reasons to believe this connection. And there are lots of narratives in our culture that seem to support the connection. These narratives though are all racialized, and have histories in White supremacy. So accepting them unquestioningly is dangerous because it means we can more easily reproduce them ourselves.

OUR JUDGEMENTS OF LANGUAGE ARE RACIALIZED

There was a funny film several years ago that I found offered a good critique of our world, particularly the overly materialistic and Capitalistic U.S. It is also a good example of just how easy it is for anyone, including me, to reproduce White Supremacist thinking and judgements, even as I explicitly try not to. In a

---

6   For more on the linguistic research on the myth of accentless English, see Lippi-Green, *English*, 44–53. Hearing accents has also been shown to be affected by racial implicit biases, cause discrimination in hiring practices, and influence perceptions; see Sylvia P. Perry, Mary C. Murphy, and John F. Dovidio, "Modern Prejudice: Subtle, But Unconscious? The Role of Bias Awareness in Whites' Perceptions of Personal and Others' Biases," *Journal of Experimental Social Psychology* 61 (November 2015): 64–78, https://doi.org/10.1016/j.jesp.2015.06.007; Alice Robb, "A Person's Accent Can Change Your Perception of What He Is Saying," *New Republic*, September 23, 2014, https://newrepublic.com/article/119546/accents-can-influence-perception.

way, the film is a cultural instance of the Southern language strategy. And I was caught in it. But upon reflection, I can see how I made such a mistake, how I engaged in fast thinking. The film is not just a film. Films are often how the tacit language war is waged. It is vital to the way White language supremacy operates, because it seems like it ain't about race or anything like that.

In the film *Idiocracy* (2006) written by Mike Judge and Etan Cohen, the two main characters are frozen in an Army experiment, forgotten, then awake 500 years later. They find a very different America, one that has mostly collapsed and is dysfunctional because people have become dumber over successive generations. The montage of images and scenes that open the movie attribute this dumbing down of America to both biology and a bankrupt culture.

High IQ couples wait too long to have children, and then can't, while low IQ (and low income) men have low IQ babies with multiple partners. The film prints the characters' IQ scores on the screen, so there is no doubt about their intelligence. Meanwhile, the culture is filled with vacuous and mindless entertainment, movies of just butts farting, and TV shows about a man being continuously stuck in the groin, called, "Ow! My Balls!" Apparently, this is the only entertainment that low IQ people want or need.

This film offers a window into influential and long-standing beliefs about standardized English that are not only false but harmful to everyone. And yet, it is easy to buy into them. The film also helps us see a central problem with our ideas about a standardized English language, one that implicates our narratives about language more generally, like Bushisms and accents, and how we judge with it. Our ideas about language and intelligence are racist and White supremacist.

Early in the movie, Joe Bauers (played by Luke Wilson), the main character, awakens in the future. A voiceover provides some explanation for what has happened to those around him, with whom he tries to communicate:

> Joe wandered the streets, desperate for help, but the English
> language had deteriorated into a hybrid of hillbilly, valley-girl,
> inner city slang, and various grunts. Joe was able to under-
> stand them, but when he spoke in his ordinary voice, he
> sounded pompous and "faggy" to them.[7]

The connection, even causal link, between language and intelligence is written into the plot of the film. The very average Joe[8] is deemed the smartest man

---

7   From the voiceover in the film, *Idiocracy* (2006), page 21. Screenplay found at: https://the scriptsavant.com/pdf/Idiocracy.pdf.

8   The film makes a point to reveal Joe as very average in intelligence by showing his IQ and other test scores, all of which make him eligible for the Army program that freezes him.

in the world after taking a set of simple tests in the future to determine what work he's capable of doing (note the centrality of testing, even in a bankrupt and degraded future). In this future, Joe's language, a White, monolingual, middle-to-working class English, sounds "pompous and 'faggy'" to everyone around him. Apparently, this is due to his longer sentences, attention to details, and appeals to logic and reasoning. By being frozen for so long, Joe escaped the deterioration of the English language.

This is a running gag in the film. He's made fun of numerous times for how he talks. It's difficult for many around him to understand what he's saying. Additionally, as the narrator in the above description illustrates, people in the future halo their negative feelings about homosexual sounding voices to that person's credibility or intentions. Because Joe sounds "faggy," he's not taken seriously early on in the film. While the audience is supposed to chuckle at this ridiculous haloing of feelings about gay sounding speech onto Joe, the movie works from other haloing of language that the film is uncritcal of, a haloing that the audience is supposed to engage in as well.

The link between language and intelligence in the film, which is the foundation on which everything happens, is not meant to be questioned. It's not being critiqued, rather it's one of the tools of critique. The film works from a premise that it expects most audiences will accept easily: Language indicates intelligence. The authoritative narrator, who speaks in a deep, masculine, California, radio announcer English, reveals biases that help create this overarching larger premise. What makes people dumb apparently is hillbilly, valley-girl, inner city slang, and grunts. This view of a deteriorated standardized English is very similar to that of Strunk and White's views, despite the White working-class Joe who epitomizes it in the film. And the key to Joe's connection to intelligence is that Joe and his language are White.

What is hillbilly English? Poor, rural White English. What is valley-girl? Privileged, California White girls who say, "like" and "gag me with a spoon" because apparently they never bothered to learn anything. What is inner-city slang? Black English. And grunts? Is that a reference to an animalistic and primal nature? Is it significant that this descriptor immediately follows a reference to Black English? The frequency of Blacks seen and represented as animalistic and savage in U.S. history suggests that this is a reasonable interpretation. Thus the narrator's description engages in the Southern language strategy, hiding the racial, gendered, and classed associations that the terms in which this futuristic English are described.

Furthermore, many of the actors playing the future citizens who speak in this deteriorated English in the movie are ambiguously Brown or Black. The country's leader, President Dwayne Elizondo Mountain Dew Herbert Camacho, is played by an African American actor (Terry Crews), who is always dressed in sleeveless shirts and spandex to show off his large muscles. President Camacho is a former porn star and professional wrestler. The character's image in the film, who is aggressive, big, muscular, menacing, and often shooting a big gun, is the epitome of the Black savage out to take White women from White men. It's a familiar image that has continuously haunted the imagination of White people in the U.S. Here it is used as the image of a dystopian, degraded, dumb, and savage American President, the leader of a helpless and stupid nation that needs a White savior who only needs to be average.

Language and intelligence, which is often set against animalistic savagery, are associated with markers of race and class. These are the familiar tools the film uses to critique. Most people around Joe are staggeringly dump and inept, putting electrolyte-filled juice on fields of crops, which kills the crops and causes a famine. No one believes the working class, White Joe when he tells them to put water on the crops. They don't understand.

In a later scene, White Joe is discussing his solution to the crop problem with White House cabinet members, attempting to reason with them. Here's the dialogue with a few of my own cues to help show what's happened on screen:

> White Joe: "For the last time, I'm pretty sure what's killing the crops is this Brawndo stuff."
>
> Secretary of Defense (played by David Herman; in a slower voice, a bit confused): "But Brawndo's got what plants crave. It's got electrolytes."
>
> Attorney General (in a hesitant voice, who is a busty woman with long red hair, played by Sara Rule, uncredited): "So wait, like what you're saying is you want us to put water on the crops?"
>
> White Joe (sharply): "Yes."
>
> Attorney General (with a disgusted look on her face): "Water? Like out of the toilet?"
>
> White Joe: "I mean, well, it doesn't have to be out of the toilet, but, yeah, that's the idea."
>
> Secretary of Defense (confused): "But Brawndo's got what plants crave."
>
> Attorney General (waving her hands in the air looking equally confused): "It's got electrolytes."
>
> White Joe (exasperated; as he talks, the camera cuts to various members in the room. All have blank looks on their faces.

They are confused by his words and logic.): "Look, your plants aren't growing. So I'm pretty sure this Brawndo stuff is not working. Now I'm no botanist, but I do know that if you put water on plants they grow."

14-year old boy cabinet member (played by Brendan Hill): "Well, I've never seen no plants grow out of no toilet."

(The camera cuts to Joe. He looks exasperated and baffled at the comment.)

Secretary of Defense (with a look of astonishment): "Hey, that's good. You sure you ain't the smartest guy in the world?"

The exchange continues, with the cabinet members, who are mostly White or White passing, simply not understanding that the plants should not be irrigated with Brawndo but with water. They repeat the two ideas that they think they know, "Brawndo's got electrolytes" and "It's got what plants crave." Their ideas about Brawndo come from the numerous advertisements all around them, dominated by a single, multinational corporation, Brawndo.

The next scene begins with Joe asking his partner who was frozen with him (played by Maya Rudolph), "How did the world ever get like this?" He's referring to how dumb everyone is. There is the film's critique. The viewers of *Idiocracy* are meant to ask this question with White Joe. Viewers are meant to associate the deteriorated English language with the thick-headed animalistic people who can't figure out that plants need water, who are frequently Black or Latine in the film, people who elect a Black, muscular, savage, former porn star, and professional wrestler as their president. And their most distinguishing marker of idiocy? Their hillbilly-valley-girl-inner-city-slang-grunting language.

When the film was released in 2006, two years after it was finished, its production company Fox did so silently to a small handful of theaters. It seems clear that Fox didn't want the film to do well, perhaps because of the critiques it made of large corporate sponsors. Starbucks offers "handjobs" with coffee. Costco is an endless, shambling, confusing place. Carl's Jr. sells "big ass fries," and declares customers "unfit mothers" when they cannot pay for their food. Since 2006, however, the film has become a cult classic.

David Fear in a 2014 *Rolling Stone* article called the film "the smartest stupid movie ever made, a Swiftian satire that, seen now in the Year of Our Lord 11 A.K. (After Kardashian), feels more pertinent than ever."[9] Bilge Ibiri of *The Village*

9   David Fear, "Darwin, Dar-lose: The Genius of 'Idiocracy,'" *Rolling Stone*, October 1, 2014, https://www.rollingstone.com/movies/movie-news/darwin-dar-lose-the-genius-of-idiocracy -51831/.

Voice finds the film more paradoxical. It is genius that "makes you dumber too." It can be attractive to both the political right and left, he explains. Ultimately, Ibiri says, "we see what we choose to in this movie."[10]

He's not wrong. He's describing the phenomenology of error and confirmation bias that gets used in fast thinking.[11] And yet, it was hard for me not to be seduced by the critique that the film presented. Our culture is filled with stupid stuff. It's gonna ruin us all. Originally, I found the thesis attractive and funny. We all can find stupid things in our culture that we don't like and feel are counterproductive or harmful. But is this just confirmation bias? Are we just looking for stupid stuff to call stupid in a world filled with more stuff that is not stupid?

Idiocracy is not simply a satirical film meant to make us laugh at its critique of our culture. It's also a reflection of common language biases and ideas about language that circulate in U.S. culture. It illustrates why it is very hard to avoid these language biases, that is, our ideas about the virtues of a standardized English language. It shows how closely associated that standardized English is to our notions of intelligence and Whiteness.

The main reason we accept that White Joe is the smartest guy in the world is because everyone around him speaks a version of English that is "hillbilly, valley-girl, inner city slang, and various grunts." White Joe's English is the primary marker that everyone in the film and those watching it use to distinguish him from everyone else—that, and of course, his working class Whiteness. The film also slyly connects the audience watching it with White Joe, and imagines or projects that viewer as White, working or middle class, and a monolingual English speaker.

White Joe's English is the language by which all logic and solutions are voiced. He is the only logical one on screen at any time. He is literally the solution to the world's problems—the narrator tells us this at one point. And all these critiques and plot turns hinge on a bundle of language biases, each of which is connected to other racialized, gendered, and class biases. This bundle of biases equate to a middle-to-working class, monolingual English language being synonymous with higher intelligence; higher than poor, White, hillbilly; higher than blank-minded, irritating valley-girl; higher than multilingual, superficial inner city slang; and higher than animalistic grunts. The critique that the film

---

10   Bilge Ebiri, "The Genius of 'Idiocracy' Is That It Makes You Dumber, Too," *Village Voice*, October 4, 2016, https://www.villagevoice.com/2016/10/04/the-genius-of-idiocracy-is-that-it -makes-you-dumber-too/.

11   I discuss confirmation bias in more detail in the appendix essay, but one might think of it as a mindbug that allows someone to unconsciously look for data or evidence of their original biases or ideas of things. If you believe that someone is not smart, you will look for and see all the markers that make that person stupid, ignoring other markers that may suggest otherwise.

offers is one based on fear, built with ideas about language that are informed by notions of Black and Brown racial inferiority, and savagery, set next to the HOWLing of White Joe, of his individualized rationality; his clarity, order, and control; and his hyperindividualism.

When we move these ideas about language and intelligence out of this movie and into schools and jobs in the real world, they become dangerous, the seeds of dissension and violence. Lose standardized English, and we all become dumb. Gotta test for it. Gotta make it a job requirement. Make sure all students are punished if they don't use a standardized English. Standardized English will save us from a dystopian future like the one in *Idiocracy*. No President Camachos. Put police in urban, Black schools. Those people are dangerous. It's obvious. Listen to them.

These false truths become in our minds a matter of life and death. The policies made long before us, our ideas about language and intelligence, the feelings we halo onto our judgements, the fast thinking that makes us and our decisions, as well as all the other structures that make us in the places we are at, all these structures—the systems around us—tell us that our differences amount to life and death. Differences have been programmed to be understood as bad by our systems of work and play. And any language that is different from the dominant White Standardized English becomes naturally unintelligent or not preferred, not rewarded in the classroom or marketplace.

Those people over there are not us over here. Those people who speak or look or think in those other ways are not just different from us but wrong, deficient, even dangerous to democracy or a civil classroom or the public good. They don't meet our personal standards. We just know we are right. We are not bad. They are. And we translate falsely all of this into a threat, without seeing how the "we" and "they" in all these false truths and logics are racialized. The threat of racial difference is perhaps the most obvious in U.S. history.

In America, we live in currents of racial anxieties. It's very difficult to escape them. They have been formalized in legal decisions and laws, from the Chinese Exclusion Act of 1882 and the Plessy v. Ferguson decision in 1896, to racist pseudoscience that upholds racial hierarchies, such as Blacks and other people of color being intellectually inferior to Whites.[12] We don't escape our historical

---

12   To read about racist and White supremacist science that has never really disappeared, see Angela Siani, *Superior: The Return of Race Science* (Boston: Beacon Press, 2019); Christopher D. E. Willoughby, "White Supremacy Was at the Core of 19th-century Science. Why That Matters Today," *Washington Post*, April 22, 2019, https://www.washingtonpost.com/outlook/2019/04/22/White-supremacy-was-core-th-century-science-why-that-matters-today/. For a discussion of how science was used to argue that White people were more intelligent than others, see Stephen J. Gould, *The Mismeasure of Man*, rev. and exp. ed. (New York: W. W. Norton & Company,

fears and worries in a generation or two. Our fears are systemic, both inside and outside of us. We don't escape such historical fears by ignoring them or not naming them as racial or racist.

White racial anxieties about Black and Brown people helped establish concerns over literacy throughout America's history. This is why one of the first moves in colonizing any group of people is to take away their language. We can see this practice in Indian boarding schools in the nineteenth century,[13] and the American public school system that was set up in the Philippines to "pacify" what the American government saw as savage and uncivilized Filipinos, "our little Brown brothers."[14]

We can see it in the British empire's educational practices in India and other former colonies, where most formal education was and still is conducted in English from compulsory to university. Asking all students from a large and diverse country like the U.S. or India to use one version of English, then grade, rank, and punish them for deviations from that standardized version is a kind of domestic, linguistic, and ideological colonizing, or maybe pacifying, or brainwashing. Whatever it is, it is certainly a language war. One group's language being used to control everyone. And that group, and those others, when we look at the outcomes of such colonizing are racialized. It's a war for White language supremacy.

No matter what you call a mandatory use of a standardized English in schools, it amounts to a White, middle- to upper-class, monolingual English used as a standard. That group has historically determined the standard. That

1996). To read about how Whiteness and White people are woven into the history of racist science, politics, and ideas, see Nell Irvin Painter, *The History of White People* (New York: W. W. Norton & Company, 2010).

13   To read about Indian boarding schools, see Becky Little, "How Boarding Schools Tried to 'Kill the Indian' Through Assimilation," *History Stories* (blog), *History*, updated November 1, 2018, https://www.history.com/news/how-boarding-schools-tried-to-kill-the-indian-through -assimilation. You can also read about the efforts that the Cherokee nation used to keep their language in Ellen Cushman, *The Cherokee Syllabary: Writing the People's Perseverance* (Norman: University of Oklahoma Press, 2011).

14   To read about the U.S. educational system in the Philippines, see Carolyn I. Sobritchea, "American Colonial Education and Its impact on the Status of Filipino Women," *Asian Studies: Journal of Critical Perspectives on Asia* 28 (January 1990): 70–91, https://asj.upd.edu.ph/media box/archive/ASJ-28-1990/sobritchea.pdf. The term "our little Brown brothers" was coined by then American Governor-General of the Philippines (1901–04), William Howard Taft, which is explained in Stuart Creighton Miller, *Benevolent Assimilation: The American Conquest of the Philippines, 1899–1903* (New Haven: Yale University Press, 1984), 134. One of the first decolonial histories of the Philippines that explains the flawed reasoning behind such paternalistic racism is found in Leon Wolff, *Little Brown Brother: How the United States Purchased and Pacified the Philippine Islands at the Century's Turn* (New York: Doubleday, 1961).

standard is what we inherit in colleges and schools. Black and Latine groups, as well as working class and poor groups, are affected negatively because of elite White racial anxieties that manifest as guidelines and rules about language standards in classrooms, boardrooms, newsrooms, and other civic spaces. And it's all done without mentioning race or having intentions toward White language supremacy. It allows the average White guy to succeed. Why? Because apparently, there is an assumption that this country, America, is his property. It is his to claim, and protect. The system seems to only promote average White Joes.

The U.S. also has a long history of narratives that promote the country and everything in it as the property and patrimony of White racial populations. Our history is one of systemic White supremacist narratives and ideas, which means we don't escape it very easily.[15] If we aren't careful, there will continue to be Southern strategic calls to "Make America Great Again," which really means make America White again.[16]

Even *The Great Gatsby* (1925), considered by many to be one of America's greatest novels, opens with popular White supremacist fears of the time. Near the opening of the novel, Tom Buchanan discusses a White supremacist text he's read:

> "Civilization's going to pieces," broke out Tom violently. "I've gotten to be a terrible pessimist about things. Have you read 'The Rise of the Coloured Empires' by this man Goddard?"
>
> "Why, no," I answered, rather surprised by his tone.
>
> "Well, it's a fine book, and everybody ought to read it. The idea is if we don't look out the White race will be—will be utterly submerged. It's all scientific stuff; it's been proved."[17]

White supremacy. Scientific stuff. Words published seem to make things scientific, proved. Solutions to civilization's problems, maybe all of them. There's a familiar connection we might hear in this passage, one drawn on by Mike Judge and Etan Cohen 80 years later. It's the great White hope theme. The right, or White, kind of language equates to proof, to intelligence and smart ideas. It's the

---

15   For a study of white supremacy in U.S. history, see Ronald Takaki, *Iron Cages: Race and Culture in 19th Century America*, rev. ed. (New York: Oxford University Press, 2000); Roediger, *Wages*; George Lipsitz, *Possessive Investment*; Matthew Frye Jacobson, *Whiteness of a Different Color: European Immigrants and the Alchemy of Race* (Cambridge, MA: Harvard University Press, 1998).

16   Former President Ronald Reagan's successful 1980 presidential campaign used the slogan, "Let's Make America Great Again," and President Donald Trump used the slogan, "Make America Great Again" (MAGA) in his successful 2016 presidential campaign.

17   F. Scott Fitzgerald, *The Great Gatsby* (New York: Scribner, 2018), 12–13.

solution, the White savior for a degraded world. Intelligence, good ideas, and language are linked to White racial supremacy. The tacit race war appears to have begun for Tom Buchanan. He could have said, "let's make America great again."

Likely, Fitzgerald is invoking a real-life author and book in the fictional ones referenced by Buchanan. In this case, the printed language that's "all scientific stuff" suggests the real-life author and historian Lothrop Stoddard (sounds like Fitzgerald's "Goddard"), a White supremacist from Harvard who grew up in a well-to-do, Eastern family. His Father, John Lawson Stoddard, was a lecturer and well-known writer of travelogues. Stoddard is a familiar elite, White, masculine authoritative voice, one easily trusted for his alleged objectivity and truthiness. He is a scholar that Fitzgerald's initial readers in 1925 most likely knew and perhaps read.

In an article that explains how White supremacy has been a part of America from its beginnings, Fareed Zakaria reveals that the sentiments of Buchanan may have voiced Fitzgerald's own racial fears. In a letter to a literary critic, Edmund Wilson, Fitzgerald writes in 1921: "The negroid streak creeps northward to defile the Nordic race . . . Raise the bars of immigration and permit only Scandinavians, Teutons, Anglo-Saxons and Celts to enter." And a bit later in the letter: "We are as far above the modern Frenchman as he is above the Negro." This letter comes four years before publishing his famous novel. Fitzgerald was racist.

In 1920, one year before the letter and five before *the novel*, Lothrop Stoddard published *The Rising Tide of Color: The Threat Against White World Supremacy*. It's the book that Fitzgerald is likely invoking in the novel. Fitzgerald's references to the "rise of the colored empires" and the White race being "submerged" call on the same language and metaphors that Stoddard uses. Stoddard was a vocal White supremacist. In the book, he argues that increasing populations of people of color around the world threaten the White geographic, economic, and political center. People of color are taking over White racial settlements, and this is a bad thing. Strategically, Stoddard notes, there are inner and outer dikes that must be attended.[18]

The outer dikes of White civilization are those places in the world that contain mostly people of color, but the inner are those places on the globe that are White settlements in which people of color are increasing. Those areas must be protected because they are the last defense of the White centers of property. It is not hard to hear a logic that associates race, intelligence, worth, value, and language in Stoddard's own words. In a chapter called "The White Flood," he explains:

---

18   Lothrop Stoddard, *The Rising Tide of Color: The Threat Against White World Supremacy* (New York: Charles Schribner's Sons, 1920), 226.

For instance: biologists had recently formulated the law of the "Survival of the Fittest." This sounded very well. Accordingly, the public, in conformity with the prevailing optimism, promptly interpreted "fittest" as synonymous with "best," in utter disregard of the grim truth that by "fittest" nature denotes only the type best adapted to existing conditions of environment, and that if the environment favors a low type, this low type (unless humanly prevented) will win, regardless of all other considerations. So again with economics. A generation ago relatively few persons realized that low-standard men would drive out high-standard men as inevitably as bad money drives out good, no matter what the results to society and the future of mankind. These are but two instances of that shallow, cock-sure nineteenth-century optimism, based upon ignorance and destined to be so swiftly and tragically disillusioned.[19]

The world I imagine Stoddard and Fitzgerald seeing in the future, one with tides of color washing over inner dikes, one with Black and Brown bodies creeping "northward to defile the Nordic race," is a world that *Idiocracy* has envisioned as well. The White anxieties of tides of color in this passage percolate underneath it. The downfall, the degradation, the erosion of Western civilization begins with language, the marker of intelligence and scientific proof of "low-type" and "high-standard men." Between 1920 and 2006, the same racial anxieties are voiced, first by an avowed White supremacist, then by a mainstream Hollywood film. And it continues to be voiced by presidents using the Southern language strategy of making America great again.

The defense of inner dikes and White property always assumes violence. In all of these examples—*Idiocracy*, Stoddard's scholarship, Fitzgerald's letters, Tom Buchanan's words in *The Great Gatsby*, making America great again—there is an implicit threat of race war, of violence. The White subject, the average White Joe, cannot sit by and do nothing. What is missed, of course, is that the world and everything in it is not his to conquer or take. It ain't his patrimony. Our fast ideas about language are interlaced with our historical ideas about race, intelligence, and the White property of literacy that White supremacist systems say must be protected from the rising tides of color.[20]

---

19   Stoddard, 150.

20   To read more about how historically in the US literacy has been seen as White property, see Prendergast, *Literacy*. To read about the way the U.S. justice system has defined White property, see Harris, "Whiteness."

This argument of precious inner dikes is still used today, only with different, less overly racialized language. Our arguments today engage in the Southern language strategy. Education, schools, and literacy in the US are inner dikes that teachers and others too often protect from the rising tide of students of color. Schools use language standards and standardized test scores to stem the tide. Racist intentions are not necessary because White supremacist outcomes are inevitable in systems built to produce such results. We have already inherited Stoddard's ideas and forgotten their origins and histories. This is why I could watch *Idiocracy* and think it was good, sound critique.

We don't think that what those ideas produce, their consequences to people, are racist. But inevitably, the ideas about language and intelligence have shaped our thoughts about language and people. They have become a part of our normal thinking. Our arguments now are about clear expression, literacy standards, good communication, but the racialized consequences are the same as they've always been.

And so, we see the same flawed, White supremacist ideas about language in our schools as we do in *Idiocracy*. Blacks, Latine, and poor Whites are harmed most, or just left out, by dike logic, not because they are the underclasses, but because they don't use or can't learn quick enough the right kind of English, the smart kind, the White kind. Material conditions of people matter to their languaging in the world. We are what we do in the places we are at with the people there.

And so, the system rewards average White Joes mostly—they appear to be our saviors. We have seductive ideas about language and intelligence, but they are racially flawed because we don't investigate them carefully enough. It is difficult to notice when our ideas about language and intelligence are racist because they are our systems, our biases, our histories. They seem so natural because they feel as if they've always been with us and in us.

PROBLEMS WITH ENGLISH STANDARDS IN TESTS

During the summer before my senior year in high school, I took the SAT twice. I had just moved to Corvallis, Oregon, where Oregon State University resides. It felt like a poshy, elite, and very White town. The school I went to, one of only two in that college town, was at the time the more affluent one, Crescent Valley High School. The first day I walked into the school, I saw a long list of student names posted in big letters in the hallway near my locker. There must have been several hundred names. It was the school's honor roll, those who had gotten at least a 3.5 GPA the previous year.

I thought, holy shit, everyone in this school is on the honor roll! While this wasn't true, what was true was that the school was quite elite, middle- to upper-middle-class, and very White. In fact, besides my brother and me, there were only three or four other students of color and only one Black teacher. Everyone else was White. The entire year that I was there, I never had a class with anyone of color, student or teacher. Then again, even in my more diverse schools in Las Vegas and North LV, I had no teachers of color.

So when the results of our SATs came in the mail, I was very nervous. It wasn't just because I felt out of place and unprepared for what I saw as a high-powered academic high school, but I knew I hadn't done well on the test. I just didn't know exactly how badly. News started going around. So-and-so got a 1450. She got a 1500. He got a 1250.

To get a 1500 is to score better than 99 percent of those who take the test. A score of 1450 means you are in the 97th percentile. A respectable score is something like 1250 (the 81st percentile). While I don't remember my exact score, I do know that I scored so low that I felt ashamed to tell anyone, not my brother, not my friends, not even my girlfriend. My score wasn't even four digits. It was three, like 900 maybe. That means that 78 percent of those taking the SAT that year scored better than me. To my friends, I said that I did okay. Made excuses. Didn't remember the number. I wasn't worried.

But really, I was frightened. I thought I had just blown my chance at college. It figured, I thought. Didn't think I was college material anyway. Who was I fooling? Trying to be like all these rich, White kids. I ripped up the slip of paper that showed my failure. I didn't even bother to apply to the one university I'd planned on attending, Oregon State University, the school that resided in that town. I only got in because my aunt, my mom's sister, who lived in Corvallis too and was married to a professor at the university (Uncle Bill), filled out all the application forms for me, even the FAFSA for my financial aid. By the time she'd finished doing it, and I had to sign them, I was embarrassed. We had to disclose that really low SAT score.

Years later, my GRE score was not much better, also embarrassingly low—and I took that twice too! Part of the reason I even found Washington State University when I applied for graduate school the second time was because their English Department didn't use GRE scores to determine acceptance into their graduate programs.[21] What luck, I thought.

But by these standardized tests, I should be a failure. I should not have done well as an undergraduate student, but I was on the honor roll from my

---

21   Previous to WSU, I stayed at OSU and got my master's degree in part because my GRE scores were so low that no other graduate school I applied to accepted me. I am grateful that I was known in the English Department at OSU already because I'd gotten my bachelor's degree there and also grateful that they were willing to ignore my low GRE scores and admit me as a master's degree student.

sophomore year on. And I was taking 18 credits each term in my final two years there, since it was cheaper to do so. In grad school, I got all A's and one B. The B happened during my first semester at Oregon State (I got my master's degree at OSU and my Ph.D. at WSU), and it was a product of a dysfunctional group project. We were all learning how to be grad students.

So how could those standardized tests be so wrong about me? They didn't predict anything about me. They didn't predict how well I'd do grade-wise in college or grad school. They didn't predict that I'd pass my Ph.D. qualifying exams with honors. They didn't predict that I'd publish a version of my master's thesis, a rare thing to do. They didn't predict that I'd be a college professor or an associate dean in one of the largest universities in the US. They didn't predict that I'd research, write, and publish numerous articles, book chapters, and books on language and racism. They didn't predict that I'd win numerous national awards for my scholarship. They didn't predict that I'd be elected as the leader of my academic field's biggest organization, the Conference on College Composition and Communication. If the SAT percentile system is accurate, then I'm in the lowest quarter of academics. That is, 78 percent of my peers should have better resumes than me and be more accomplished.

More likely, my experience with those standardized tests explains how I am actually different from most successful academics, how my academic norms, my habits and dispositions with language, are not always well-fitted to conventional, White, academic standards exclusively used in tests like the SAT and the GRE. My low scores likely show how I was unable—or maybe unwilling—to HOWL like a good student. I have not waded into the waters of the academy cautiously, but I do swim in the current well now. I have made waves and created new currents for others after me to follow in or paddle against.

In my case, my ill-fitting habits, my strange orientation to language and the entire academic enterprise, did not mean something more tragic, like failure or dropping out of college, although it could have very easily. I did drop out of college twice. I was lucky to have a supportive aunt who took it upon herself to make sure that my application for college was in on time. I was privileged enough to have an uncle who was a professor at the same university I would graduate from. I was lucky to have a mom whom I loved and who loved me, who sat on weekends reading Harlequin romance novels by the dozens. I was lucky to halo my feelings about my mom to my feelings about words and books. I was lucky that I was a Brown kid who had White women helping me at every step of the way, White women who spoke White, middle-class English and knew enough about college systems to sneak me in. I was lucky to have a twin brother who played D&D with me. I was lucky I had Schmindrake to show me how to cast spells, to be a hero, a mage. I was lucky to be poor, lucky to find ways to make ends-meat.

But really, I wasn't lucky in the conventional sense. These were my conditions in which I learned language. I was able to find ways to use them to keep moving through, to be the exception, but my movement wasn't always easy. Like everyone else, testing in school was a part of my conditions. Like the SAT, tests are usually gates to other places, like college, jobs, and other opportunities and rewards. Gates are usually guarded. In most cases, the testing gates are guarded and locked by standards. Standards in tests are perhaps the most obvious front in the language war.

There are at least three deep problems with tests of English language proficiency and the standards that they are based on. For most, these problems are not easy to see. When left unaddressed in large scale tests and course curricula, these three problems amount to English language standards that reproduce White language supremacy and racist outcomes in schools and society. They are the hidden ways that the tacit language war is won. They are how White language supremacy occurs without anyone being White supremacist. The first is a straight forward problem, while the other two are less so.

PROBLEM 1. THOSE WHO HAVE MORE POWER GET TO MAKE STANDARDS OF ENGLISH IN TESTS

I've discussed this in various ways, particularly when it comes to style guides. Those who end up ruling make the rules. But let's think about this more deeply. When we talk about standards of English, regardless of the context or people, we are rarely referencing exactly the same things. We've all experienced this in classrooms. A teacher asks for a clear summary of another text, but then they say your summary is not clear, nor does it have the appropriate information in it. You are confused. You thought you were clear and included all the necessary information. Both your teacher and you were working from the same two criteria for the summary: Be clear and include the appropriate details from the original text in your summary.

Because we usually default to the teacher's standard, the teacher's view of things, we give up our original one. This can be okay, but let's not forget that we were still working from the same criteria, the same standards. We just had different ideas about what "clear" and "appropriate details" meant and how to accomplish those things in a summary. The teacher, because they have more power in the classroom (and because you've acquiesced to that power, usually out of necessity—that's actually coercion if you had no say in the choice), gets to decide whose version of the standard is appropriate or correct. But this difference in power doesn't make one view of the same standard better than the other. It simply means that the teacher gets to decide for the same reasons Strunk and

White got to decide good language practice. The politics of the classroom are in the teacher's favor, and students must accept this.

There are good reasons to accept the teacher's ideas about clarity and appropriate details in summaries of texts, but the student should have an opportunity to negotiate what the goals of their learning in that classroom will be, which will then dictate how to use a teacher's and students' different standards. Of course, I'm arguing here not just for a new kind of student-centered teaching and learning. I'm arguing for a classroom that structures power differently. It's a classroom that does not validate or reinforce only a teacher's power over standards that get used against students. It doesn't take for granted, or assume, one standard for language. It's a classroom that negotiates a teacher's authority with a student's informed goals for the class in order to figure out what to do about standards, how to use the various ones that exist in the classroom already in equitable ways, and how to give those who have not controlled standards of English more control.

PROBLEM 2. TESTS CREATE WHAT THEY TEST

F. Allan Hanson, a professor emeritus in sociocultural anthropology at the University of Kansas, has argued that "tests do not simply report on pre-existing facts," instead "they actually produce or fabricate the traits and capacities that they supposedly measure."[22] His book details numerous ways this happens, and has happened throughout history in various tests in our contemporary lives, from SATs and classroom testing, to IQ tests and drivers licensing.

He opens the book with the historical practice that occurred from at least the fourteenth to the seventeenth century in Europe and later in America called "swimming a witch."[23] The test of witch swimming was to determine if an individual was a witch or not, and it had theological implications to the community beyond the deadly implications to the individual accused. There needed to be a test that could not simply determine if an accused woman was a witch but root out the Devil (capital "D") in the world and maintain God's (capital "G") superiority. This test, much like our associations with language, was meant to show us a person's moral value, their goodness or evilness. But it clearly had a lot of haloing happening with it, and it worked from the fast thinking of the WYSIATI heuristic.[24]

---

22   F. Allan Hanson, *Testing Testing: Social Consequences of the Examined Life* (Berkeley: University of California Press, 1993), 284.

23   Hanson, 36–42.

24   The WYSIATI, or "What You See Is All There Is," heuristic is another mind process of Kahneman's. It's fast thinking that is similar to the availability heuristic. WYSIATI happens

The test was simple. In most cases, the accused was tied right thumb to left big toe and left thumb to right big toe, then lowered into water by a rope around their waist. If they floated, they were a witch. If they sank, then not a witch (sometimes it was the opposite). Today, we can see right through this test. There are no such things as witches, at least not the kind that the folks of sixteenth-century Europe were worried about. We also know that a person's buoyancy says nothing about any supernatural powers they may have, putting aside the fact that supernatural powers don't exist.

One's buoyancy has to do with their body's density compared to the density of the water they are dunked into. Salt water, for example, is denser than freshwater, and colder water is denser than warmer water.[25] A person's density will also be affected by how much air is in their lungs, how big their lungs are, the amount and kind of clothing they have on, how much body fat to muscle they have (muscle is denser than fat), etc. The point is we can see today that this test didn't test one's witchy-ness, rather it tested more directly how buoyant the accused person was relative to the kind of water they were being dunked into that day. Like Williams' phenomenology of error or hearing accents and Bushisms, this test tells us more about the biases of the test makers than about the qualities of the test takers. They saw witches. They just needed some kind of evidence to confirm it.

Putting all that aside, witch swimming was still a test. It measured the construct of a witch as defined by the test, or something equivalent to one's buoyancy. That is, as Hanson explains, the witch construct is created by the test itself. Without the test, you don't have witches. What is a witch? Well, witches are the people who float (or don't float) when tested in this way. The test literally creates witches. This same dynamic occurs in classrooms, IQ tests, and SATs. Take IQ. That test, or rather that battery of tests, offers a score typically between 69–130, but most score between 80–130, with 90–110 being considered average—that's the middle category created by the test and demonstrated in a large distribution of scores on the test. Those average IQ scores of 90–110 are within one standard deviation from the mean or middle score of 100. This part of the distribution of all scores creates that average IQ score range.

The point is, what does an IQ score actually measure? Is it really something called "intelligence" that can be understood in a linear fashion or by a score? Is

---

when someone operates from the assumption that the information in front of them is all they need to make a more complex or global claim or argument. In lay terms, it could be thought of as jumping too quickly to conclusions, or judgements, from limited data. See Kahneman, *Thinking*.

25   Here's a test: put an egg in a glass of water, then take it out, put a few tablespoons of salt in the same glass of water, mix, and drop the egg in. The water's density has changed.

someone who scores a 120 dumber or less capable than one who scores a 121 or 122 at whatever tasks or problems we are talking about? Does IQ really tell us something about how smart we are? If not, what is IQ? That is, what is the construct the test calls IQ? What exactly is the "intelligence" in "intelligence quotient"? Before 1904, IQ was meaningless because the IQ test didn't exist. So what was intelligence before IQ tests? We've lived with IQs for so long that the idea of someone possessing a high or low IQ seems real and natural. It's become a part of our systems, our conditions, but we've made this idea up.

Stephen Jay Gould, in his famous book *The Mismeasure of Man*, explains how scientists throughout history, particularly in the sciences of measurement and the testing of people's intelligence, have created such concepts like IQ, then measured people by them. Gould explains two fallacies that occur when we test intelligence, measure it with a single number, then rank people by their numbers. The first fallacy is one of "reification," or when we "convert abstract concepts into entities" then refer to those entities as if they were real in the world, as if they existed materially.[26]

In other words, we take a test that is meant to account for a large collection of cognitive and other capabilities that are complex and diverse, that create things and solve problems in the world in particular human situations and environments, then call what the test measures "intelligence," or in this case, IQ. Further, we use that new thing, IQ, as if it were real like a chair is real. We reify a bundle of actions, ideas, competencies, and cognitive skills that are allegedly all accounted for in the test, then rank people, or bestow privileges and opportunities, based on their scores or rankings.

Cathy O'Neil, a data scientist with a Ph.D. from Harvard in mathematics, explains this same phenomenon from a math and programming perspective in the world of big data. O'Neil discusses the ways that the hidden (to most) biases in the models used for programs that mine big data on people today do more harm than good. They tend to increase inequality in groups of people while increasing profits in corporations and entities that use big data and statistical algorithms to make decisions. These data models, with bad, unchecked biases, O'Neil calls "Weapons of Math Destruction" or WMDs.[27]

The SAT and GPAs in school work the same way. Is someone with a higher SAT score or GPA in school smarter than someone with a lower score or GPA? We often think so or make decisions from this fast thinking because we've accepted the reification of intelligence by equating it to such scores. We've also accepted

---

26   Gould, *Mismeasure*, 24–25.

27   Cathy O'Neil, *Weapons of Math Destruction: How Big Data Increases Inequality and Threatens Democracy* (New York: Broadway Books, 2016).

the models of intelligence, good languaging, and good students hardwired in the biases of the test's models, that is, the constructs each test uses to design tasks and their appropriate answers. But maybe most people with higher GPAs or SATs have them because their conditions afford them such scores, because they come from the same places in society, use the same kinds of languages, as those who make the models and constructs. Their biases are similar.

But our reifications may still be useful predictors, some may say. Even if they don't measure anything real, some argue that tests like the SAT can be predictive of future college performance when used with other factors, like GPA. But this isn't how most of us think about, refer to, and use such scores. We don't talk about GPAs or SATs as merely providing a degree of future success. In my experience, most people make loose equations between the score and intelligence. The smart kids are the ones with the 4.0 GPAs. Even if we accept that these students are smart, it doesn't mean that those with lower GPAs are not.

And yet, we often make such loose equations between test scores and GPAs to intelligence. These ways of quantifying intelligence have racial implications because GPAs and test scores are connected to conditions that afford higher or lower results. In our systems, because those systems are already made racist, most quantified ways of representing intelligence and language ability have White supremacist outcomes. We can see this in how folks talk publicly about such tests and scores.

William Shockley, a 1956 Nobel Prize-winning physicist, argued publicly that Black people were biologically less intelligent and used IQ to make this argument. On William F. Buckley's "Firing Line" TV show on June 10, 1974, Shockley stated, "My research leads me inescapably to the opinion that the major cause of the American Negro's intellectual and social deficits is hereditary and racially genetic in origin and, thus, not remediable to a major degree by practical improvements in the environment."[28] The problems in Black people and Black communities, he's saying, cannot be helped by any changes in their environment, like changes in schools or more jobs in the community. The problems of Black people, Shockley says, is their genetic inferiority seen in IQ tests.

Do you hear the racial implicit bias in this? The fast thinking? The White supremacy? Do you hear how Shockley has not considered that the IQ test he's basing much of his conclusions on may be racially biased against Black people, like all standardized tests of intelligence and language have been before then (and since)? Can you hear how he has not considered that Black social scientists

---

28   *Firing Line with William F. Buckley Jr.*, episode S0145, "Shockley's Thesis," recorded on June 10, 1974, https://www.youtube.com/watch?v=7JOIqkh2ms8&t=3116. For a discussion of Shockley's ideas and life, see Joel Shurkin, *Broken Genius: The Rise and Fall of William Shockley, Creator of the Electronic Age* (London: Macmillan, 2006).

have not had a chance to make the IQ test or the methods used to interpret its results? Can you hear him HOWLing, assuming his view, his language, his values, his conditions as universal ones?

So blinded by the reification of IQ as something real and objective in the world that tells him something real about people's capabilities, Shockley appears to have a difficult time considering that IQ itself is flawed and White supremacist when used in the ways he does. But then, Shockley promoted eugenics. He saw a dystopian future if low IQ people were not sterilized. The difference between Shockley and Stoddard is small. The consequences of their ideas on society are large.

Around the same time, Arthur Jensen, the noted professor of educational psychology at the University of California, Berkeley, made similar claims about the genetic inferiority of African Americans.[29] In 1994, Richard Herrnstein and Charles Murray published *The Bell Curve: Intelligence and Class Structure in American Life*. In it, they argue that many social problems like out of wedlock births, low IQ, and illiteracy were inherited, at least in part.[30] Many critics, such as Stephen J. Gould, Noam Chompsky, Thomas Sowell, and Joseph L. Graves, among others, criticized the book's statistical analyses and dubious findings.

My point is: White supremacist ideas and biases have not only been with us, but have always been the material by which those in power have made ideas like "intelligence" and standards of behavior or language. Tests made from such systemic biases create worlds and outcomes like this. Tests create what they purport to measure. Beware of tests and their singular, universal standards. Through their results, they are made by and make in the world the biases of their makers.

The standards of most standardized tests favor White people, so White people get higher IQs. People of color get lower IQs. These are the patterns White people create through tests White people make. These White tests and standards all have racial and other biases baked into them, only most call such standards neutral, or apolitical. Nothing when deployed in society by people is apolitical. The anxiety of the dystopian future of *Idiocracy*—the anxiety of a President Camacho—is inevitable in our world because such anxieties have always been with us. Our tests and the reifications that they create and test reflect this.

IQ scores are not simply a novelty. There are lots of other tests of so-called cognitive abilities and general intelligence used in schools, jobs, and other areas of society. The NFL, for instance, has used the Wonderlic test since the late

---

29   Arthur R. Jensen, "How Much Can We Boost IQ and Scholastic Achievement?" *Harvard Educational Review* 39, no. 1 (1969): 1–123, https://doi.org/10.17763/haer.39.1.l3u15956627 424k7.

30   Richard J. Herrnstein and Charles Murray, *Bell Curve: Intelligence and Class Structure in American Life* (New York: Simon and Schuster, 1994).

1960s.[31] SATs, ACTs, GREs, and even GPAs, all have this same problem, which is why I could score so low on all of these tests and still be quite successful at almost every step in my education and academic career. The ability to communicate effectively and accurately in any language is not a straightforward set of skills or competencies, nor are they easily tested. When we test for it, we have to make up the thing we test for, which will inevitably contain our biases.

PROBLEM 3. LANGUAGE NEEDS MORE LANGUAGE IN ORDER TO JUDGE LANGUAGE

Even if we agree on a particular standard for English usage to be tested, there is still another thorny issue. Any language standard that a test uses is language itself. How do you describe the standard so that it can be tested properly, or understood more carefully by anyone, test takers and test makers? Standards are only as strong and useful as they are descriptive and explanatory in what they refer to. They are only as good as they allow us to agree on the same things in the same ways.

To see better the problem of language needing more language, consider clarity of expression in English. What is clear English expression? As a standard, it is not so easy to identify and explain in some precise way that a variety of people will understand and agree with. How would you describe it to others so that they would not only understand exactly what you mean, but be able to use that understanding of clear English to judge instances of language for clarity in similar ways?

Notice that we can talk about clarity of expression in English, but you don't actually know precisely what I'm speaking of. We are talking about an abstract concept, a reification, that I have not really defined. In order to do so, I have to use more language. I mean, am I talking about clarity of spoken English, or written, or both? Is it really possible to have a standard for clarity of English expression that covers both spoken and written language? They are not the same, so let's focus on written expression. This way, we avoid having to consider things like someone's voice, or aural tone or pitch, as well as the speed of their speaking, among other features of spoken language like accent.

Okay, so we got the standard of clarity's general gist, but that's not the standard itself. It's the label for the standard. The actual standard for clarity is something more descriptive, something that makes up what we think of as a description of written language that is clear. Often, standards are lists that

---

31　The Wonderlic test is a test of cognitive abilities and general problem solving capacities and has been used in a number of fields; see Wikipedia: The Free Encyclopedia, s.v. "Wonderlic test," accessed March 4, 2021, https://en.wikipedia.org/wiki/Wonderlic_test.

describe features or dimensions that can be seen or heard in the language. These dimensions of the standard reference the key attributes or features demonstrated in a text or collection of texts.

How would you describe the characteristics or features of an instance of English that might fit your definition of clarity of expression? Does it include ideas about order or organizational structures, or certain kinds of words, the length of sentences, or their variation when put together? Does it include what is stated (subject matter) and in what order ideas are offered? Does it include some logics and exclude others? What does it say about linear and chronological logics, or associative, inductive, deductive, or other logics? Likely, you might be able to answer most of these questions to your own satisfaction, but can you describe what those answers mean to others' satisfaction? Can you describe it so others can use your descriptions as a way to judge instances of language for your idea of clarity? And can they do it *consistently*—that is, would numerous readers agree with you about the degree of clarity in any given passage, according to your standard?

Take the first feature I mentioned above about order and organization. Let's assume that most of this construct, one we are calling "clarity of expression," is based on that. How would you describe that feature to someone so they could spot it in examples too, or even employ it to write something clear for you? Does my chapter fit your ideas of order as clarity? Why? How would you explain the clarity of my prose in terms of how I've ordered words, sentences, paragraphs, or organized language? Could there be other ways to order a similar discussion in words that you'd see or hear as orderly or organized? How would you account in your description for these other, perhaps unexpected, ways to order words and sentences?

Let's get even more specific and look at an example. We'll use clarity in *word choice* as our primary criterion for clarity since it seems simple and knowable. What words are clearer than others? What words are inherently unclear? Consider these four statements that attempt to express our criterion of clarity as good word choice:

1. The draft *articulates* its ideas in careful ways.
2. The draft states its ideas in careful ways.
3. The draft voices its ideas in careful ways.
4. The draft *gives* its ideas in careful ways.

You may think that all of these versions of a standard for clarity work equally well. But some readers may think the second one is clearer than the first because it uses a more common, less fancy word. It is reasonable to suspect that more readers would have an easier time with the second sentence than with the first.

We might also say that since it is three syllables shorter, it is clearer, so a good example of what it describes. Brevity equals clarity.

But do the two words "articulates" and "states" mean the same thing, and are both equally close enough to the intended meaning of the sentence? Both mean to express or say something explicitly, but "articulate" has an additional meaning: to form a joint. It also refers to a place where two or more sections of something are connected and flex.

In Great Britain, what some in the US call semi-trucks or semis, they call "articulated lorries" because there are two sections, a back trailer with wheels and a front cab or lorry, which are connected and articulate, or flex. So if one was wanting this nuance or meaning to the above idea, then the first statement is clearer if clarity means a fullness, or accuracy, or even precision in meaning. That is, if the standard for clarity is not just stating an idea carefully in a draft, but leaving flexible ways to understand or interpret key ideas connected carefully together, then the first is more accurate and precise, since it includes more of the intended meaning.

One might argue, then, that the first sentence is therefore clearer in these ways than the second sentence. The word "states" is not clear enough about the flex in ideas in the draft. The second statement is just more accessible to more people. I could make a similar case for the embodied dimensions of "voices" in sentence three, or the associations with gifting and exchanging things with other people that I hear in sentence four, but you get the idea.

I go through these examples in detail because what I want to demonstrate is two things. First, our assumptions about something so seemingly obvious as clarity is not so easily defined, agreed upon, and captured for others to understand, use, or apply in their own language and judgement practices. It is hard to explain standards so that they work for most people in the same ways. In fact, I'd argue it's pretty much impossible. When it comes to standards in language use, we just work from the assumption that we can have this kind of near universal agreement, even though we don't and we never have.

Second, the language of standards is inherently shifty and ambiguous. The meaning in the descriptions of standards, in the words themselves, floats. Words can only mean what we want them to mean, or what our conditions in life that created our literacies afford those words to mean to us. So when we have language about other language, as in standards, we compound this slipperiness of exact or precise meaning. We might agree generally about the goodness or necessity of "clarity," but we will never fully agree about what exactly that looks, sounds, and feels like, or how well clarity is achieved exactly in any given expression of language.

In order to judge language with a standard, you have to have still other language to do that judging. Not only do you need language that describes the standard of language, but language that judges some other instance of language. It's taken me many paragraphs to explain a seemingly simple standard of language that most would agree with, clarity of expression. And I've not covered a number of obvious dimensions in this kind of standard. The trouble with standards is that they are words about words that necessitate more words in order to use them. And all these words are shifty and articulate, flex, depending on who is using them and reading them, and where and when those words circulate.

Stepping back from these three problems, I wonder about the consequences of White language supremacy in the testing of language more broadly in society. I have certainly felt the consequences. Here's what we know. Elite, White, male groups of people have had the most power to decide language standards. Tests created by elite White male groups themselves create the standards those tests allegedly measure. We need additional language to do any measuring of language apart from the language of any standard. This additional language has been controlled exclusively by the habits of language and judgement of elite, White, male groups. Our language and judgements reveal how much our ideas about language float and are inherently ambiguous. And these facts create an overdetermined set of overlapping systems of language, schooling, testing, and judgement that create our ideas of intelligence and ability, which are implicitly and historically associated with race.

THE COIK OF WHITE LANGUAGE SUPREMACY

Part of the problem with standards of English language is that in common conversations, we use the language of standards, or rather we invoke it, but we are not being precise. We aren't referring to the same things. You receive an email or letter. You judge it as bad or unprofessional because it is "unclear"—that is, it is unclear to you, but it was clear enough to the writer; otherwise, they would not have written and sent it. No one writes or speaks in order not to be understood. But what exactly do you think you see, or not see, in front of you in the email? This is what we often skip when we reference our own standards. We just jump to the judgement. We don't realize that if we didn't jump, what we jumped over, our reasons and evidence for our judgement, may be something else. That is, we shouldn't jump to judgements so quickly.

This may happen because most standards for English language already *seem to* make sense to us. However, as we've learned, this fast thinking is dangerous and too often racist. This racism comes from only having one language group forming standards, and only having our own singular perspective (no matter who we are) to judge from, and not realizing or admitting that we all are using only our singular

141

perspective to judge language by a standard that comes from a White, elite group of language users. Lots of mind bugs can occur in this situation.

Ask yourself: Do I think I'm a good writer? Can I write something, give it to another person without qualifying or justifying how bad the writing is, or how I wanted to spend more time on this part or that part, or how I know the opening needs some work? These insecurities about our languaging tell us that we don't even match up to our own standards. Why do you suppose we are all so insecure about our language use? Could it be because most of us do not share the same material relations to language as those who control the standards we've been taught in school and other places? Could it be that this condition in our lives makes most of us feel like we are not good language users, and therefore not very intelligent? Have you ever not given someone some of your writing, or not written an email to someone because you didn't want them to judge you as not very smart, as a bad communicator? I have had relatives who told me that they refuse to email me because they are worried that I'll think they aren't smart because of their alleged bad writing.

When we jump to our judgements about language, this can keep us from reflecting on our own unspoken standards of language and what they reproduce when we circulate them. This can make each of us unconscious reproducers of racism and White language supremacy, no matter who we are or where we come from. In other words, it is one thing to say that an email is unclear *to me*. It is another thing, perhaps a racist thing, to say an email is objectively unclear, then make another decision from that judgement, such as not give an applicant a job or turn down an opportunity for that person that you hold the power to bestow.

The second judgement assumes that the language practices of the email are *inherently* unclear, that the language itself is unclear language, and this judgement is linked to our notions of intelligence, which have always been associated with race and class. We transfer this unclear language onto the person, saying that the person is an unclear communicator and so not fit for this opportunity. But that language is not the only thing that makes it unclear to you. It is also your reading of the language, your experience of the email that creates the email as unclear. So why are we blaming that other person? What we might notice first is that they use language differently from us.

I'm not saying we shouldn't be able to identify when we don't understand a bit of language, or when we don't find someone's argument compelling. I'm saying that our not finding an argument compelling is more complicated than saying that the communicator is not good at communicating, and that the reasons for this often have to do with the racial politics of language and how we use them to judge instances of language around us. We need to slow down our thinking, realize that we all are implicated in White language supremacy.

Most of the time, we operate from a simple test: Is the language in front of me clear to me or compelling (choose your standard)? If yes, then okay, it is clear language or a compelling argument. If not, then it is unclear or unconvincing. When I was a technical writer for companies like Hewlett-Packard, Mitsubishi Silicon, and NASA, the rule or logic for this kind of test was called COIK—"clear only if known." If you know what a compound sentence and a relative clause are, then when I ask you to get rid of your compound sentences and convert them to sentences with more relative clauses in them, you'll likely know what to do. The instruction or feedback I've given you is clear because you know the terms already. But if you don't understand those two terms and how they apply to sentences, then what I asked of you is unclear.

Another way to define COIK is to think of it as the logic of I'll-know-it-when-I-see-it. For instance, COIK operates in the HOWLing that Strunk and White use to describe the different "languors" of Hemmingway and Faulkner back in chapter 3. As they themselves explain: "Anyone acquainted with Faulkner or Hemingway will have recognized them in these passages and perceived which was which. How different are their languors!"[32] COIK logic is why my reading of their style guide was so difficult to do in college.

In my previous email example, the communication is unclear or unconvincing because, well, I don't understand it, or I don't like the argument or evidence used. But my rationalizing of why I don't find it clear or convincing—that is, the deep structures of my thinking, my habits of language that afford me meaning in this instance—is not really identified. That is, we often, when pressed, will simply restate our opinion, not offer evidence for that opinion. This suggests that we don't usually think in terms of evidence for our claims and judgements, particularly our judgements of language. Psychologists have researched this phenomenon and found most study participants only offered explanations for their positions, not actual evidence, even when pressed.[33]

The key here is that *I* don't understand the email—that *I*, the person reading the email, don't like the argument. My judgement is more about me and how I'm using my linguistic and other biases and assumptions than about the person who wrote the email. I'm sure we've all had an exchange like this one:

> "This is such a great book," Karen says.
> "Why is that a good book?" Jose asks.
> "I don't know, I just like it. The book is clear and forceful,"
> says Karen.

32   Strunk Jr. and White, *Elements*, 68.

33   Deanna Kuhn, *The Skills of Argument* (Cambridge, England: Cambridge University Press, 1991).

It's clear to Karen why she likes the book, but likely not to Jose, at least not in any precise way. Does he know what "clear and forceful" looks or sounds like to Karen? No. She hasn't offered that. But much like my discussion of clarity in the previous section, this kind of an exchange can seem like some standard has been communicated, but it really hasn't. Remember, words float, and such standards require more floating words to help others make precise sense of them.

Clear and forceful are ideas that float around, meaning whatever Jose wants and whatever Karen wants. It's COIK. The habit of language, if we are not careful, turns into the Southern language strategy. COIK language explanations and standards are fine in many everyday situations, but once rewards, opportunities, and punishments get attached to our judgements of language and people, then our own private standards become racist because of where they come from in history, culture, and society. In those important places like schools, law firms, governments, and the like, we should be asking: What do our language conditions, which generate and circulate our standards, afford us to judge in any given instance of language?

I'm not saying, however, that some people are not as smart or language savvy as others. I'm not saying that White people are better and smarter with words than, say, Black people in the US. I'm saying that in our historically segregated society, racial groups and the languages that follow those groups have different material conditions. Those conditions create different English languages with different habits and norms. Each version of English has its rich and potent ways of understanding, thinking, and being in the world. They are not always compatible or transferable.

Knowing Black English may not help you learn White English, and vice versa. In fact, Black English often presents markers in your language that teachers and employers may judge harshly, or translate negatively through other racial implicit biases, as well as through mind bugs like the halo effect. They may hear a version of *Idiocracy* in your Black English, or Spanish-inflected English, or Chinese accent (heard by them). We often fall back on COIK ways of justifying our language judgements. Most of our mind bugs are not caught. The racial language biases go undetected. And White language supremacy is affirmed as neutral, as universal language practice, as proper English.

CHAPTER 6.

THE ECONOMICS OF RACISM

Growing up on Statz and in Pecos trailer park, the economics of racial groups mattered and muddied things for me.[1] In my youth, like many folks in the US, my own race-judgements were often economically motivated. Money, the abundance or lack of it, always complicates our abilities to understand and fight against things like racism or sexism or ableism, even when we think we are doing good work like antiracist practices. If you have adequate monetary means and are White, then you have more privilege and freedom to fight things like racism or simply to stand aloof from racism in your attitudes and decisions.[2] But turning one's back to racism, ignoring it, is not the same as fighting against it.

Not engaging in racist behavior or practices doesn't mean you've actually done any antiracism work yet. Abstaining from racism is still complicity with racist systems and policies. It allows the systems to continue and grow. Ibram X. Kendi, the Director of the Center for Antiracist Research at Boston University, speaks at length about this.[3] There's an analogy that may help. I think of economics as one set of rules and conditions in a larger society's game of tricks and fake-outs, a game in which the outcome is always White supremacy.

PLAYING ANTIRACIST GAMES IN RACIST SYSTEMS

If you are rich enough, then you don't have to shop at Walmart, but if you're poor or on a limited income, it may be the only place where you can afford to

---

1   To read about racial hierarchy in Western societies around social contract theory, see Charles Mills, *Racial Contract*; to read about racial formations and hierarchy in the U.S., see Michael Omi and Howard Winant, *Racial Formation*; to read about the pressure that working class White racial formations have placed on other formations of color, see David R. Roediger, *Wages*, or George Lipsitz, *Possessive Investment*; to read about racist hierarchical thought and behavior, see Ibram X. Kendi, *Antiracist*.

2   I realize that a person of color cannot be racist in the same ways that a White person can since the systems of racism are set up against us (people of color), even when some of us may have economic or other kinds of privileges. However, a person of color can hold values and make decisions that reproduce racist systems and outcomes in the same way that a poor White person can vote for political candidates or initiatives that work against White economic or other interests; thus anyone's decisions and ideas can work to oppress them further regardless of racial or class or gender status.

3   See Ibram X. Kendi, *Antiracist*. For a language- and literacy-based argument along the same lines, see Asao B. Inoue, *Antiracist Writing Assessment Ecologies: Teaching And Assessing for A Socially Just Future* (Fort Collins, CO, and Anderson, SC: WAC Clearinghouse and Parlor Press, 2015), https://doi.org/10.37514/PER-B.2015.0698.

shop. It's prices are low enough that you can get by there. But Walmart has been known to engage regularly in harmful practices that destroy local communities' small businesses and that pressure companies to sell their products cheaper to them, which depresses other local economies that produce those goods and lowers workers' wages in those places. They use employment practices that are unethical and harmful to their own employees, such as denying full time work, health insurance, and other benefits.[4] Buying from Walmart supports them in these practices and the oppressive ways they harm communities and people all over the globe.

Now, if you're rich enough, you can afford to be more ethical in your own shopping practices. You can boycott Walmart and shop at more expensive local stores. You have that privilege. Your money allows you to turn your back on Walmart. But if you are poor, you don't get that privilege. That's not how capitalism is set up. Capitalism is set up so that the more money you have, the more you're able to exercise your ethics. All the while, the folks who have to shop at Walmart help that company continue employing its bad practices. It's not simply an irony. It's a built-in contradiction, a paradox that perpetuates the badness of the system. It is a systemic bias that makes Walmart both good and bad. It is an inexpensive place to shop and a place that oppresses its workers and others around the world in order to provide low prices to people like their employees, not so ironically all because of the lower prices they can offer.

Walmart's badness continues to oppress poor communities, the very communities Walmart preys on with its low prices and less-than-full-time jobs. Meanwhile, the folks who have the privilege to choose not to shop at Walmart and not have to work there haven't done anything to stop Walmart's unethical and oppressive practices. And ironically, they are likely the ones most in positions to do so. They have economic privilege to stand aloof from that bad place.

In this analogy, in my youth, I was the Walmart shopper who, through his own racial oppression, hated the Mexican Walmart shoppers around me, in part because I was seen as one like them, which paradoxically I was and wasn't. I wanted the privilege to not shop at Walmart—both literally and figuratively.

---

4   Walmart's unethical business practices have been the subject of much discussion over the years; see Chris Osterndorf, "10 Reasons Walmart is the Worst Company in America," The Daily Dot, last updated March 1, 2020, https://www.dailydot.com/via/walmart-labor-unions-bad -company/; Nicholas Conley, "Shady Secrets Walmart Doesn't Want You to Know," Grunge, last updated July 31, 2019, https://www.grunge.com/26656/shady-secrets-wal-mart-doesnt-want- know/; Barbara Farfan, "Walmart Ethics Shown in Class Action Lawsuits," The Balance Small Business, last updated December 12, 2019, https://www.thebalancesmb.com/walmart-classic -action-employee-lawsuits-3974960; Philip Mattera, "Wal-Mart: Corporate Rap Sheet," Corporate Research Project, last updated December 7, 2020, https://www.corp-research.org/wal-mart.

I thought naively that simply turning from racism was antiracist, all the while holding racist ideas about Mexicans.

Meanwhile, the good White people around me, the ones with liberal and good intentions, such as my White teachers or my college friend Erik, who had more power to aid me and alleviate some of the systemic racism in our schooling, did nothing to actually stop the racism around us. What they did was avoid shopping in the Walmart of racist ideas and practices, but the racist system itself was still operating and thriving. And all I wanted to do was be like those rich White liberals and avoid racism in the system without seeing that it was the system itself that I was trying to avoid.

I thought escaping racism was a game in which to avoid racism, individuals avoided oppression, but it isn't. Thinking racism or White supremacy is an individual sport, that the game is about how each of us play it, is a hustle. It's a line the system sells us. It's just like the fact that you don't get to determine what products are available at the grocery store, nor what stores are available to you, when they are open, or anything about those stores. You have choices in what you buy or avoid buying, yes. However, be careful with that kind of thinking. It's a hustle too.

You are pitched the narrative that you have free choice, the power to choose where to shop and what you want, but what you want and where you want to shop are limited to what the system dictates is available to you. You can only see the choices you've made and the ones presented to you. It's great to have choices for shopping, but do not confuse your ability to choose the best possible free range, organic, non-GMO chicken with the freedom to choose the healthiest chicken to eat, or whether it's a good idea to eat chicken at all. Your shopping habits and choices are determined by the system that makes stores and food possible. The freedom to make a choice in a system is not the same as the freedom to choose just anything.

The game of racism is much like this constrained and determined system of judgements and choices. And it works better if we all think that the key to success, the key to not being racist, or to avoid racism, is to take care of one's own decisions and judgements, to not be prejudiced, to play your game well. But antiracism is not simply an ethical game individuals play. It is not solely a team sport. Individuals alone do not win the game of antiracism.

It is also not won solely on the field of play. It is won before the game, when the rules and guidelines of play are determined. It is won by those who decide which grocery stores are built (or not) in your neighborhood. It is won by Walmart. It is won by those who architect our society and decide on language standards. It is won in the places where privileges and roles are decided, and who gets them, and who doesn't.

When I speak of privilege, particularly White privilege, I am not saying that White people do not struggle, or that they have higher grades, better jobs, and more opportunities handed to them with little effort. We all work hard. But too often, White people's hard work is worth more than people of color's, even though there are plenty of poor and disadvantaged White people. Everyone is capable of achieving, but we shouldn't be fooled into believing that our own individual paths toward success or achievement can be others' paths, that everyone's hard work is rewarded in the same ways. Our material and economic conditions, which are patterned by race in the US, are often dramatically different.

Despite what it sounds like I'm saying, hard work and merit are not abstract concepts in real life. For most people, they are gritty, sweaty labor that is experienced in context and through specific material conditions that define them. But they are not experienced in the same ways by everyone. We are not all running the same races, or starting in the same places, to use an often invoked metaphor for racial inequality. Most of us are also not in the room before the race begins, deciding on the rules of the race.

If you don't believe me, likely you are White and middle class. Your hard work generally has benefited you. You've had choices. That's not an insult. It's a real privilege to think that everyone has the same chances at things, that life is fair, and success is mostly about hard work, and dedication, and being a good person. If you believe this, it likely means your hard work, and dedication, and goodness in the past have paid off, that you've seen your friends' and family's hard work pay off. That's really wonderful. It should be the norm for everyone, but it is not.

Because your view, like everyone's individual view, is limited and situated in your life, it may be hard to see that it's only your view, not a universal one. This is fast thinking, an incarnation of the availability heuristic. And yet, many often act as if their view is a universal one—that's HOWLing. When someone says things like, "Surely you can see that . . . ," or "Obviously, this is the case . . . ," they assume their listener is seeing things just as they are, but that is not a certainty. It's the trap that Strunk and White fell into so easily, thinking that their readers were just like them. What I'm describing are two habits of HOWL that often get used in arguments about race and racism: hyperindividualism and a naturalized orientation to the world that is universalized or is assumed to be everyone's orientation. Together these HOWLs justify all kinds of racism in society by those who get to have a voice, those with social and cultural power to speak or be heard.[5]

---

5   In discussing the way science creates its ideas, Donna Haraway says that the language of science too often offers universals, which leads to thinking in terms of "god-tricks," or visions of

To compound this limitation, the stories you've been told reinforce the idea of abstract merit and hard work, that everyone's hard work will be rewarded as yours have. I'll say much more about this narrative of success that is central to the US in Chapter 10, but it's worth a few words here. We've been told stories about how anyone can pull themselves up by their own bootstraps and make it in the world, that life is essentially fair, or at least rule-bound. And if we know the rules, we can follow them and win. The rules are objective, not biased, the same for everyone. One of those rules is that hard work pays off for everyone in the same ways.

We make movies about this story. We wish for it, because this kind of story is comforting, and gives people faith in tomorrow and their own laboring in the world. It tells us that, yes, we too can be successful, can make it. It's the opium we all take in teaspoons daily.[6] Meanwhile, these stories allow us to ignore or downplay the counterstories and statistics that disprove this harmful narrative of merit and the pulling up of bootstraps.

This is a White story told and sold by White elites. It's told and sold in those grammar and style guides for English. It's told and sold in schools. It's told and sold in churches. Then it's purchased by many poor and working class Whites and people of color. We might even have seen some around us succeed through their hard work, the Oprah Winfreys and Barack Obamas of the world. But these few exceptions fool us because we can see them, and we think "I too can be a Barack Obama." But there can only be one Barack Obama with his particular set of circumstances and material conditions. That's how the system works.

Most of us find that our hard work pays fewer dividends, but we still have hope because we've bought the story of hope in all of its audacity.[7] But does this story simply keep people in their place, keep people hoping and working hard

---

knowledge and our world that projects a particular group's view of things, which historically has been a White, Western, male view. This view is called objective and universal, and if we buy into it as objective, then all other views of things are subjective. To read more about situated knowledges, see Haraway, "Situated."

6   This is a reference to Karl Marx, "Introduction," A Contribution to the Critique of Hegel's Philosophy of Right: Works of Karl Marx 1843, ed. Matthew Carmody, last updated 2009, https://www.marxists.org/archive/marx/works/1843/critique-hpr/intro.htm. In the Introduction, Marx makes a structural or systemic critique of religion as human-made. He says: "The foundation of irreligious criticism is: Man makes religion, religion does not make man . . . Religion is the sigh of the oppressed creature, the heart of a heartless world, and the soul of soulless conditions. It is the opium of the people."

7   More about audacity and hope can be found in Barack Obama's second autobiographical book, The Audacity of Hope: Thoughts on Reclaiming the American Dream (New York: Crown Publishers, 2006).

with stories of hard work and dreams deferred?[8] Believing in the story has the effect of keeping money and power in the same groups of people if the story doesn't come true for enough people.

And the story doesn't work for most of us. It didn't work very well for my Black neighbors on Statz, nor my White, working-class neighbors in the trailer park, nor the nearby Latine communities, nor my mom. Why? Because none of us sets the terms for success and what that hard work is worth in the marketplace or classroom. We play a game we cannot win. All we can do, right now, is keep playing with our hands tied behind our backs, keep playing and hoping. Keep having faith in a system not made for our success. Meanwhile, those White, rich, elites make the rules about hard work because they own stuff and have lobbyists who help make laws that benefit them and the kind of hard work they do, but not the kind most others' do.

Again, hard work is not abstract. It's contextual and contingent on the material conditions you live in, just like our languages. Our words come from our material conditions. The minute someone mentions "hard work" or "merit," you should ask what conditions make such a thing and what it looks like. In other words, whose conditions get to define hard work and merit? Who benefits most from that definition? If it ain't clear, likely the story is meant to be swallowed in one gulp, unproblematically. It's meant to be unquestioned and undefined, as if no one has questions about what it means to work hard, or how much work merits something else. If it isn't defined and situated in someone's life story, then it's just an empty slogan, or what some language theorists call a "floating signifier," a term that the reader or listener is supposed to fill in with meaning.[9] It's meant to convince, not inform. It's meant to mean anything you want it to. It's the Southern language strategy.

Using and reading terms like "hard work" are race-judgements, among other things. And to complicate this, our own hard work generally defines us as individuals within communities that have understandings of things like "hard work." That is, we are what we do in the places we are at with those there. And who we are, and what we do, and where we are at are floating concepts in another way. They are biased by those who use them. That is, they are

8   I'm reminded of Langston Hughes' poem, "Harlem," which begins: "What happens to a dream deferred?/Does it dry up/like a raisin in the sun?/Or fester like a sore—/And then run?" See, Langston Hughes, "Harlem," Poetry Foundation, accessed March 8, 2021, https://www.poetryfoundation.org/poems/46548/harlem.

9   To read the original discussion of "floating signifier," see Claude Lévi-Strauss, *Introduction to the Work of Marcel Mauss*, 61–62; for a very good discussion of race as floating signifier, see *Race: The Floating Signifier*, directed by Sut Jhally, (Northampton, MA: Media Education Foundation, 1997), DVD.

raced, gendered, classed, sexed inherently because they come out of our lives and life stories.

And so, these stories that we tell ourselves, when taken as hyperindividual-ized and universal orientations for everyone equally, hide the way economics is a part of the way racism is reproduced in our society.

RIGGING THE RACIST GAMES WE ALL PLAY

Tax laws in the US are a good example of the way the game of literacy we play in school, business, and civic spaces is already fixed to create certain unfair out-comes. The federal income tax rate is a progressive tax, meaning as you make more money by your labor, portions of your income are taxed at a progressively higher rate. In 2019, this rate started at 10 percent and went up to 37 percent. Meanwhile the tax for capital gains, that is monetary gains made by owning assets, like property or stocks, were between 0 percent and 20 percent. You get taxed less for income you make from having lots of money and buying things that make you more money and that appreciate in value. These tax laws benefit the hard work that rich people do, not the hard work that poor or working class or even middle class people do—that is, wage labor. And within one's racial group, who is statistically more likely to be poor or working class in the US? Who is more likely to have a wage, to work by the taxable hour? People of color. Who makes up most of the rich deciders in the US? White people.

So if you are White, statistically you have economic advantages that most people of color do not have—I'm speaking of the racial group as a whole, not individual cases. Exceptions that any of us can name, like myself, do not dis-prove the rule. This is why we call them *exceptions* to the rule. But systems are not made up of exceptions. They are made up of rules and patterns. Another way to see this racial inequality is to compare wealth among racial formations in the US. In 2016, White households had 41 times more accumulated wealth than Black households and 22 times more than Latine ones.[10] Black households that were at zero or negative wealth, meaning they had more debts than assets, had risen to 37 percent of all Black households; meanwhile, the same proportion of White households in the same category was 15.5 percent.

These gaps are the outcomes of historical inequalities—the material con-ditions that each group lives in and learns to communicate in. They are the

---

10   "Wealth Inequality in the United States," Inequality.org, The Institute for Policy Studies, accessed March 8, 20201, https://inequality.org/facts/wealth-inequality/; see also, Kimberly Amadeo, "Racial Wealth Gap in the United States: Is There a Way to Close It and Fill the Divide?" The Balance, updated November 23, 2020, https://www.thebalance.com/racial-wealth -gap-in-united-states-4169678.

outcomes of what people have done in the places they were at with those there. They do not just go away in a generation or two. You inherit a range of opportunities because of who your parents are, what they did, and where they were able to live and raise a family. You inherit where you went to school as a child. You inherit who your family's friends and connections are. You inherit the language your parents use, and the schools they got you into, and those with whom you associate, your friends. All inheritances.

None of these things you choose as a child. They are part of an historical system, a game the rules of which have been determined by racism and White supremacy before you were a player. Do you think E. B. White or William Strunk were in full control of their opportunities to go to Cornell University, an elite, Eastern university? Do you think they would have met if their fathers hadn't been a lawyer and a president of a company?

And paradoxically, the economics of racism is not simply a predetermined system, one in which people do not have any agency or control. People generally do have some control. Sometimes agency ain't enough, though. I made it out and up, but surely the game was more rigged for me than my Black neighbors. While I didn't get to start where Erik started, inherit what he got, I did have some inheritances that the system accepted.

My mom crawled, scrubbed, and scraped her way out of the ghetto. She took us south from North LV to North Pecos Street in Las Vegas, the trailer park. While it was just a short 2.7 miles south of Statz, following roughly Boulder Highway (I582), I remember Pecos Trailer Park feeling very different. It seemed miles and miles away, almost a different city. The streets, the neighbors, the texture in the air was dramatically different. When we moved into the trailer at Pecos, I felt rich, like we'd made it, Jeffersons' style.[11] I'm sure my friend Chris did not feel this way about that place, having moved from a home in a middle-class area on the other side of town.

Even today, these economic conditions persist in the neighborhoods of my youth.[12] Today, the average household income for those living on Statz Street is $26,000. If you are Black, it's $20,000. The average rent is $680 a month. Go 2.7 miles to North Pecos Street, and the average household income goes up to

---

11   My brother and I loved *The Jeffersons*, a TV sitcom (1975–1985) developed by Norman Lear and written primarily by Don Nichol, Michael Ross, and Bernard West. The show starred Isabel Sanford and Sherman Hemsley, a Black couple who owned a chain of successful dry-cleaning businesses and moved to a rich, White part of town, Manhattan. It was a spin-off from *All in the Family*.

12   All data in this and the next five paragraphs I take from The Opportunity Atlas project, which was formed by a group of researchers from Harvard University, the Census Bureau, and Brown University. See https://www.opportunityatlas.org/.

$31,000. If you're Black, it's only $24,000. Average rents in the area rise to $845. It could all seem like economics, like capitalist markets working as they should. Such markets, even if they work as they should, become stubborn and persist generation after generation. They become racialized barriers and walls, but barriers and walls are paradoxical. For some, they are more permeable than for others. Barriers and walls keep people out while trapping people in.

Today, Statz is 93 percent residents of color, while Pecos is 80 percent. That's pretty much what it was in my day. And of course, just like when I lived in these places, more White residents coincides with higher household incomes, higher rents, and higher property values. This is why my trailer park neighbors hated me so much, wanted us out of the White trailer park. There were lots of Brown folks around the trailer park in the adjacent streets. But my Pecos trailer park neighbors were walling in Whiteness as much as walling out Brownness. It's why they kept asking me: "Why are you here?" It's why they kept their elaborate strike system *just for us*. My Brown body lowered their property values, degraded the value of their trailers. This is how the economics of racism works. It creates inherited conditions that beget certain kinds of racialized outcomes from one generation to the next. My neighbors' racism toward me was in part a product of our economics.

In the middle of high school, my mom would move us even more south, following Boulder Highway another seven miles to Ithaca Avenue, still in Las Vegas. Today, the average rent around Ithaca is at $1,000 a month. This neighborhood is 67 percent residences of color and has an average household income of $36,000. But if you're Black, that income is only $25,000. That's only $1,000 more a year than the Black population at Pecos. So, the more south one goes on I582 today, as was the case in my youth, the better people do economically, the better funded the schools are, the Whiter it gets, except if you're Black. If you are Black, you may live in the area, but you don't really make more money than those Black residents north of you. In fact, the White and Latine residents on Statz make $1,000 a year more than you on average if you're Black.

There are other things related to economics that follow this same path south. Other life conditions change as one goes south out of North LV to Pecos to Ithaca. All are skewed by race. For instance, the percentage of married households increases. Teenage birth rates lower. On Statz, this rate is 40 percent, but it's 49 percent if you're Black. This means every other teenage Black girl gets pregnant and gives birth to a baby. On Pecos, the overall teenage birth rate is 39 percent, with the Black rate greater than 50 percent.[13] On Ithaca, it's 26 percent, and in that place, there are too few Black residents to report any data.

---

13 The data given on The Opportunity Atlas website simply says, ">50%".

Perhaps the most damning statistic is incarceration rates. On Statz, the over-all average incarceration rate is 4.4 percent, but that's deceptive. When broken down by race, a very different picture develops. White rates are at 3.1 percent, Latine are 3.8 percent, but Blacks are 20 percent. That is, two out of every ten Blacks from the area are incarcerated. A similar picture develops at Pecos: Whites incarceration rates are 1.2 percent, Latine are 1.6 percent, and Blacks are 8.7 percent. And on Ithaca, only 1.4 percent of Whites, 1.9 percent of Latine, and 2.1 percent of Blacks are incarcerated.[14]

All these differences are not just from how much money folks make, but lots of other inherited factors, conditions that are mostly out of people's control but connected to our systems of economics. There is only a $5,000 bump in household annual income from one neighborhood of my youth to the next. Does $5,000 really make that big of a difference to one's life? My mom struggled to make each jump and had to get married in order to make the last jump to Ithaca. Two incomes. The barriers for us were more permeable. And yet, in the end, she'd lose that house to foreclosure.

So, all of us inherit many privileges, practices, and opportunities that make us, that allow us to play life's racist game in the ways we can, or maybe, give us a different game to play with better rules and chances at winning. Language is central to our inheritance and the game. I inherited a poor, single-parent house-hold in North LV, a mom who only had words and love to feed me at times. But she spoke and used a standardized English, a White English from Oregon, an advantage, a White privilege. And my little success in that reading contest was enough for me to see that words could be mine. I could not change a lot of things, but maybe, I thought, I could language my way out and up.

And this assumption about the exchange value of a standardized English in the US has its tradition. I didn't make this idea up. Ta-Nehisi Coates, in his essay, "The Case for Reparations," recounts *The Chicago Tribune*'s comment on reparations to African Americans in 1891.[15] Among the trade-offs that the newspaper argued was fair was English. The article states: "They [African Amer-icans] have been taught Christian civilization, and to speak the noble English language instead of some African gibberish. The account is square with the ex-slaves."[16] So one might exchange slavery and "African gibberish" for Stan-dardized English. The assumption is: lift up. And of course, there are lots of contemporary reports and articles that proclaim English as the lingua franca of

---

14   For a deep history of the U.S. prison and justice systems, see Michelle Alexander, *The New Jim Crow: Mass Incarceration in the Age of Colorblindness* (New York: The New Press, 2010).

15   Ta-Nehisi Coates, *We Were Eight Years in Power: An American Tragedy* (New York: One World, 2017).

16   Coates, 178.

the international business world.[17] It is common sense to say that one universal key to success in life in the US is fluency in English. Standardized English means more money in your pocket.

I translated this need for Standardized English as reading and writing like White people—talk White and go to college. But I was bucking social trends that were not in my favor. My mom never went to college, nor did her parents. My grandma had an eighth-grade education. I'm not even sure if my grandpa graduated from high school. We are talking about my mom's side of the family. On my dad's side, I don't know. I didn't know them, didn't know my dad, but I know that he didn't go to college. I know his family were farmers in Hawai'i, immigrants from Japan.

I was the first to get a college degree in my family, a first-generation college student on both sides. I am the first college graduate in my family that I know of. A 2018 study by the National Center for Education Statistics shows what we would expect: The more years in college parents have, the more likely their children are to go to college and graduate.[18] First-generation students have the lowest chances of going to college, staying in or persisting, and graduating. The White supremacist language system we live in, that some of us bear through, is overdetermined. It's one of the rules of the racist game, and much of those rules are written by economics. This means that the college game has multiple, overlapping, and redundant ways to be racist. There are many ways to keep Brown and Black people poor, in debt, underemployed, and uneducated. Most of those ways can be accomplished without direct reference to race.

So being in college, staying in it, and graduating is a privilege. Those privileges are racialized—that is, they follow racial patterns. They also follow economic patterns and social patterns that travel with those who have already gone to college or those who could not. If you go (or went) to college, chances are your parents did first. They helped you in significant ways to get there, stay

---

17   English as the dominant language for international business has been reported on over the years; see Tsedal Neeley, "Global Business Speaks English," *Harvard Business Review*, May 2012, https://hbr.org/2012/05/global-business-speaks-english; Dorie Clark, "English—The Language of Global Business?" *Forbes*, October 26, 2012, https://www.forbes.com/sites/dorieclark/2012 /10/26/english-the-language-of-global-business/#447eeeabb57e; Christine S. Sing, "English as a Lingua Franca in International Business Contexts: Pedagogical Implications for the Teaching of English for Specific Business Purposes," in *Business Communication: Linguistic Approaches*, ed. Franz Rainer and Gerlinde Mautner (Berlin: De Gruyter, 2017), 319–356.

18   Emily Forrest Cataldi, Christopher T. Bennett, and Xianglei Chen, *First-Generation Students: College Access, Persistence, and Postbachelor's Outcomes* (National Center for Education Statistics, U.S. Department of Education, 2018), https://nces.ed.gov/pubsearch/pubsinfo. asp?pubid=2018421.

in, and graduate. They even may have made sacrifices to pay your tuition or helped you with food or rent. But don't let your family's sacrifice blind you to your privilege.

While many White and elite families sacrifice much to help their kids go to college, it is important to remember that such families have enough means to make such sacrifices. Sacrifice is part of most people's college experience, but too often, people of color must sacrifice more than others. Furthermore, the ability to sacrifice for college is an exercise of privilege for some, and historically in the US, sacrifice, particularly economic sacrifice, has been a White privilege. Think the Walmart example.

If your family has negative wealth, there is nothing left to sacrifice. College is not a realistic option, which perpetuates the cycle of poverty, low household wealth, and negative wealth among many people of color in the US today. But if your family just has to give up some luxuries, take fewer vacations, or make extra loan payments that they can afford, then the sacrifice is a privilege, less of a sacrifice than others' sacrifices, yet still a sacrifice. Do you see the paradox? It's not a pissing contest. We should recognize that we all get pissed on but not equally. Some of us are drenched in it. Others just get sprayed a little. But we all stink of urine.

To make matters worse, college ain't gettin' any cheaper, but it was more doable when I entered. In 1989 when I started college (the first time), the average annual tuition for a state university like the kind I attended was around $3,200 in 2017 dollars. In 2017, the average tuition for a four-year public institution was almost $10,000.[19] That's triple the cost in just tuition alone, before the cost of books, food, housing, and any medical or transportation expenses. And these are not the only barriers that keep many from college today.

Inflation, a devaluing of the dollar, also hits poorer people harder than those in higher tax brackets, keeping more poor folks from college. Their fewer dollars in their wallets or bank accounts are worth less. According to the Bureau of Labor Statistics' consumer price index, a dollar in 1989 was worth $2.08 in 2019.[20] That's a 108 percent increase. This means today's dollar buys less than half of what it did in 1989.

But everything, all systems, are connected. The economics of racism are also influenced by environmental racism. Environmental racism is the condition in which the areas where people of color live are disproportionately contaminated

19   Emmie Martin, "Here's How Much More Expensive It Is for You to Go to College Than It Was for Your Parents," CNBC, last updated November 29, 2017, https://www.cnbc.com/2017/11/29/how-much-college-tuition-has-increased-from-1988-to-2018.html.

20   Ian Webster, "Value of $1 from 1989 to 2019," CPI Inflation Calculator, accessed 22 March 2019, https://www.in2013dollars.com/us/inflation/1989?amount=1.

and toxified.[21] The father of environmental racism as a concept and area of study is Dr. Robert Bullard, who is Distinguished Professor of Urban Planning and Environmental Policy at Texas Southern University. What environmental justice activists and researchers, like Dina Gilio-Whitaker, Kandi Mossett-White, Mustafa Ali, Jamie Margolin, and LeeAnne Walters, have found over the last few decades reveals more inherited barriers to life, clean air, water, and housing for people of color. And ultimately what all these inherited toxic environments mean is a decreased access to college. If you're sick, you cannot get to or survive long enough to go to college. Just to illustrate, here are some facts:

- Seventy-eight percent of all African Americans live within 30 miles of a coal fired power plant.
- The closer one gets to a superfund site (a site of toxic, abandoned, accidentally spilled, or illegally dumped hazardous substances) the more likely you will encounter Black families living there.
- Black people are exposed to 1.5 times more particulate matter than White people.
- Latine people are exposed to 1.2 times more particulate matter than non-Hispanic Whites.
- In over a 20-year period, more than half of the people who live within 1.86 miles of toxic waste facilities in the United States are people of color.
- In a 2009 report, 11.2 percent of African American children and 4 percent of Mexican American children are poisoned by lead, while 2.3 percent of White children are.
- Communities of color have more contaminated water than White communities.[22]

---

21   You can read about environmental racism in a number of places; see "Environmental Racism in America: An Overview of the Environmental Justice Movement and the Role of Race in Environmental Policies," The Goldman Environmental Prize, June 24, 2015, https://www.gold manprize.org/blog/environmental-racism-in-america-an-overview-of-the-environmental -justice-movement-and-the-role-of-race-in-environmental-policies/; Nina Lakhani, "'Racism Dictates Who Gets Dumped On': How Environmental Injustice Divides the World," *Guardian*, October 21, 2019, https://www.theguardian.com/environment/2019/oct/21/what-is-environ-mental-injustice-and-why-is-the-guardian-covering-it; Renee Skelton and Vernice Miller, "The Environmental Justice Movement," The National Resources Defense Council, March 17, 2016, https://www.nrdc.org/stories/environmental-justice-movement.

22   To read more about each of the listed outcomes, see, Chloe Reichel, "Toxic Waste Sites and Environmental Justice: Research Roundup," Journalist's Resource, September 24, 2018, https://journalistsresource.org/studies/environment/superfund-toxic-waste-race-research/; Anne M. Wengrovitz and Mary Jean Brown, *Recommendations for Blood Lead Screening of Medicaid-Eligible Children Aged 1–5 Years: An Updated Approach to Targeting a Group at High*

The point I'm making is that in order to have access to the kind of language practices that I saw as a child as worthwhile and valuable in school and the world, the kind that would take me out of the ghetto, a person usually needed to go to college. This means that you gotta inherit a number of things, among them are White racial language habits and economic conditions that give you a chance to afford college or make some sacrifices to go. And on top of these things, you have to also be well enough to go and learn. You have to have lived in a healthy enough environment, one that didn't make you sick.

College is still the primary place one goes to gain good language practices, or so we tell ourselves. But it's harder to get to and more expensive the poorer and Blacker you are. College has become more and more difficult to get into and persist in for too many people. Those barriers to entry keep more poor Black, Latine, Indigenous, Asian, and White students out than White, middle-class students.

I'm oversimplifying the problems, but that doesn't negate the problems. There are more issues than just race and economics that keep people from college. But I simplify the issues in order to magnify—in order to show more clearly—one part of the problem of the politics of language and its judgement in the US, which I lived in contradictory ways, in ways that were presented to me as paradoxes. That part of the problem is the tangle of economics in White language supremacy. One of the gates to economic success is taking on dominant White language habits, habits which one uses to get into and persist through college, which then allows one to have better chances at good jobs and places to live free from harm or disease.

Somehow, I made it. I'm one of the exceptions, and by all accounts, I succeeded quite well. My language has been good to me. But most people of color like me do not make it, and this is the problem. We should not judge a system by its exceptions, by those few who seem to thrive in the system. We should judge the system by its rules, by what happens to most.

And yet there is another complicating factor for many students of color to make it to and succeed in college, one you likely can guess. We are what we

Risk (Morbidity and Mortality Weekly Report, Centers for Disease Control and Prevention, U.S. Department of Health and Human Services, 2009), https://www.cdc.gov/mmwr/preview /mmwrhtml/rr5809a1.htm; Jasmine Bell, "5 Things to Know About Communities of Color and Environmental Justice," Center for American Progress, April 25, 2016, https://www.american progress.org/issues/race/news/2016/04/25/136361/5-things-to-know-about-communities-of -color-and-environmental-justice/; James VanDerslice, "Drinking Water Infrastructure and Environmental Disparities: Evidence and Methodological Considerations," *American Journal of Public Health* 101, suppl. 1, December 2011, https://doi.org/10.2105/AJPH.2011.300189; Van R. Newkirk, II, "Trump's EPA Concludes Environmental Racism Is Real," *Atlantic*, February 28, 2018, https://www.theatlantic.com/politics/archive/2018/02/the-trump-administration-finds -that-environmental-racism-is-real/554315/.

do in the places we are at with those there. That is, we language the way we do because of the places we are at and the people around us. North LV was not a place where the Standardized English of schools and colleges was used, neither was Pecos trailer park. As educators and linguists know, after a certain point in one's life, usually around adolescence, our ability to learn new languages, new ways with words, is a lot more difficult.

The linguist Rosina Lippi-Green describes this phenomenon as each person's "linguistic sound house," in which our childhoods greatly determine the boundaries of our language practices for the rest of our lives.[23] This doesn't mean that we are stuck with one way of speaking or using English after childhood, but our childhood determines most of the default language structures we use to make language. Our linguistic sound house is the language foundation we work from, add on to, or alter throughout our lives, but our original sound house is mostly stable.

This makes it even more difficult for many to get into college. Their sound houses aren't built for the White, middle-class, monolingual English habits of language expected in college, and yet everyone is built for college, built to learn and to language. So it's the rules of the college language game, the standards used to judge people and their language practices, that are set up as universalized, and when one doesn't match up to those standards, the failure is blamed only on the individual, not on the conditions in their lives that fostered the languages they use already, conditions that are conveniently not racialized but economic. But this makes economics an important part of the racist game we all play.

I'm glad neither my mom nor I knew the statistics of first-generation college students. I'm glad she had the audacity to think I could go to college, that I was worth that. We just accepted those false narratives of merit and hard work, despite them not working for most of the people we knew. I bought into them completely, even though I wasn't convinced I could get into college.

During elementary and junior high, I remember talking to my mother about what people do after college. What does one do with college? And while she was not that familiar with college, she offered me an idealized and romantic version of what college graduates do. They work in offices, make good money and important decisions. They wear nice clothes, drive new cars, and have health insurance. They get to go to the doctor and dentist regularly. They don't have to worry about the ends of meat. They get all of the meat. They take vacations away from home in faraway places. They have the privilege to sacrifice for their children.

---

23   For a discussion and further research on the influence that childhood plays in language use, see Rosina Lippi-Green, *English*, 48–51.

I often thought about college as a young kid, despite feeling it was likely an unrealistic goal. Even after I got accepted to the only university I applied to, I didn't think I'd make it all the way, graduate. I'd already flunked out of one community college and dropped out of another. I had also withdrawn from the same university during my first quarter there. In my first attempt, I lasted less than eight weeks. And yet, I had been preparing for college for as long as I could remember. I would plan my academic class schedule in junior high and high school with an eye toward what classes would prepare me best for college. No wood shop or extra P.E. classes. French and Spanish were more useful, I thought.

What we didn't understand was that there were few good ways to prepare me for college in the places we were at. The system, the game, is not set up to do this for a boy of color like me. I would have to be an exception—exceptional—if I was to make it to and through college.

CHAPTER 7.

A LANGUAGELING OF COLOR

During the first half of the third grade, I idolized my White teacher, Mr. Hicks. He was kind to me. He'd pull me aside on days we had a party, like the Halloween party, and ask me, "We should make sure this candy is okay?" He talked like that, in questions that were statements. Then we'd eat a few pieces while everyone was at recess. I don't know why he was kind to me during the first half of that year. Maybe he saw something about me that seemed like I needed it. Maybe he did this for everyone. But I don't think so.

Looking back now, I can see how I was searching for a father figure, a male role model. Mr. Hicks was the first man I really knew in my life. My biological father was gone. I never knew him. My mom was raising my brother and me alone. The rest of my teachers and the grownups in my life were all women. Maybe Mr. Hicks sensed this absence in my life.

So, when Mr. Hicks found a drawing of what was supposed to be him that was not flattering and that had scrawled on it bad names and swear words, all naming him, he turned on me. My mom was called in for a parent-teacher conference. She asked me, "Son, did you do this?" I told her what I told Mr. Hicks earlier. No, I didn't do that. I wouldn't. It's not my picture. I knew who did it, because I saw him do it the day before, then shove it in my desk. I don't know why I didn't take it out or tell Mr. Hicks when it happened. Perhaps it was because it was the end of the day. We were leaving school. Maybe I didn't think it was that big of a deal or that Mr. Hicks would find it.

What I remember most vividly about the parent-teacher conference, the grilling and questions, was my mom's thumb on the picture and the swear words underneath it. I kept saying, I didn't do it. I didn't do that. It's not my paper. It's not mine! That isn't me! I remember the feeling of helpless misunderstanding, of neither of them really believing me or my words, that those were not my words. It felt like a pool of mud rising all around me that I could do nothing about. All I could do was watch the mud rise. I wasn't sinking into it. It was enveloping me, expanding around me, constricting me, holding me tight and still, getting higher and higher until I wasn't sure I could breathe. All the while, my mom's beautiful, delicate thumb was on that picture.

Eventually, I just stopped trying to convince them. I could see it didn't matter what I said. My words didn't seem to matter. It was those words on the page that mattered, someone else's words that were not mine and that now mattered because they were in my desk. It didn't seem possible that maybe some other kid, a White kid, could have put them there, that this act didn't seem to be like what I was like, or did it?

They had already figured me out, and these were the grownups who were most on my side, the ones I loved most. What I was coming to understand, even as a third grade boy, was that words matter. It matters who others think said them. And these things are not always agreed upon by all parties. Surely, the White kid who actually did this bad thing couldn't have done it. It is more likely that the Brown kid without a father did it. It's more likely, isn't it? Isn't it? I looked like I did it, at least to Mr. Hicks.

I wish I could remember how my mom responded, whether she defended me or pleaded with Mr. Hicks, or whether she said something like, "I cannot believe that my son would do this thing. He did not do it. I'm sure of it." But I don't recall. Some people get to have more power to decide what the important words are, what they mean, and who is responsible for them. What I was coming to understand was the politics of the English language. I was coming to understand that race matters to language. We are always talking about race by not talking about it.

LEARNING TO READ LIKE A WOMAN

I grew up in rooms filled with White women. Almost every significant learning experience I can remember from my childhood until deep into college—regardless of what it entailed, where I was, or what I learned—was an experience that involved a White woman, my mom, my aunt, my nana, a teacher, my first girlfriend. I had few significant exchanges directly with men through high school and none with a man of color. White men made me nervous, and men of color were a mystery. They were absent. I did not understand men. They were big, loud, brusque, and threatening to me.

So it should be no surprise that I associated the act of reading with the women in my life. Most of my teachers were women. All of my caregivers and family members who watched over me and taught me how to be me were women. I can recall many Saturday afternoons sitting on the floor in my mom's room in our trailer. I was maybe twelve years old. She would be lying on her bed, still in her nightgown, reading harlequin romance novels, a box of them at the foot of her bed. She would pick up a dozen of them at the library or go to used book stores or Goodwill and get a box of them for a few bucks, read them all in a weekend, then return them for cash back and do it again the next week. It was likely my mom's escape from our life. But I knew she loved reading and was good at it.

I would watch her read and eventually snuggle up to her, feeling the safety of her warmth. The rest of our life and the world would melt away lying next to her. No more bills that could not be paid. No mean neighbors. No cockroaches. Just my mom reading, warmth, and softness. I liked to watch her read, her green-hazel eyes moving quickly back and forth across the pages, her delicate, graceful fingers turning page after page.

My mom's hands have always been beautiful. They are lean, graceful, and delicate. They have just the right amount of muscle over bone. Even her wrinkles in her older age are few and supple. These are the hands that loved me, fed me, took care of me. So even the sound of her turning the page with her delicate fingers soothed me. To this day, I love the sound of a page being separated from the one behind it and turned with a soft crinkle.

I thought my mom was superhuman in her ability to read so quickly. She didn't even move her mouth. Today I still find myself mouthing words I read or write. I compose and read most everything out loud, even emails. I cannot help it. Reading just doesn't feel right if I don't feel the words being pushed by my tongue, sliding across my lips and out of my mouth. I need to feel and hear words in the air as much as I need to see them in front of me in order to conjure meaning.

As a languageling, words have always been a multi-sensual experience for me. They are auditory and tactile. Tactile. Now, that's a word that feels like its meaning when I say it, TAC-TILE. It's an onomatopoeia to me, which is another word that feels good in my mouth. ONO-MATO-POEIA. Words are vocal, visual, and even vibrational to me. Many words I can feel vibrating places in my head, face, ears, chest, or throat. Have you ever felt a word vibrate one of your sinus cavities, those open places hidden under your cheeks or in your forehead?

The word, "nana" does this for me. Nana. It means love, and warm hugs, and gifts, and smiles, and false teeth in a glass by her bed. It means being rocked in a green chair to the sounds of "Amazing Grace." It's like a soft, heavy, cool quilt, like the kind my nana made. Words have many dimensions for me.

Today, I realize that my mom just had a different relationship to words than I did. Her story of literacy is different from mine. And yet, hers helped me make mine.

"How long does it take you to read a book, mom?" I asked her.

"It depends on the book. This one? Maybe a couple of hours," mom said in a soft, gentle voice, one that still soothes me today. She doesn't even look up from her book.

"A whole book in a few hours?" I'm shocked. It takes me weeks to finish a book.

"They're just stories, son." A soft crinkle, turn. She doesn't say it with sarcasm. That's not my mom's way. She says that sentence with tenderness and nonchalance.

Just stories? There is no such thing as *just a story*, I think. For my mom, it seemed words were to be devoured, not chewed and carefully digested. At this moment in my life, I was discovering Greek and Norse mythologies, stories about gods and heroes, stories that made worlds. I loved the story of Odysseus in Homer's *Odyssey*. Our school library had a retelling of the epic poem in story form for kids my age. It was illustrated. I loved it, loved all the adventures, all the monsters. I loved that Odysseus was clever, that he outwitted his opponents with his mind, not muscles. I loved that it was a series of adventures in different places.

Later in college, I would learn in one of my English courses that this is an important element of his character. He is wily and doesn't give up. He is the only significant character of the Trojan War who survives and makes it home, even if it took him ten years to get home after spending the previous ten years at war— twenty years away from home! Talk about persistence and grit!

To survive and thrive in the world, it is not usually, nor even mostly, about how strong you are, I learned. If you want to make it home, you don't want to be an Achilles or a Hector. They die because all they have are their muscles and their masculine brutishness. There is always someone stronger or younger than you. That isn't a game most will win most of the time. Hanging your hopes on being the strongest or fastest or some other -est is foolish. Instead, you want to be an Odysseus, clever and wily enough to get home. You want to use your words to gain advantage, survive, and thrive. This was one of my first literacy lessons.

Around this time, I was also reading science fiction and fantasy novels. This is when I learned about Asimov, Clark, Heinlein, Brooks, Tolkien, Bradbury, Lewis, and a few years later, Zimmer Bradley and Le Guin. In my foolish youth, I didn't even realize that Bradley and Le Guin were women. I thought fiction like the kind I couldn't get enough of was written solely by men. I could not escape the chauvinism or masculine biases that travelled with my reading, even as I read in rooms filled with women.

And I'm sure I was a product of my patriarchal culture, one that could not let a boy like me imagine that some of his favorite storytellers were women. This would seem to be an irony given that I mostly related to women, felt most comfortable around them, not men. But it is not ironic if you consider the male-dominated material conditions in which young boys in the US in the 1980s got their literacy, a world with male role models like Arnold Schwarzenegger and Sylvester Stallone, men of action, men who solved their problems through brute strength, men like Hector and Achilles, not Odysseus. And so, tensions existed for me.

Reading was understood to be a girl's activity. It was inactive, passive. It was a leisure activity, one that required no muscles. It wasn't macho to be smart or to read. Sports were what I was supposed to like, and I did like them, especially football. Reading and writing were girls' activities, weren't they? And yet, I thought only men could write good stories. I wanted to write stories too, but I wanted to be a man as well. The world didn't seem big enough for a man who loved words, a male languageling who enjoyed the indoors and questions and football.

I was also just a year away from discovering the ultimate storytelling, language game, D&D, and that would change my literacy practices dramatically. It would combine words with action, language as adventure. Even at this earlier moment in my life, I knew a story was not just a story. The singular importance of words was always apparent to me, always. Stories made things. Our stories make us, as the native scholar Tomas King has said so eloquently.[1]

I got my mom's meaning in her casual reply to me, though. My mom meant that she didn't have to think too hard about her books, that what there was to get out of them was mostly apparent in the reading itself, not in the thinking about them afterwards. She didn't want to think in this reading moment. She simply wanted to revel in the story unfolding in front of her. For her at that moment, the point was the labor of reading itself. And this was the first gift of literacy she gave me, the gift of appreciating the labor of reading, the practice of it, of noticing how much fun and engaging it is as you do it. This I could hold on to.

For my mom, her reading labor was her break from all the thinking she had to do in the bank, a male-dominated world that never appreciated her in any real way. In all her years as an underpaid bank teller, my mom never got a raise nor a promotion; instead, she watched as younger, less experienced men did. Consequently, she was also a janitor and even delivered papers in the early mornings so we might have some school clothes or just rent.

My mom had to be an Odysseus in a world of men-monsters. No, that's not accurate. She was a Penelope, Odysseus' wife, waiting all those years faithfully for her husband to return. But that's not what makes my mom a Penelope. Penelope had to be wily and persistent herself, had to be smarter than all the men-monsters around her trying to marry her and take over her kingdom. She had to weave a burial shroud for Odysseus' father each day, then unravel it at night in order to keep doing it to avoid having to pick a suitor. It was a trick to stave off the suitors.

Penelope was a master trickster. She had to take care of the kingdom while her husband was away. She kept shit moving for 20 years, kept everything running and working, making "ends-meat" for her son Telemachus and her kingdom. Penelope was perhaps more wily and crafty than Odysseus himself. She had to do everything he did but do it with less social and cultural power. She had to do it as a woman in a man's world. She was the real fucking hero in that story. Odysseus doesn't get his belated happily-ever-after without her 20 years of hard, wily work. Thank you, Penelope.

---

1   King, *Truth*, 2.

Ironically, much of my mom's wily ways and sacrifices were done to nourish and support me, a potential man-monster myself. I do not want to be a man-monster who makes only demands and underappreciates the women in his life, the women who make his life possible, who love and cherish him, who sacrifice for him, who deserve their own stories. To be a man-monster would insult the love and labors my mom gave me. So, for my mom, this reading time was not a time to think, but a time in the week when she could take the luxury not to think about being clever, or how to get home in one piece to her family, or how to both weave and unravel her own funeral shroud in order to stave off the man-monsters in her life. It was a time just to read for reading's sake.

For me, however, there was always thinking after reading. Words usually beget thinking, questions, ideas. As a languageling, I need and thrive on language. I am made of it. Often, it is all I can see or hear or feel. Language. Words. Everywhere. This is my male privilege, a privilege bestowed upon me in part by my mom and her wily ways. I get to feel words around me without having to worry about all those man-monsters. I'm grateful to stand on my mom's shoulders.

HUSTLING AND LOOKING FOR DAD

At this time in my life, I was not old enough to get a job. Paper routes, which paid good money, were hard to come by. So I hustled. Most of the time, I would sell my free or reduced price lunch tickets at school and not eat lunch. After a week, I might have five or even ten dollars saved. This is how I paid for books that would come each month through my fantasy and science fiction book club membership. I literally starved myself for books.

At a time when food was still a bit scarce in my life, I exchanged eating for reading. That's how important reading was to me. I could survive on language. Without constantly being fed words, I knew I'd die. But the book club was a scam, really. Each month, I'd select the books I liked, then the next month they'd mail them to me for free. If I liked them, then I paid for them. If not, just return them. No charge. Of course, it is harder to return a book once you've received it. It's more hassle. So I ended up with many books I didn't want. The next year, when we discovered D&D, well, that's what I spent my extra money on.

Of course, there were more paradoxes. Despite the fact that White women taught me almost everything of consequence in my early life and that I associated them closely with school, reading, and even my own literacy, I cannot recall a time in my life when I didn't yearn deep down for a male role model, for a man in my life whom I could look up to, a father figure to emulate, someone to tell me how to act and feel, how to be in the world. I did not get to have this.

So if my mom was Penelope, the struggling but crafty single parent, I was Telemachus, the boy who spent the first four books of the *Odyssey* searching for his father. I never knew my biological dad, and my mom purposefully stayed away from relationships until I was almost into high school—more of my mom being the Penelope.

At that time, my mom married a White, working-class diesel mechanic from New Jersey with flaming red hair, a former Navy mechanic, a good, hard-working man, a man I loved, who died of cancer this past year. They were married for over 35 years. His name was Bill Peterson. He had worked full time since he was 14 years old, mostly to escape an abusive father of his own. Later, because he and my mom needed money, he spent several years as a civilian diesel mechanic in Iraq and Afghanistan working with the U.S. Army. He was close to the fighting and came home with PTSD. For years afterwards, he had difficulty sleeping, had nightmares. It was the shelling and explosions that did it.

Bill was loving and kind with a deep sense of duty to his family, and he had his own problems, too. But he was good to my mom, and we all miss him. But Bill came at the tail end of an important part of my literacy story. I was already a languageling in the ways that would matter. I couldn't call him dad or father, even though he was that to me. I called him Bill because I didn't know how to relate to men or to a patriarch.

I wish I could have called him dad just once to his face. I wish I could have told him that he was all I really needed in a father, that I was young, and stupid, and ignorant, and so interested in not being poor or even working class that I couldn't see his divinity much of the time. I wish I could have told him that I didn't know how to relate to men until it was too late for us. I was too interested in what I thought literacy would give me and make me into, so I often turned away from my own working-class roots and him, who was the epitome of that.

I turned to visions of who I thought I wanted to be, my mom's sister's husband. I idolized this man because he was not working class. My uncle Bill was a college professor at Oregon State University, the only university I applied to and eventually graduated from. Uncle Bill was my only model for what a college graduate and successful man was. I idolized him throughout my childhood and into college.

He was a microbiology professor, seemed to know everything, worked in labs, and travelled all over the world. People asked him for his advice. He was exotic, successful, rich, and smart. He made important decisions. He took his family to faraway places, New Zealand, Florida. He drove a Jaguar and a Cadillac. He lived in a two-story house on a hill outside of Corvallis, Oregon. He was White and upper middle class. He was everything I wanted to be and everything I knew I'd never become.

For several years, he came to Vegas for conventions, I think. When he visited the first time, he gave my brother and me each a dollar bill. We called them our "Uncle Bill dollars." Putting aside the fact that we rarely ever had as much as a dollar in our pockets, having such a thing given to us was an amazing and extravagant occurrence. That dollar was valuable in a number of ways. We saved that dollar in our wallets for the entire year until Uncle Bill came back the next year and gave us a new one. We were seven and eight years old.

There are lessons in those dollar bills, I know it. And if I could give my own sons one gift, it would be to know the feeling of possessing an Uncle Bill dollar, saving it for twelve months, even as you want so badly to spend it. However, my sons have grown up in a home with more privilege and money than I did. I've been lucky enough to give that to them. And yet, I'm to blame for their inability to see the value in such consequential things. Still, I would not trade it for the poverty that revealed the lessons in those Uncle Bill dollars. More paradox. I cannot give my sons this gift of delayed satisfaction or the value of a single bill. I'm lucky I had two Bills in my life. My sons will have their own lessons to learn and share, their own Bills, perhaps.

Uncle Bill was special to me. He was the vision of prosperity. I associated college and the language of school and books with my uncle's success, with that kind of manhood, with being a professor in a university, with exotic adventures in faraway places, with being smart and rich, getting out of poverty, having the means to give others a dollar for shits and giggles. These were the things that I wanted for myself, the things I thought delivered people. These were the signs of thriving. Even Odysseus was a king.

What I wanted was to be White in the ways Uncle Bill was. This meant that I didn't want to be White in the ways that my mom's husband was, the other Bill, the one man who was really the only dad I've known. It was a form of colonizing that I did to myself, but it was the only option I could see in the ghetto of my youth. Classrooms and books presented this to me. It's the rules of the racist, sexist, and classist game. You don't strive to be a diesel mechanic who travels around the world to dangerous places. You strive to be a college professor who travels around the world to exotic places. Now, I'm not sure I see the differences.

I would not be able to admit this until I was in graduate school at Oregon State University getting my master's degree and writing a thesis on identity and race. I had been searching for a male role model my entire life. I was a Telemachus without realizing it. I felt unmoored, like if a strong current came along, I'd be taken out to sea, lost, wrecked on the rocks. All the loving and caring women in my life simply could not save me. They could all be standing on the sandy shore calling to me, but I would be in my dinghy looking the other direction with my hand shielding the sun from my eyes, scanning the far horizon, hoping to see a glimpse of a ship called dad.

My master's degree at OSU was a time of deep reflection and problem-posing for me, a time of discovering myself as a languageling and becoming more self-aware of my own insecurities and needs. It was also the first time I had a significant male role model in my life who shared the same passion for language that I had. He was my thesis director, Chris Anderson.

Chris was the director of composition, so he was also the first person to teach me how to be a writing teacher. This was at a moment when he was training to be an ordained deacon in the Catholic church. He was White with working-class roots from Eastern Washington. Chris was not what I thought an English professor was supposed to be like. He was self-effacing and unassuming. He was gentle, kind, and encouraging as a teacher, rarely lectured; instead, he would ask us to write, and write with us. We would read our words, and Chris would engage us by speaking in soft, almost quiet tones, yet with lots of authority. Sometimes, he'd even curse, say "fuck" and "shit," not a lot, but enough to show us that he was real and not stuffy or prudish. I admired everything about him, especially his writing. I had read his beautiful book on living near the McDonald-Dunn forest in Oregon, called *Edge Effects: Notes from an Oregon Forest*. It was what I thought I wanted to do, too. It was a book about him, about a managed forest, and writing. In some ways, this book you're reading now is a reflection of him and that book.

The book's discussion of writing as a forest still strikes me as an appropriate way to understand my own literacy experiences, my life with words, and the words that have made my life. Near the end of the book, Chris writes:

> Essays grow from careless seeds, from the varieties of life,
> slowly accreting, nourished by the matter stored in the mind,
> and gradually, intuitively, expand into flowers and fruit—or
> grow up into the canopy, their crowns bristling like imper-
> fect bottle brushes. All the dead and dying ideas, all the ideas
> abandoned or modified in the course of the writing, are left
> lying on the page, not revised away, the tentative conclusions
> rising up from that previous thinking. The levels are there.
> Gaps open.[2]

In one sense, this literacy narrative, this book in your hands (or on your screen), is a collection of careless seeds sown, the imperfect flowers and fruit of my literacy life, fed by my life's material conditions, by the many forests of my

---

2   Chris Anderson, *Edge Effects: Notes from an Oregon Forest* (Iowa City: University of Iowa Press, 1993), 160.

youth that have nourished this made-forest in front of you. The flowers and fruit here have been fertilized by my poverty and want, by a second grade reading contest and racist words thrown, and fists shaken in my direction, and my mom's beautiful hands, and her fast moving hazel eyes. And in the act of putting these words down about my literacy journey, I have gradually urged them into something that may be meaningful to you, even though they have always been meaning-filled to me. These words are magic and forest.

Literacy as forest, as ecosystem. Literacy as an organic organism. I like Chris' metaphor and how he offers it in a generous way in the book. It is so like him in real life. It does not feel masculine to me, not in the toxic ways that I felt uncomfortable with growing up or that I embraced as a young man. But maybe I read his words in this way because by the time I'd read Chris's book, I already knew the author. He was my professor. I was his graduate student. I could hear his real voice, soft, gentle, speaking these words in a generous fashion.

This did not feel like language from the working-class, White men I knew growing up, not the mean ones who accused you of things you didn't do, the racist ones, the ones with shaking fists, the ones who would hurt you with their words or hands. It wasn't like the ones yelling, "Go back to where you came from, you fucking Wetback!" This was a more feminine voice. It felt like my mom's hands, soft, warm, offering me tentative questions and turned pages. It was like Nana's "Amazing Grace," soft sweater language. Chris' voice asked me about myself, language that begs language. The book read like an invitation to write, and I did.

The summer I read the book, I wrote Chris a letter, thanking him for writing such a beautiful book. I told him in the letter that the book made me want to write, that his words invited me to my own page. I sealed the letter, put a stamp on it, and mailed it. I don't know why I started doing this, writing to authors I admired or found wonderful. This was the first of many letters I'd write over the next 25 years.

It is a custom that I enjoy mostly because I know as an author the value of words given to others. I know that when you put down words on a page, little pieces of yourself, proclaiming yourself as a languageling, then send those words out into the world, what you really want is for others to read them and respond in some meaningful way. You hope they smile, or laugh, or feel that deep moving sense of goodness in their bellies when they read your words. Or maybe you hope they get excited and move to some action. Maybe you hope they change their minds or the world.

Words given are rarely a one-way exchange. And giving thanks to someone for their words is a deeply joyful act that can complete the exchange, showing the writer that there is a willing receiver who is changed. You give joy to the author, and you get it as a giver. I like doing this because I think of my wife and partner Kelly, my mom, and her sister—my Aunt Sue, all deeply giving White women. Their lives have been filled with days of giving to those around them. I have received much of that giving. Their words have fertilized my literacy forest, and I am so grateful that I can sacrifice a few in their honor.

And maybe this is what I love about that metaphor of a forest as literacy. Forests give us much. From my vantage, forests are the picture of living compassion. Usually, we humans only take from forests, take their trees and their inhabitants, which we call lumber or food. Conversely, forests give fresh air, and green beauty, and clean waters freely. They ask for nothing but time and place, perhaps some respect.

As ecosystems, they are incredible generators of life on the planet, necessary, vital. They are creative places. But walk in one for a spell, and it can feel as if you are the only one left in the world. There is a quiet, low vibration in a forest that when I pay attention, I can feel. It wakes me up and calms me down at the same time. Maybe it's the seeming absence of life in a place so filled with it, or maybe it is the silence, the slowing down, the stillness. Some, like Chris, might call it its sacredness.

INESCAPABLE WHITENESS IN OUR LANGUAGING

And yet, I have misgivings about Chris' words now, 27 years later. His language habits are those of a Western, Whitely, masculine voice in many respects, a voice that has hurt me and my students of color, and paradoxically, a voice I know I have taken on to some degree. If a reader isn't careful, the "I" in Chris' words can sound like a universal "I," like an objective "I" who makes sense of the world as if there is but one sense to make. His exposition often proclaims from nowhere, objectively, as if he is not *subjectively making* that sense from his unique position in the world, constructing, picking and choosing details that he is uniquely qualified to find from a universe of other details.

I'm being unfair to him. I know Chis does not believe this—he certainly does not live or teach in ways that suggest it—but his language habits betray this intention. That's how White language supremacy works in systems that make it almost exclusively. We all live in paradox. Chris is no different.

Chris draws on the traditions of Michel Montaigne and Henry David Thoreau, White, male writers who proclaimed the subjectivity of their ideas in contradictory ways. Thoreau begins *Walden* with, "I should not talk so much about myself if there were any body [sic] else whom I knew as well."[3] But he doesn't

---

3   Henry David Thoreau, *Walden and Resistance to Civil Government*, 2nd ed., ed. William Rossi (New York: W. W. Norton & Company, 1992), 1.

speak just about himself. Thoreau offers universal truths from his experience, even if qualified. He says, "The mass of men lead lives of quiet desperation," and "while civilization has been improving our houses, it has not equally improved the men who are to inhabit them."[4] Thoreau acknowledges his subjectivity only to continually take on an authoritarian and objective sounding stance, making claims as if we all believed them already, as if they were self-evident. Nothing can be self-evident inherently, can it?

Don't get me wrong, I love Thoreau. He's taught me much. But Thoreau and Montaigne are White, European men of considerable means. Montaigne was a Lord, born on his family's estate in the south of France. Thoreau was born in a more modest family from Concord, Massachusetts, but a family who had relatives who also, like him, graduated from Harvard. Chris comes from a masculine, White, European literary tradition, but we all do if we've been trained in U.S. schools and colleges. I don't blame Chris for his training, but we must pay attention to the effects of our languaging and where it comes from, especially because we all, no matter who we are, teach others language in our daily exchanges. What do I have in common with Thoreau or Montaigne? If I am to take something from their words, it likely needs to be extracted with tweezers, not dug up with a shovel.

Donna Haraway, a White, feminist scholar researching science and technology, calls this kind of orientation to the world a "god trick," or the trick of "infinite vision" where one's vision of the world and science is disembodied, or ignores the embodied and situated nature of all knowledges.[5] It presumes we can know things from a perspective outside of our gendered and racialized bodies that manufacture that very knowledge. For writers, it is a stance of supposed neutrality, objectivity, and apoliticality that then produces objective knowledge from only one's own experiences. These experiences are recollected from inside the writer. It's also the habit of hyperindividualism that extracts universal truths for everyone. Haraway, however, counters this objective knowledge with "situated knowledges," an orientation to the world that remains embodied in people and their material conditions that make that knowledge possible.[6]

Like many places in Chris' *Edge Effects*, the above exposition also assumes that the reader is in the same proximity to the details and ideas that the writer, Chris, is. This orientation is similar to the proximity assumed by E. B. White, who mastered the stance well in his essays for the *New Yorker*. That stance is a Whitely stance that not only assumes that any knowledge can be discerned

---

4   Thoreau, 5, 23.

5   Haraway, "Situated," 581.

6   Haraway, 579.

through one's hyperindividualistic experiences in the world but that all readers have the same access or proximity to that knowledge or world, an unseen, naturalized, universal orientation to the world.

Drawing on Franz Fannon, an influential French West Indian scholar of color from Martinique, Sarah Ahmed offers a compelling way to understand the phenomenology of Whiteness as an assumed universal orientation to the world that is made by its own proximity to things, ideas, people, and places. Whiteness in this way is inherited, an inheritance of proximity. It comes from our access to things around us, language, people, spaces, money. Ahmed is worth quoting at length to explain this:

> Such an inheritance can be re-thought in terms of orientations: we inherit the reachability of some objects, those that are "given" to us, or at least made available to us, within the "what" that is around. I am not suggesting here that "Whiteness" is one such "reachable object", but that Whiteness is an orientation that puts certain things within reach. By objects, we would include not just physical objects, but also styles, capacities, aspirations, techniques, habits. Race becomes, in this model, a question of what is within reach, what is available to perceive and to do "things" with.[7]

But this is what academics are supposed to do, right? Professors are trained and required to profess and offer knowledge to the world, aren't we? We can reach certain ideas and things, which we then offer to those who cannot. It's what I'm doing in this book, isn't it? But am I being paternalistic? Am I being snobby in the way Strunk and White seemed to be? Do I acknowledge the multiple ways that knowledge exists and gets created in the world? Or am I just professing so-called universal truths? Ahmed warns us to be careful that we do not assume that our proximity to things, to habits of language, for instance, are assumed to be universally reachable by all. We should be careful of our HOWLing.

Chris' habits of language were very attractive to me as I entered graduate school. I tried hard to emulate them in those early years, some of which I've kept. I like these habits of White language. Just as Chris sounded both masculine and feminine to me, I have HOWLs myself that make these same moves, but I also have habits that ain't so fuckin' White nor classy. And I ain't never been mistaken for a White person, White writer, White teacher, or White academic.

In fact, even today, I get wounded by racialized slights that colleagues slide into our conversations. Some call these slights microaggressions, but if I'm being

---

7   Sara Ahmed, "Phenomenology," 154.

honest, they don't feel micro. Most do not mean anything malicious or racist, but they cannot see through their own Whiteness to stop doing them. They cannot see that their own proximity to things, to words, is not universal nor should it be. Besides, "not meaning to" don't make it hurt any less.

Recently, I was in a meeting with a colleague who holds the same position I do, an associate dean of another college at the university where I work. She was probably ten years older than me. She is White, travels abroad every year to exotic places, with pictures and mementos on the walls of her clean and neat office, pictures of Greece. She tells me about a few of her trips to Athens. I tell her about my trip to Greece, how Kelly and I worried about a member of our touring group, a young woman who hadn't brought any sunscreen to Delphi. She wore a thin shoulderless top, no hat. She was very pale. She was gonna get sunburned that day. We gave her our sunscreen. I said, "She was young, maybe late 20s," suggesting that she was just being young, not thinking ahead.

And with a chuckle, my colleague says to me, "You're not *that* much older than her." I brushed it off with a laugh. I didn't want to have to explain to her that I'm almost twice that young woman's age, that I could be her father, that I have a son who is almost her age. When the hell I do get to be respected for my years on the planet? This isn't an isolated incident. It happens all the time, the small comments about my youthfulness or being mistaken for a college student.

A White, male colleague who is my junior in every way, from age, to rank in the institution, to position, in passing tells me casually, "You're young; you've got lots of energy." The implication is that I'll learn what he knows already. I've got the time and energy. I know these White people would not say these things to White colleagues. Their memberships give them more respect than that, more respect for a colleague (a superior even) than to brush away years of experience and wisdom with a clause that begins a diatribe on what he is doing in his academic unit, Whitesplaining to me about shit I've been doing for two decades.

I know this seems like it's about age, not race. But how do you separate those two things? Our perceptions of age are connected to racialized bodies in time and space that each of us are in contact with. Aging and its markers are not separate, or separable from, the gendered and raced bodies that age around us. Aging never happens in the abstract. It is often a Whitely orientation to the world, an assumption of a universal proximity to the markers of age. It's assuming that all people age like White people do. The sayings like "Black don't crack" and "Asians don't raisin" refer to the ways many African Americans and Asians seem to age well and not have many of the hard age lines as they get older that mark older White folks.

Some dermatologists and scientists have attributed this phenomenon to the increased amounts of collagen and melanin in the skin of people of color.[8] Melanin protects the skin from UV damage. Collagen keeps it firm. Furthermore, a longitudinal study by Rutgers Medical School showed that many African Americans have denser facial bones, which can help maintain facial structure longer in life.[9] This means that older Black people can look more like their younger selves longer because their facial structures stay the same longer than White people's can generally. My doctors and dentists have told me for years, "You have such dense bones. Your jaw is very dense. You are a good candidate for the tooth implant. There's plenty of bone to anchor the titanium screw to."

Using a White racial standard for beauty and age is no different than using a White racial linguistic standard for everyone's languaging. We are all languagelings. We are all racialized. We also all live in systems that have an orientation to the world that uses an unspoken White standard for age or language as universal ones. This means those systems often take Whiteness as objective, neutral, and universal. "You look young" is relative to what youth looks like, to a White, European standard assumed in the statement.

And what youth looks like is tangled in the physiological markers associated with race and gender. It only seems that I'm being paid a compliment, but that compliment comes at the cost of disrespecting my years and ignoring the wisdom that goes with them. I get infantilized. And again, I feel like the little Brown boy who must go to his special reading classroom. One day I'll grow up or catch up with the others.

This false universal White orientation to the world has other aspects to it, all of which have hurt me as a languageling of color in rooms filled with White languagelings. Several years ago while I was the director of university writing at the University of Washington Tacoma, I was in a meeting about student success. I was the only person of color in the room, which was typical. Despite the fact

---

8   To read about how melanin and collagen affect the aging of skin, see Charlie Brinkhurst-Cuff, "A Dermatologist Explains the Science Behind the 'Black Don't Crack' Stereotype," VICE, February 19, 2016, https://www.vice.com/en/article/mgmzva/a-dermatologist-explains-the -science-behind-the-black-dont-crack-stereotype; or Soo Youn, "Black Don't Crack? Asian Don't Raisin?: The Truth Behind the Clichés," AARP, October 23, 2017, https://www.aarp.org/disrupt -aging/stories/ideas/info-2017/cliches-that-are-true.html. To read about the unfair pressures this stereotype places on African American people, see Patia Braithwaite, "'Black Don't Crack' Is Stressing Me Out," Refinery29, August 7, 2019), https://www.refinery29.com/en-us/black -woman-aging-black-dont-crack.

9   David Buziashvili, Jacob I. Tower, Neel R. Sangal, Aakash M. Shah, and Boris Paskhover, "Long-Term Patterns of Age-Related Facial Bone Loss in Black Individuals," *JAMA: Facial Plastic Surgery* 21, no. 4 (2019): 292–297, https://doi.org/10.1001/jamafacial.2019.0028.

that at the time most of the students on that campus were students of color, there were few, very few, faculty or administrators of color there.

I suggested that we might gather data on the racial identities of student respondents to a survey we were discussing. We might add a few questions about the racial climate in classrooms. We might even ask about Whiteness, about students' perceptions of it on campus. I brought up the fact that in classrooms with White teachers, many students of color who have travelled through classrooms with mostly or all White teachers may find it difficult to confide in the well intentioned White, liberal college teacher in front of them. Racial trauma follows you. The survey could be a good opportunity to understand the ways Whiteness is experienced on campus by our students of color.

As my voice was slowing down, pausing, one of the meeting's attendees, an older, male, graduate student from Ireland spoke up—rather, he interrupted me. We all knew him. He was very involved in several committees and other activities on campus. He was liberal, kind, and had a wonderful Irish sound to his words. He was doing an interdisciplinary master's degree that was social justice oriented. He had a previous life in the tech sector, owned a business that he sold for a lot of money. He'd lived in Washington for over a decade. Now that he wasn't running a business, he had time to go back to school and get a graduate degree.

In the meeting, he reiterated what I had just said and suggested the survey questions. He even re-explained what I was saying just moments before, as if I'd not said anything. He looked right at me, as if he was teaching me things about being Brown in an all-White school. I remember his passion and my own anger at his racialized mansplaining. No one seemed to notice that he had just taken my idea and my rationale with no reference to the words I had just spoken. He was robbing me of my words, and the White people in the room were not noticing, just nodding in agreement. I said nothing.

I offer this kind of interaction, which has happened to me on several occasions in different ways, as a version of Whitesplaining. Usually, folks refer to an incident of Whitesplaining as one in which a White person condescendingly explains to a person of color how their complaints of racism or White supremacy are unfounded, how the person of color is too sensitive, or sees race everywhere. In this case, the Whitesplaining that my Irish colleague engaged in was a kind that I see happen with liberal White academics and others. It's where good intentions are not checked by context and who you are talking to. It's the White person thinking that expertise in a subject like racism can be purely academic, that you can learn enough of its depths in a book alone, or by mouthing ideas that you heard from someone of color without acknowledging that.

This White man had never been in any situation where he felt threatened by the Whiteness of an authority figure, like a teacher, in front of him. But because he read about it, or had just been told about it, he took ownership of the ideas because he agreed with them. And as White people in authority have done throughout history, he assumed authority on the subject at hand, assumed an authoritative posture. His orientation was one that said authority and expertise on a subject is abstract. It's all about knowledge possessed. It is not about a body experiencing it.

At best, he acted on the idea that his expertise and authority on racism and White supremacy was based on the interchangeability of abstract knowledge and experience. His habit of language, a common Whitely one, was that you can have either abstract knowledge or experience of racism in order to speak in the way he did, in the presence of a body of color, even after that body had just said the same thing.

What made this meeting difficult was that I didn't want to embarrass this man, who was technically a grad student and my junior in authority, even if he was a few years older than me. Despite him slipping into a White authoritative stance, one I've seen many times in my life, ones that always infantilize me, I did not want to wound him in such a public way. We were both trying to do right by our campus' students. I was trying to be nice to him. I was doing what people of color, and many women of all kinds, do out of habit and necessity all of our lives, softly cradle the gentle egos and brittle spirits of the White people, or men, around us. It can get exhausting.

This, over time, is at the cost of our own egos and spirits. I didn't want to have to be the Brown guy bringing up racism again—too much responsibility, too much burden, day after day, even for a guy like me. Calling it out in a meeting where everyone was trying to solve this very problem on campus just felt like I would be read as the bad guy, making everyone feel bad for nothing. I didn't want that fight that day. And yet, I should have. That would have been the compassionate thing, the antiracist thing, to do, but not the easy thing.

Even back at OSU, I knew my lack of Whiteness was a problem in school. I knew that no matter what I did, I was not really in the club. I knew that my membership had restrictions. I cannot pull off what Chris did as a teacher or writer. But given my history with language and others' judgements of me that never squared with my own views of myself, I knew then, as much as I admired, learned from, and loved my first mentor in school, his mentoring was incomplete for me. I just didn't know how to articulate this yet. I didn't realize that the material conditions that travel with racialized bodies really mattered to the man I could be mentored by. I needed a man of color who could understand my journey and struggles, but I was still in love with the idea that I could be White, that I could take on the master's language so well that he would accept and reward me.

CHAPTER 8.

UNSUSTAINABLE WHITENESS

There were cracks in my desire to be White, which I'm thankful for now. In graduate school, it wasn't sustainable for me to think in this way. If I'm being honest though, it's only today that I recognize this. Then, while I may have been uncomfortable, it took time with my words, time with others, time away from it all to realize that what I yearned for was Whiteness and that it was mostly unattainable.

CRUMBLING WHITENESS

While getting my master's degree at OSU, I was also a teaching assistant, a TA. In that English department, this meant that I was the teacher of record for a first-year writing course, what many refer to as "Freshman English." It was the required writing course for all students at the university. I was one of about fifteen TAs, all grad students like me. The master's degree was a two year program, so you taught one or two courses a term (three terms in an academic year), and you could apply to teach an extra class in the summer between those two years. There were often extra sections needing an instructor in the summers when most of the professors were gone.

The summer after my first year of teaching as a grad student, I got one of those summer teaching assignments, a first-year writing course. Chris had given us a three-day orientation on teaching writing the summer before as we entered the program, and we'd all taken several grad courses that helped us with our teaching, so I felt quite prepared and excited. I could do this thing I loved doing, make money that summer, and not work at the gas station. I felt like a real, professional teacher, earning his way.

In the writing course that summer, I had a student who was a veteran, an older, White, working-class man from Oregon. He served at the tail end of Vietnam, then came home and worked in the lumber industry for maybe 20 years. Recently, his job had been eliminated. He was middle aged and in school to be retrained for something else. He seemed unsettled, quite unsure about the whole college thing. He said little in class, a class filled with students who could have been the age of his children at that time, although I don't know if he had a family. What I remember about him was his paper.

I asked the class, as was the custom in our writing program at the time, to write an essay on some experience they felt they could explore and perhaps understand in some way. It didn't have to be a big, ground-breaking experience. It could be a mundane experience in their lives, as was the case for many of the essays we had read in preparation for our writing. In fact, I'm almost positive we read E. B. White's essay, "Once More to the Lake," an essay that does this very thing. In class, we talked about the ways those writers, as in White's essay, move from showing an experience to making sense of that experience, describing details in a scene then carefully analyzing them, drawing out big things from small details. This is the same move that Thoreau and Montaigne make in their writings. Chris taught it to us too.

Chris was the director of composition at the time. He trained us in teaching this kind of writing, the personal. We even used his edited collection of readings, a collection of essays and poems by a variety of authors, called *A Forest of Voices: Reading and Writing the Environment*. It was a thematic reader about nature, place, forests, and activism. I still like this reader, but I wouldn't use it in the ways we did then. I wouldn't use it to ask students to confess things, to draw on their experiences in order to learn some truth about the world or themselves or their pasts.

These moves in personal essays too easily come off as writers offering universal truths from calm, dispassionate reflections of their pasts. They rehearse HOWL as if they are the best habits of language, the best ways to language ideas. They too easily seem like they are the best ways to make sense of one's experiences. Like in White's essay, the move from personal experience to some big truth, with no other outside information considered, is a hyperindividualistic habit of White language that assumes most truths can come from inside the individual.

It is a version of what René Descartes gave us in his *Meditations* and his *cogito ergo sum*, or "I think, therefore I am."[10] His *cogito* is a hyperindividualized precept that Decartes develops purely from his reasoning, his rationalizing. It's a truth from the inside of his mind, applied to the outside, the external world. The habit of hyperindividualism in this case is also linked to another White habit, an individualized, rational, controlled self. It's the rational self, the "I" in the essay, that produces universal truths for everyone through only the manipulation of words. Its central logic: thinking will give you the answers you seek. It considers one aspect of the dialectic of words, the power of meaning-making and logic, of reasoning, but ignores other aspects, the magic, the way words can bewitch, the context, the people.

---

10   In "Meditation Two," Descartes says, "Thought exists; it alone cannot be separated from me. I am; I exist—this is certain,"; see René Descartes, *Discourse on Method and Meditations on First Philosophy*, trans. Donald A. Cress (Indianapolis: Hackett Publishing Co., 1998), 65.

While there were a few readings in the collection that discussed things in deeply contextual and historical ways, most readings we used in our writing program did not. I don't recall much in the curriculum that helped students work out how to contextualize and historicize the poems and essays. I don't recall anything that helped us consider the ways that our thinking about our own language experiences are structured by the conditions from which we each come to the classroom. What logics and thinking structures are we using to make sense of our personal experiences? Where did they come from? What do they afford and deny us?

Instead, we asked students to describe experiences, then analyze them and come to some conclusions or meaning from them, as if the most important meanings and logics are internal, inside each of us, accessible to us all in similar ways. But those conclusions were often universalized in all the writing in those classrooms—they were in mine—because we didn't contextualize our thinking and histories with language. We never asked students to situate their ideas, views, or assumptions in their lives and histories. We never asked them to consider the systems, structures, conditions, and histories that enable individual writers to make particular kinds of meaning. We never asked about the politics of language and our lives.

We never examined, for instance, under what conditions might someone have the tools they do to make the meaning they can from the experiences they believe they have reinvented on the page. We never asked how race, economics, gender, or the history of ideas in our lives have structured our ways of being in the world. We never asked how our being in the world affords us the methods we have to say what we think we can say and think what we think we can think.

The curriculum of that program, as good as it was in many ways, did not assign these kinds of readings. The writing program had a lot of strengths. It was doing a kind of writing curriculum that was popular at the time, but this was a Whitely weakness of the field and our writing courses. It turned away from politics and locations of writers and readers. This was changing in the field at the time, but not in our writing program.

From this instruction, my veteran student, a big burly man with bulging, hairy forearms, wrote a confusing paper about being in the jungle. It was the image of the jungle I most recall and his own jumbled sense that he made of it. In the paper, he is in one place, then in a very different place. Others are around him. Then they are not. He's somewhere else. Things are happening, but he's not being very specific. The language was confusing.

Many of the sentences were not sentences. They didn't even read as fragments. They read like oddly put together phrases. Corn slight cracking. Lifter toading careful. Cheat rub red. Those phrases were not in the paper, and I don't have the paper anymore. I gave it back to him. But they are the kinds of languaging I recall the paper filled with. He was describing his feelings in abstract ways only, I think. He was explaining how confusing the experience was, how there were arms and voices everywhere, how it was hard to recall, how it was hard to explain the feelings. As a young teacher, I was not prepared for this.

I had set up appointments with each student after reading their drafts. In those meetings, the student and I would talk through their draft, and I'd offer feedback so that they could revise. It was meant to be a dialogue. It was good pedagogy. Still is. My student sat down next to me in the conference room on the second floor of Moreland Hall. It was a warm summer day. Moreland had no air conditioning. The windows in the empty classroom across the hall were open so that an occasional breeze would caress my back and arms. I was dressed in a button up shirt and khakis. This was my typical teaching uniform because I looked young. I was young. I needed to look older than I was. I needed to look more teacher-like.

"So what is going on here? I can't tell what you are writing about. Can you tell me what experience you are trying to show in your paper?" I looked at him. I was a little nervous. He was so much older than me. I was just twenty four at the time. He sat silent, looking into his hands, which were in his lap. He had put his cap on the table, half obscuring his paper.

"I-I-I . . ." I could hear him breathing through his nose harder and harder. The utterance took ten seconds, but it seemed to my inexperienced ears like ten minutes. I thought, maybe he isn't sure what he's writing about. Maybe he has several experiences here, and we needed to focus on one of them. I couldn't see the distress that he was under, not yet. I was too busy trying to think of a way to help him clear up this paper, running through options in my head. I was too busy trying to enact the Whitely professor for the benefit of this White man. I was too busy thinking I knew what was wrong here. I was not attending to him.

"Maybe we can start with this first paragraph. Just tell me what you are trying to say here." I flicked his cap a few inches, revealing the first paragraph, and put my finger on the first line of his paper. He just looked at it. I watched his mouth, waiting for his explanation, waiting for his language move, for the move from this paragraph of jumbled words to a coherent idea, to something that I could understand and respond to.

"It's . . . It's about w-war—friends." His voice was hesitant and seemed to fade in and out with each word, as if he was inventing the words right then for the occasion. I could feel a cool burst of air come through the doorway behind us. "I guess. . . I was trying to write about my experience. . . of the war, and how I. . . ." He choked up, and I thought he was sobbing. I didn't know what to say or do.

I sat waiting for some other language move of his, feeling like shit. I had fucked up somehow as the teacher. I knew it. The khakis didn't work. It took maybe three more seconds, and this middle-aged, White, veteran of Vietnam, former lumberjack with his large forearms, still wearing his rolled up flannel shirt in summer, just openly bawls, sobs, weeps in front of me, and I feel compassion for him. But I am lost. I don't know what to do. I don't want to be there, and I desperately want to help him, a preposterous, presumptuous, and Whitely impulse on my part.

In my immaturity then, I thought: What could have possibly happened to him? Now, I think: What didn't happen to him? How is this not an expected outcome of an ill-fitting writing assignment like that one? Write about an experience that matters to you? Motha fucka, really? Imma ask this of a Vietnam veteran and recently jobless lumberjack? Imma tell this guy how to make sense of his experience?

For an instant, I thought, I ain't got it so bad. I ain't never had it this bad. Then: How do I help him? Do I wait for him to stop crying? Do I wait for this much older man who has seen things I simply do not understand? Do I say I'm sorry? Is this paper really that fuckin' important? Can I give him something else to write about? Will he even listen to me?

Somehow I mustered up enough to tell him, "I think this may not be the subject that you can write about at this time. It would be okay if you picked something else, something less emotional for you." He nodded in agreement, and picked up his hat, and tugged it on firm and low, and left.

The problem with my suggestion was that all our readings and discussions in class had hinged on one fact: Write about something that means something to you, that you care about. Write about things you want to learn or discover. Write about the gaps in your forest, the unexplored levels of flora and fauna. Use writing to know yourself, to learn, to grow. Language yourself into being. Re-understand yourself through words. It's good writing advice but also dangerous and reckless if you follow it in spirit without care and guidance.

He was following instructions very well. This was his gap, but there was no sunshine streaming through it. There was no rising from a chair, no words whispered in his ear that could help him do it, at least none that I knew of, none I was prepared to help him find. There was only: Corn slight cracking. Lifter toading careful. Cheat rub red. Now, I wonder: Must I always understand what my students write when that writing may emotionally unhinge them? Why should I expect to have full access to him and his languaging?

My suggestion was also contradictory, or maybe paradoxical, to the initial good advice the class worked from. This thing in front of us was what he cared about personally, and yet I forced him to start caring about it publicly by asking him to write about it to me. And yet isn't it often the case that we must be forced to do things that are good for us? Is *that* my place as a teacher of writing? Is my job to encourage—or is it urge, or is it coerce—students to confess their secrets to me, submit their private languaging for my evaluation? Does my habit, my Ph.D., my regalia, robes, and other vestments, entitle me to demand or even ask for such disclosures from any of my students? I am not an academic priest in the cathedral of higher learning, only a mage-professor trying to cast spells, and some are just illusions.

My student's emotional response to his languaging kept him from writing in a way that I could understand for the purposes of our class and his own education. Yet again, is not emotional writing—*pathos*—an element of much good writing? Teachers want their students to deeply care about the things they write about. That's what makes good writing good, isn't it? That's what made his choices so important, so meaningful to him, even though they were meaningless to me—that is, they were difficult for me to see the meaning in them.

We don't write about things we don't care about, not really. And if we care, then we have emotional attachments, even if unexamined and undigested. But must we always digest our emotions? What was so wrong with him crying in my presence? Because he was my elder? Because that's not what dudes do in public? Because men don't give access to those kinds of emotions to anyone, and certainly not their teacher? Because we were in this educational exchange that is too often assumed to be one devoid of emotions, one conducted dispassionately? These are questions about Whiteness and its dominance in our thinking and in our ways of teaching English.

One thing that I can see now that I could not then, but I felt it, was the apparent contradictions in this teaching moment. They were contradictions that made it appear and feel like a teaching failure. Now, I'm not so sure. He was an older, middle-aged, White man, coming to kneel at the feet of a 24-year-old, graduate teaching assistant of color in order to learn how to write. There are no movies or novels or teaching stories that depict this scene, not because the White man is crying, nor because he was a war vet, but because the crying White man, the military veteran, was crying at the feet of a young man of color, who is and is not the authority, the higher power, the teacher, in the scene. I'm supposed to be Robin Williams, and he Matt Damon.[1]

We were both out of place. Nothing seemed to hold together, not his languaging, not my instructions, not our dialogue, not our feelings. If either of us had met anywhere else in Corvallis—at the store, a restaurant, the DMV—my

---

1   In the film, *Good Will Hunting*, Robin Williams plays a college teacher of Psychology who helps a younger student, Matt Damon, who is math savant, but has deep problems.

words would have no power over him, and he would likely think nothing of me, maybe even ignore me. We were not men who would know each other or share a cup of coffee together. I could not say it at the time, but I felt like a failure because deep down I knew that I could not help this White man, even though I wanted to and he wanted me to, I'm sure. There was too much around us and before us that bound us, walled us in our own histories and lives. The systems and conditions of our lives and languaging did not allow for this.

He was a White man, old enough to be my dad at that time, always entering rooms where he is the authority, always watching and hearing stories where he is the hero. I was just a languageling of color who had grown up in rooms filled with White women. I was just a Brown boy faking his way through White places, realizing that I was not of these places, and they would not let me be so.

CHAPTER 9.

NAMING

Our names are important signifiers that change over our lifetimes. They are loaded with our histories and our families and our feelings about ourselves. Names are dynamic because they are words that travel with ever-changing people in their ever-changing lives in an ever-changing world.

Names represent us to others too. They let others speak us into existence in our absence. Your name can be placed on a piece of paper or a plaque or a statue or a stone, left somewhere for a long time, centuries, then discovered by people you don't know. And poof, you exist again as a time traveler. These people in the far future do not know you like your family today can know you, yet they know some bit of you. They have your name. They have your words. Naming is a conjuring. Naming is powerful. We need our names, but they can also be other things.

ON BEING NAMED TWICE

In my own life, I was named twice. During my childhood, my family and friends called me by a nickname, an Anglicised name that was easier for people around me to remember and pronounce, but no one told me it was a nickname. I thought it was my real name. I thought it was me. And of course, it was my name, and it wasn't. In the third grade, I brought home my report card and my name was not on it. On the card was this weird, foreign, vowel-heavy name, one that looked like a girl's name to me at the time. And in fact, my first name can be a female name.

ASAO INOUE.

This name looked foreign and strange to me. I thought maybe I'd accidentally picked up someone else's report card. My mom assured me, "No, sweetheart. That's your birth name." Huh? My birth name? What does that mean? Why doesn't my brother have two first names? Why hadn't anyone used this name? Why didn't anyone tell me this? I didn't even know how to say it. No one had said these words in my direction before. What was I supposed to do with this name? It felt like a horrible secret, a terrible betrayal, like someone had just taken away something sacred from me, a piece of me, and replaced it with something else, something unrecognizable.

At first, I felt as if all the adults around me were in on an elaborate trick, a lie that I had to find out myself. Yet when confronted with this lie, no one seemed to see the severity of what they had done. I wasn't who I thought I was. I was some-one else. I was no-man, nobody. I didn't know this foreign name, yet it was me. Or was it? Names are important, aren't they? Names conjure us, even to ourselves.

Even to this day, my own birth name feels a little loose, not snug and well-fitted like I imagine everyone else's name feels to them when others call them by it. Do you remember when you were confronted by your own name written down for the first time, say on some official document, maybe a report card? Do you remember having to learn to pronounce your own name and it feeling awkward and ill-fitting in your mouth? Have you ever heard someone call your name and it *not* feel right, not feel like a well-worn and comfortable shoe? I do.

So during the period of my growing up when I won that reading contest, I was not only learning English as textual words on pages, but learning that my name was some other textual reference, a foreign one. I was not who I thought I was. I learned that all the grownups in my life, including my teachers, had kept this big secret from me. I was also being confronted with my racial identity every day, or rather others around me confronted me with my identity as a racialized one, one associated with negative terms, like wetback and beaner.

I was consciously swallowing the Black English I learned on Statz, imitating the Standardized English that was expected of me. I was confused because I thought in Black English, and yet that English was slowly vanishing from me as I stopped using it, as I left Statz, as I read more and more books, as I tried to take on the Standardized English of school and the books I loved, as I embraced the language of my White mom, of my White uncle Bill, of school and success. At the same time, I was wanting to be Japanese. I was proud of my Japanese heri-tage. So you'd think that finding out that I had this very Japanese name would be a boon. You'd think I wouldn't reject it. But the spell of Whiteness was too great.

Today, when I hear the word "Japanese," sometimes I'm taken back to mid-dle school, to a song. In 1980, the British new wave band, The Vapors, released a hit song, "Turning Japanese." I heard it everywhere on people's lips. Everyone loved it. They sang its chorus: "I'm turning Japanese, I think I'm turning Japa-nese, I really think so."[1] It's fast and up-tempo. I recall not being able to escape the song. It was everywhere, at least that was my perception.

I couldn't describe why I didn't like the song, but I didn't. I fucking hated it, but I was forced to hear it everywhere, on the radio, in stores, at school, from others' mouths as they squinted their eyes. The song incorporates a stereotypical "Oriental" riff in it, and it's easy to sing. At the time, I remember people saying the song was about masturbation, about how one squints when masturbating and climaxing.

---

1   David Fenton, "Turning Japanese," The Vapors, 1980, United Artists, compact disc.

The song begins, "I've got your picture/Of me and you/You wrote 'I love you'/I wrote 'me too'/I sit there staring and there's nothing else to do." Sexual innuendo? Somehow I didn't see or hear me in that song. I was turning Japanese, for sure, but not that way, not that kind of Japanese. Still, as an eleven year old, I could hear the racism, the cultural appropriation. I didn't want to be that kind of Asian. I wasn't a joke. I didn't know any Asians like that. Or did I?

When you live as a racial outsider all your life, it starts to feel normal, and you stop seeing it—or rather, I think you protect yourself by not engaging with it. It's like being at a party where everyone is having a good time, talking in a big circle, but you are outside that circle, trying to get in. No one will let you in. You ask politely. You do all that you are supposed to, but they say, "Sorry, no room here. Try down there." You try down there, but again, no room. You just keep trying in circles. You think this is what everyone does, or there's something wrong with you, not the circle. The circle is just the circle. You jump up, trying to look over the backs of everyone's heads. You can't fully hear the conversation, but people in the circle are laughing and patting each other on the back. The party, the club, is in the circle. That's what being Japanese, but being mistaken for Mexican, all the while trying to be White, felt like in the US in the 1980s to me.

It didn't help that all the Asian representations during my growing up were not much better than Mr. Yunioshi. They were usually someone with so-called "broken English," like Long Duk Dong from *Sixteen Candles* (1984) or *The Karate Kid's* (1984) Mr. Miyagi.[2] Because reading and writing in English were important activities for me, this hurt. Most of the time, I dissociated myself from the racial stereotypes meant to poke fun at Asians' expense, but not from the language.

It was like someone saying, "this is what you sound like," then spending millions of dollars to show everyone in the world that you sounded like that, that you are a buffoon when you clearly are not. And they gather in a circle you can't enter and talk about you, mimicking some strange and foreign version of you, a Mr. Yunioshi, a White dude playing a fictitious Asian guy. But you are not Mr. Yunioshi. Mr. Yunioshi is not Mr. Yunioshi. But the White kids in the circle cannot see or hear the difference. And you ask yourself: Is everyone fucking nuts?

Language marks people racially. Language makes us and our world. Names are important in our racialized language-world. But we often hear what we want to hear or what we are prepared to hear. This is to say, we hear what our material conditions prepare us to hear. There is often only one Mr. Yunioshi at the party, and everyone laughs and thinks they know Japanese Americans.

---

2   Both actors, Gedde Watanabe (Long Duk Dong) and Noriyuki "Pat" Morita (Mr. Miyagi), were required to play their famous characters with accents, even though neither actor speaks with an accent.

At this time in my life, I saw English languages as markers of goodness and badness, darkness and Whiteness. Talking White was a way to fit into the racial binary, to be named White without actually being White. If I could do that, then I wouldn't be a Long Duk Dong or a Yunioshi. I could elbow my way into the circle. I could be a back clapper and laugher too.

So I initially rejected my Japanese name. It was neither White nor Black. It was foreign and foolish. I didn't use it in social settings. My birth name did not fit into that racial landscape. And it didn't fit my vision of me at that time. I had two names, yes, but I used just the White one.

While I didn't understand the problems with what I was doing, I don't know what other choices I had at the time. No others were presented to me. I was required either to learn Standardized English or perish in school, or be mistaken for a foreigner, a real-life Long Duk Dong, or worse (in my mind then), be seen as a Mexican. My name was central to this self-creation. What I didn't understand then was that even taking on such a standardized English and a White name would not save me from others seeing me as the darker foreigner, the not-quite American, the non-standard, the guy with the questionable background. I was still inscrutable to many.

My name, this very Japanese, ill-fitting, awkward-in-the-mouth sounding name, did not help me make the argument that I was "American." It didn't help me with the argument that I belonged with my White peers, that I could be in the circle too. Today, however, I will not speak that nickname. I went by it until sometime during my master's degree at Oregon State University, when I used my birth name in my classrooms. I was slowly shedding my childhood name and taking on my adult name. It was a time of transition and finding my career and myself. I did not want to be a child anymore, a White languageling. I wanted to be more. I wanted to be a Japanese languageling, a languageling of color, and speak the White language of school.

NAMING STORIES

Most cultures across the globe have spent lots of time and energy thinking about names, finding the right ones for the next generation. Lots of websites and books are dedicated to baby names, the names that will populate tomorrow's classrooms, offices, and civic spaces. In the Yogyakarta region of central Java in Indonesia, there are elaborate naming practices, which happen throughout one's life.[3] The

---

3   See, Jean-Marc de Grave, "Naming As A Dynamic Process: The Case of Javanese Personal Names," *Indonesia and the Malay World* 39, no. 113 (2011): 69–88, https://doi.org/10.1080/136 39811.2011.547730.

naming of children is important in Java and thought to affect children's lives. The name of a Javanese child in this region signifies the context and environment in which they are born, and part of the name is determined by their parents' social position.[4] Children's names describe things around them at their birth. Their names often use time, objects, and animals in them. Names refer to the world of the child and their family, their material conditions that make them from dirt and farms to animals and objects.

In fact, children's names are like "protective prayers." When a parent gives a child a name, it is as if the name-giver is trying to safeguard them from evil, and help them toward a good life. A good name can aid a child in being "good, honest, helpful and devoted to people," as well as help them "fulfil tasks and missions God assigned" them.[5] In adulthood, new names are given to Javanese at weddings, when someone begins their career, starts an important job, or begins an important transition in their life. These adult names are usually different from the childhood ones.

Adult names often "refer to norms or to ideal states."[6] For instance, the fourth president of Indonesia, Abdurrahman Wahid, derives his name from his father, Wahid Hasyim, who was an independence fighter and minister. In Arabic, Abdurrahman means "servant of the graceous" or "servant of Allah." Wahid means "One" or "Absolute One." I can only imagine that in an Islamic context like Java, when you are named "Servant of God the Absolute One," you are named after both your ideal state and a social norm.

I don't think that my mom was influenced by Javanese cultural traditions, but the Javanese naming rituals give me one way to interpret what has happened in my life with my two names. The first Anglicized name, my childhood name, was a start, describing the world my mom thought was around me, even if that wasn't my experience all of the time. It was hers. It was her hope for me, or maybe it was the Whiteness she saw in me.

My birth name, the one I took on explicitly as I started my career in teaching English, was my own wish, my vision of my ideal state. It was what I chose to see in me and project to the world. While this name was given to me by my parents, mostly my biological dad, my name is also my own choice. I chose to use it exclusively. It was a conscious choice because I knew it had power. It was special and bestowed powers upon me. It made me more Japanese to others.

---

4   de Grave, 70.

5   R.D.S. Hadiwidjana, "Nama-nama Indonesia," *Jogjakarta* (Spring, 1968): 13, quoted in de Grave, 70.

6   de Grave, 73.

Many cultures have stories and myths about the power of names. In the ninth book of *The Odyssey*, Odysseus, the hero of the story, is trying to get home to his kingdom and Penelope, his queen and wife.[7] He docks his ship on an island with a giant cyclops, Polyphemus. The name means "abounding in songs and legends." His name speaks of other words, of conjuring. He is a true languageling, but flawed, evil. He is big and strong, a giant. He relies on his strength. He is a man-eater who can tear the tops off of mountains, pull whole trees out of the ground. Polyphemus is the son of the god of the sea, Posiedon, and a nymph, Thoösa. The cyclops has trapped Odysseus and some of his men in a cave. He eats the men, one by one, snatching and gobbling.

But Odysseus is wily, crafty, a true languageling. When Polyphemus asks who he is, Odysseus says that his name is "Outis," "Nobody" or "No-man." It's a con, a joke that hinges on the false-name and its meaning. You don't just give someone like Polyphemus your name. After being tricked by Odysseus with bowls of wine, Polyphemus gets sick, throws up the wine and "the gobbets of human flesh on which he had been gorging."[8] He faints in a drunken stupor.

Odysseus and his men gouge out the cyclops' one eye with the red hot end of a beam from the fire pit. The poem offers a grizzly description of this event worth reading, but it isn't for the faint of heart. In a rare, proud moment, knowing that he's tricked Polyphemus, Odysseus tells the giant his name so that he would know who tricked him. This was a mistake. Odysseus' pride got to him. He forgot that names conjure. They are magic, have powers.

Polyphemus, immediately pronounces a curse on Odysseus using his name. The poem describes it this way:

> he lifted up his hands to the firmament of heaven and prayed,
> saying, "Hear me, great Posiedon; if I am indeed your own
> true-begotten son, grant that Odysseus may never reach his
> home alive; or if he must get back to his friends at last, let
> him do so late and in sore plight after losing all his men, let
> him reach his home in another man's ship and find trouble in
> his house."[9]

Polyphemus' curse comes true. There is power in names, power in the words that conjure people. You don't just give your name away. Knowing a name matters. It can mean years at sea, men dead, and a house filled with suitors trying

---

7   Homer, *The Odyssey*, trans. Samuel Butler (Internet Classics Archive, 2009), http://classics .mit.edu/Homer/odyssey.9.ix.html.

8   Homer, n.p.

9   Homer, n.p. I've incorporated an alternative clause at the end of this translation and converted the Latin (Roman) names in this translation.

to marry your wife and take your kingdom, as it did for Odysseus. All because he was not nobody and he wanted Polyphemus to know it, to know him by his name. Somehow our names tell others about us, tell of our essence.

But names may hold our secrets too, things that others just don't get to know, or shouldn't. Our secrets can be the things that undo us or that so integrally make us that we cannot let others know. It's not their business. In Egyptian legends, the sun god, Ra, was tricked into giving his true name, a secret name, to Isis. She used this knowledge, the supernatural knowledge of Ra's true name, to gain power and honor like his, and usurp his throne.

In ancient Hieroglyphs, Isis is described as "a woman who possessed words of 'Power'" and "the lady of words of magical power." [10] Isis knows that the secret name, the name of Ra that is his alone, is the source of his power. One might own that power if one possessed the name. And again, like Penelope to Odysseus, like my mom to my absent dad, the woman is twice as wily as the man. If only Ra had grown up in rooms filled with Egyptian women, perhaps he'd have seen through Isis' wily ways, not tricked out of his name.

The Akan people of the southern parts of Ghana have an equally wonderful story of Anansi, who often turns into a spider. It's a story about stories stolen, or rather stories gotten through trickery. How else would you pay for stories but through guile and trickery? The tale has several variations, but typically it starts with the world before stories existed. That is, the Sky-God, Nyame, possessed all the stories. Anansi wanted to get them, so he makes a deal with Nyame involving four tasks that would retrieve four dangerous creatures: Onini the Python, the Mmoboro Hornets, Osebo the Leopard, and Mmoatia the fairy. Additionally, to sweeten the deal, Anansi says he'll also trade his own mother, Ya Nsia.

Four dangerous creatures and his mother in exchange for stories—It is an impossible set of tasks, especially for a weak spider. Nyame knows this. He feels safe in making the deal. Through a series of tricks, Anansi gets all four creatures and his mother to agree as well. He takes them to Nyame who is impressed since he didn't believe the spider was strong enough to achieve such feats. He doesn't understand that there are more powerful ways in the world than muscles and size. There is guile, trickery, and of course, the magic of language. The stories are exchanged.

In most versions of the story, Anansi is aided by his wife, Aso, who usually tells him how to trick each creature and trap them. She's vital to the story. Anansi cannot trick his way to the coveted stories without her help. Anansi the spider

---

10   This account of Ra and Isis is found in E. A. Wallis Budge, *The Gods of the Egyptians or Studies in Egyptian Mythology*, (London: Methuen & Co., 1904), 360–363.

is the trickster, but Aso is the more wily. She's the one with the ideas, but she doesn't have to go out and risk her life. She stays home.

What I love about this story of stories is that it is not the strong who get to possess the stories, who turn out to be the big winner. It is the trickster, the wily and crafty spider, who is aided by a woman, his wife, Aso. Most of the tricks that the spider accomplishes are word-tricks, lies, half-truths, or faking his intentions, faking his identity. He goes by many names. Anansi is always shifting his identity from one thing to another. He's not who he says he is much of the time, or maybe he is one thing at one moment and something else at another. Who better in the world to hold on to stories than the wily spider, always weaving its web, always someone else, always a new name?

I see myself in Anansi, Aso, Ra, Isis, Odysseus, and Polyphemus. We all know the power of names and what they do for and to us.

Even when names are funny or comedic, they still have similar things to teach us. The Japanese have an irreverent and comedic story of a boy with a long name, *Jugemu*, which tells satirically of the power of names, allowing us to both laugh at and admit to this truth. It's a story told in a Japanese theatrical tradition called Rakugo. In this tradition, the storyteller is alone on stage and is seated in a seiza sitting position with just two props, a paper fan (sensu) and a small cloth (tenugui), often used in a subtle fashion to wipe perspiration. The tradition emphasizes words spoken with subtle body movements. It's mostly a storyteller, seated in front of an audience, talking to them, telling them a story. Almost everything you get from the experience is meant to come through words.

Rakugo itself showcases the magic of words. But this story is particularly interesting because it's about the power of a name. There are lots of variants to the story of *Jugemu*, all centering around the comedic, long name that "Jugemu" is just the beginning to. One common variant tells of Jugemu falling down a well and dying because all of his would-be saviors passing by take too long pronouncing his name. Thus ironically, Jugemu's true name kills him.

Another version tells of Jugemu getting into a fight. He causes a bump on the friend's head. The friend goes to tell Jugemu's parents, who after pronouncing his name several times in the course of the dialogue, look for the bump on the friend's head, but it has healed. Jugemu's name saves him from blame and punishment.

And why does Jugemu have such a long and comical name? Because his father could not decide on just the right auspicious name for his son. Names are important. They conjure. They have power. They bestow things onto those who possess them. The dad knew this. Several options were given to the father by the priest, but he could not decide, so he took them all.

Each part of Jugemu's name is meant to offer him some benefit in life, but together, too many benefits make for a burden. Here's the full name with some translations, which help show the comedic irony in the name that is so burden-some and too auspicious:

- Jugemu-Jugemu ("limitless life")
- Go kō no surikire ("five kō," or 20 billion years of "no frills"; a bless-ing for a long life)
- Kaijari suigyo ("gravel in the sea and fish in water"; lots of good fortune)
- Suigyōmatsu ("where water eventually goes"; boundless wellbeing)
- Unraimatsu ("where clouds originally come"; more boundless wellbeing)
- Fūraimatsu ("where wind originally comes"; more of the same)
- Kuunerutokoro ("places to eat and sleep"; will not want for such things)
- Sumutokoro ("places to live"; similar to previous)
- Yaburakōji-no burakōji ("marlberry bushes"; boundless energy)
- Paipo, Shūringan, Gūrindai, Ponpokopī, Ponpokonā (made up names of royalty who lived a long time)
- Chōkyūmei ("long and lasting life")
- Chōsuke ("blessed for a long time")[11]

It's a funny name, especially when you hear it repeated in the course of a story or dialogue over and over. Listening to any variation of *Jugemu*, you realize quickly that we use names a lot. Hearing this long name recited, often rapidly, gives one a sense of the tremendous verbal feat it is to recite such a long name. It's impressive, which brings another dimension of joy to the listening of the story. But if we had heard on the evening news that a boy had fallen into a well and died because the people trying to save him took too long pronouncing his name, it would be more than just a tragedy. It would be a crime. We would be outraged. And yet, a performance of *Jugemu* is fun and hilarious. Only language can achieve this kind of magic.

There are many versions of this story in English, perhaps inspired by the much older *Jugemu*. To me, most appear to be influenced by the Japanese tale, as these later versions each have strikingly similar story lines, and all work from an impossibly long name of the central character. The 1950s and 1960s folk group, The Four Brothers, have a song, "Sama Kama Wacky Brown," whose cen-tral character is Eddie Kucha Kacha Kama Tosa Nara Tosa Noma Sama Kama

---

11   These translations are taken from, Wikipedia: The Free Encyclopedia, s.v. "Jugemu," accessed January 3, 2020, https://en.wikipedia.org/wiki/Jugemu. There is a good version in English of *Jugemu* on YouTube performed by Katsura Sunshine; see "Rakugo in English—Jugemu, January 20, 2014, YouTube video, 4:21, https://youtu.be/nJ8Tq5EotaE.

Wacky Brown.[12] In the song, Eddie falls into a well and dies because everyone who tries to save him takes too long pronouncing his name.

It's not hard to hear a racist element in this song with its vague and nonsensical Japanese words in the name, which are meant to be funny. But in *Jugemu*, each element of the boy's long name means something. In the Four Brothers' song, the name means nothing. It is four White guys in a circle pretending to imitate a Japanese character. It's Mickey Rooney in yellowface. It's the original version of what The Vapors did. It's the White party that gets all the Japanese wrong, but no one notices because it's funny. It's Japanese cultural appropriation and racist humor. We might ask: What exactly are we laughing at? Our own ignorance?

In a US context in 1960, it might seem self-evident to laugh at Japanese characterizations because of their Japaneseness, even if the characterization was off, inaccurate.[13] I mean, the academy award winning movie *Breakfast at Tiffany's* came out the next year (1961). Based on the novella (1958) by Truman Capote, it starred Audrey Hepburn as the flighty and whimsical Holly Golightly, with her buffoonish neighbor, Mr. I. Y. Yunioshi, who is clearly attracted to her and is the butt of every joke in every scene he is in. He is played in yellowface by Mickey Rooney.

In each of his scenes, Yunioshi is upset at Golightly's impositions on him. His mantra is, "I musta protest!" Golightly takes advantage of him at every turn. The audience is meant to see this Asian character with his accent, large teeth, big glasses, clumsiness, and impotent protesting as funny. He is not to be taken seriously, but he is also not to be trusted. One scene in the movie shows him in his apartment with elaborate camera and lighting equipment around the room, which he trips over. It's all next to his bed. Is this meant to be suspicious, funny, or perhaps inscrutable?[14]

12　Edward C. Warren and George Goehring, "Sama Kama Wacky Brown," The Brothers Four, 1960, Columbia, vinyl recording.

13　Linguistic plays with words was not new in Western cultures. The ancient fifth century Greeks' term for "barbarian," *barbaros*, came from their own imitation of what they thought the language of the Persians, their enemy, sounded like. It's a kind of onomatopoeia (a word that sounds like what it is to describe), and was meant to make fun of Persians. While it is not accurate to call the use of the term racist in contemporary ways, it was a culturally derogatory term; see Edith Hall, *Inventing the Barbarian: Greek Self-Definition Through Tragedy* (Oxford: Oxford University Press, 1989), 4, 17.

14　There are lots of books written about the racist practices, laws, and language used against Asians in the US. For a history of Asians in America, see Erika Lee, *The Making of Asian America: A History* (New York: Simon & Schuster, 2015); for a history that incorporates Asian groups with Latine and Black groups, see Ronald Takaki, *A Different Mirror: A History of Multicultural America* (New York: Little, Brown & Company, 1993); for discussions of Asians and "Oriental-

In an early scene, there's an implication that the two have talked about him taking pictures of her, a subtle nod to his yearning for sexual activity (are these nude pictures he wants?). But it's clear: She ain't interested. He's not a real suitor for her. The White guy, Paul Varjak, played by the almost blonde but dapper George Peppard, the kept man in the next apartment, the gigolo, the writer, the man of White words, is the clear love interest. It doesn't matter that he's being paid for sex. With a name like Paul Varjak, how are you not a love interest to Audrey Hepburn?

So when you move *Jugemu* to a Western context in 1960, you not only get Japanese cultural appropriation, but racist humor that infantilizes Japanese men. The Four Brothers' song, "Sama Kama Wacky Brown," does all this, but it also emphasizes the transnational power of names. At least our understanding that names are important is universal.

And yet, instances like these send other messages to Japanese boys like me in the 1970s and 1980s. They tell me that my Japanese name is fodder for jokes. They suggest that I won't be taken seriously, that I am not a love interest to women. Who ever heard of a Japanese man loving a White woman? What girl would ever take seriously Asao?

Maybe the best Western version of a *Jugemu* story is one by Monty Python's Flying Circus. It is a hilarious skit that centers on a forgotten Baroque composer named thusly:

> Johann Gambolputty de von Ausfern- schplenden- schlitter- crasscrenbon- fried- digger- dingle- dangle- dongle- dungle- burstein- von- knacker- thrasher- apple- banger- horowitz- ticolensic- grander- knotty- spelltinkle- grandlich- grumble- meyer- spelterwasser- kurstlich- himbleeisen- bahnwagen- gutenabend- bitte- ein- nürnburger- bratwustle- gerspurten- mitz- weimache- luber- hundsfut- gumberaber- shönedanker- kalbsfleisch- mittler- aucher von Hautkopft of Ulm[15]

The skit is set up as a news broadcast that centers on Johann and his only living relative, Karl (played by Terry Jones), who shares the last name of Johann and is interviewed by a British reporter (played by John Cleese). Karl is very old and dies during the interview as the reporter is compelled to say Johann's full name several times during the interview.

---

ism," such as the themes of being inscrutable and mysterious as well as the practice of yellowface, see Robert Lee, *Orientals: Asian Americans in Popular Culture* (Philadelphia: Temple University Press, 1999); or Vijay Prashad, *The Karma of Brown Folk* (Minneapolis: University of Minnesota Press, 2000).

15 "Johann Gambolputty" episode 6, season 1, *Monty Python's Flying Circus*, produced by Ian MacNaughton (November 23, 1969; London: BBC, 1969), television broadcast.

Having grown up watching and loving Monty Python, I am conflicted today. I wonder now, what do Germans think of this skit? Is the name too ridiculous? Is Karl's family name as stereotypical and over the top as Sama Kama Wacky Brown? Is the representation on screen of Karl as impossibly unreal as Yunioshi? Or does this version of *Jugemu* simply reveal how racism in Western traditions only translates to non-Anglo representations, in this case Asian caricatures, and not German? Does it reveal how powerful Western colonialism and imperialism and capitalism have been to our understandings of names? Is English a part of capitalist colonial empire building even today?

Nothing but age lines, a grey beard, and whispery voice distinguishes Karl from the reporter, who is clearly British and White. The skit doesn't seem to be making a joke at the expense of Germans. It's not joking about the essence of being German. But I'm not German, and I've not lived on the European continent, so I could be wrong.

Regardless of the criticisms we might level about these stories, the comedic aspect of each of these retellings of *Jugemu* hinges on the importance of saying the full name. While they are meant to be funny and lighthearted, the comedy only works if we understand that names mean something, that each of us has one that, like Ra's true name, is unique to us and holds power. We are compelled to use them.

In fact, as Odysseus and Polyphemus show us, our names hold our destinies, contain magic that will help us either live well or die too soon, be a love interest or a buffoon. The names in these comedic stories are still doors to life and death. And depending on who is named and how they get named tells us things about the politics of our possibilities. And race is clearly an element in the naming.

I won't say I understood all this when I choose my own Japanese birth name over my Anglicized childhood name. What I can say is that I was not going to be a joke at my own expense, nor was I going to pretend or fake Whiteness anymore. Names are powerful. They conjure us. They make us known to others and ourselves.

CRACKING WHITENESS

During the summer between my first and second year in my master's degree program, my good friend Erik, the one from Berkeley, had just graduated. In talking with him one evening over dinner, I found out that Chris had asked Erik to watch his home while Chris and his family were away for a few weeks. I didn't even know that Chris was going on vacation. I realize there are lots of reasons for why Chris would ask Erik and not me. He could ask anyone he liked, but it felt like I was overlooked, ignored, because Chris and I had a strong and pretty close relationship at that point. I talked to him every week. I figured I'd be the first he'd ask to do such a thing, or at least he'd say that he was going on a several week vacation. Maybe I was being overly sensitive. I was probably being a bit possessive of Chris, thinking I was somehow more special to him than Erik. That wasn't right.

As I looked across the table at my White, Norwegian friend from Berkeley, with the corporate lawyer father, I understood that as good and kind of a White man that Chris was, I would not be his first choice to watch over his home. I am not from his tribe. And I know Chris would not say this. He is a deeply ethical man, but I don't think we have to be able to acknowledge our racial biases in order to use them to make decisions. Our racial biases come from the systems around us. This makes them invisible, tacit, seemingly neutral and natural.

It likely was difficult for Chris to imagine a Brown kid watching over his family's home while they were away. But it was much easier to see the White kid from Berkeley do it. This is how Whiteness works oftentimes, through implicit biases, biases we cannot even see or hear or feel in the act of using them.[16] I hold no grudges for Chris's decision. If anything, I'm grateful for having the opportunity to be confronted with my own biases in this way. The incident helped me see what I really was looking for in a mentor, one who was not White, one who would understand me, share some racialized experiences.

There is lots of research on Whiteness that informs what I've been saying about my first mentor and his habits of White language and judgement.[17] Every semester, I ask my writing students to consider with me the ways that language and its judgement in school and civic life are dictated by those six habits of HOWL—that is, habits that travel with White groups of people in the language they use, the language that gets to be the standards that everyone is judged by, regardless of where they come from. We read this research together. We investigate language as political. We try to learn about writing in English as writers

---

16   There is lots of research on implicit racial and other biases that everyone has, regardless of who they are or how they identify themselves; see Mahzarin R. Banaji and Anthony G. Greenwald, *Blindspot*; for decades of research on how brains make decisions, which speaks to the ways biases are used by our brains, see Kahneman, *Thinking*.

17   I discuss and define habits of White language for use in college writing classrooms in Asao B. Inoue, "Classroom." There have been many before me who have discussed Whiteness as an orientation or stance in the world; see Sara Ahmed, "Phenomenology"; Frantz Fanon, *Black Skin, White Masks*, trans. Richard Philcox (New York: Grove Press, 2008); Ruth Frankenberg, *White Women, Race Matters The Social Construction Of Whiteness* (Minneapolis: University of Minnesota Press, 1993); George Lipsitz, *Possessive Investment*; Marilyn Frye, "White Woman Feminist"; Krista Ratcliffe, *Rhetorical Listening: Identification, Gender, and Whiteness* (Carbondale, IL: Southern Illinois University Press, 2005).

who write in a particular set of historical and political conditions, that is, a set of conditions that are designed by White people and institutions—Whitely systems—in history.

How else can you really learn how to write effectively or meaningfully if you don't understand under what conditions those rules and practices of so-called good writing exist? These conditions create advantages and disadvantages, rewards and punishments. These rewards and punishments are doled out to students based on how those students match up to the preferred dominant habits of language—that is, habits of language that are cultivated from conditions in which White men have learned and used English.

In the writing classes I teach today, the point is to confront the paradoxes inherent in learning and using our literacies in U.S. schools. The point is to understand that English languages are political. To communicate is not a neutral act but one about power, an act that is always engaged in by people who do not stand in the same positions in the system, an act that is situated in pre-existing conditions with rules for communication, rules invented and maintained by groups of people who have the power to do so. The point is that understanding how people judge language as "effective" or "clear" or "compelling" is to understand who has the power to determine such things. To learn to write or communicate persuasively or effectively is to ask: Whose persuasiveness or effectiveness am I going to learn?

When I say, "political," I mean that learning English has to do with who has power, how much they have, how they get that power, and what that means when people use language to communicate among other people who do not have the same access to power, or who cannot make the same choices or receive the same rewards for the same languaging. This is why I think most feminine gendered people,[18] who tend to have less power in social exchanges than masculine gendered people, tend to be mediators, collaborators, and question-askers, not statement-givers or dictators.

---

18   I say here "feminine gendered" and "masculine gendered" people because social scientists identify such gender cultures in this way. This accounts for some biological men being more feminine in gendered communication habits and some biological women being masculine in their gendered communication habits. This is not an either-or identification but a way to understand gender cultures; see "Gender Differences in Social Interaction," LibreTexts, last updated February 20, 2021, https://socialsci.libretexts.org/Bookshelves/Sociology/Book%3A_Sociology_(Bound less)/11%3A_Gender_Stratification_and_Inequality/11.02%3A_Gender_and_Socialization /11.2H%3A_Gender_Differences_in_Social_Interaction. Deborah Tannen has written a lot of books on gender differences in social interactions and language practices, see Deborah Tannen, *You Just Don't Understand : Women and Men in Conversation* (New York: Ballantine, 1991); or Deborah Tannen, *Talking from 9 to 5 : How Women's and Men's Conversational Styles Affect Who Gets Heard, Who Gets Credit, and What Gets Done at Work* (New York: W. Morrow, 1994).

Most will not accept as a matter of course a statement of fact from a feminine gendered person without some explicit reasoning or evidence. So, feminine-gendered people adapt in order to communicate. They ask questions, mediate, look for middle ground. That's the best exercise of power available to them much of the time. They don't demand or make universalized statements or expect everyone to see things from their view. They know that their view is not the only view possible. Their world shows them this all the time. None of this is fair, but that's what I see, what I've experienced. The women in my life, who have been feminine gendered, have mostly been givers, while the men, who have mostly been masculine gendered, are takers and dictators.

Despite my criticism of Chris' discourse now, I am thankful for him. I'm grateful that I got a chance to learn at his feet. I'm grateful for learning the habits of White language, even though I struggle today to release myself from them or at least not hold them against others. Chris and I still keep in touch, email each other occasionally, and go to coffee when I'm back in Corvallis. I enjoy his company. I respect his ideas and opinions because I know he wants the best for those around him.

He is kind in the best ways that you'd think a Catholic deacon would be. I asked him to read my first book before I sent it to the publisher. He gave me rich feedback, but said, "I don't think I'm the right reader for this book." My discussion of Whiteness and racism in the teaching of language was difficult for him to accept. But he was gracious and helpful nonetheless.

Since I left Corvallis, Chris has written many beautiful books of poetry, which is really what he is suited to. It allows him to be a languageling who mixes nature and spirituality, the ordinary and the sacred. His poetry is more homiletic or sermonic than a professing of truth. And I mean this in a good, tentative, I-don't-have-all-the-answers way. Good poetry, I find, is rarely preachy. It's usually a compassionate kind of discourse, a languaging that suffers with its readers over small things that are really big and small things. It sits with details with little need to tell us exactly what they all mean. It is perfect for revealing mystery and paradox, without being overly religious or didactic, while also being religious and didactic.

Chris's poetry, like his prose, is much like a forest: dense, layered, with many canopy gaps where the sun shines down on the detritus and ferns. But it's the details in his languaging that still get me today, that sound generous and inviting in their specificity. In a poem titled, "Piper's Dad," Chris centers on a father who is dying in his bed, his daughter next to him. [19] The old man has not been a good

---

19   Chris Anderson, "Piper's Dad," *The Next Thing Always Belongs* (Monmouth, OR: Airlie Press, 2011), 65–66.

father, instead a "bitter man all his life [who] abused" his daughter and wife. Likely, it was "combat in a war" that made him so cruel. The daughter sits next to her dad as he dies. The narrator comes into the "dark, fetid room" and reads the Psalms to him, which "seems to soothe him/for a while. He doesn't shake as much." Afterwards, the dying man opens his eyes and says two words to his daughter, "You bitch."

Here is how Chris follows this detail: "Who knows what this man was thinking/or what he was seeing. Maybe he wasn't talking/to his daughter, maybe he was talking to Death,/but this is what he says, *You bitch.*" The daughter rises, leans from her chair and whispers in her father's ear, "Daddy, I love you." And then, he dies. There is more to this poem, but this part I really like for the generous compassionate response that the abused daughter enacts, and that the narrator of the poem notices. I like how it resists making any firm conclusions. In my reading of it, the paradoxes that the details open for me are unresolved and unresolvable. How do you account fully for such meanness and compassion lying next to each other?

While the poem continually focuses its words on the dying man, it is the compassionate woman who is centered for me. She makes a mean and bitter father's last few moments better. He certainly didn't deserve it. Or did he? The filth that he spits out creates an occasion for a beautiful act of compassion and love. Both are needed here, and both need each other. At this moment in the poem, Chris does not try to make sense of this paradox, rather the poem presents it to me in the woman's act of compassion.

But maybe I want to see the woman as the center of this story. Maybe I want to see her as a Penelope and ignore the Odysseus in the room. Maybe I invent women as centers of stories like this because I grew up in rooms filled with White women, ones likely a lot like Piper. Maybe my ignoring of the poem's father is a way of getting back at my own father for abandoning me, never knowing me, and so abusing me in a very different way, abuse by absence. At least Piper's dad was there to abuse her.

This poem centers, for me, on five words spoken in this order: *You bitch I love you.* Two words by the father, and three by Piper. Two-fifths masculine, mean, and ugly. Three-fifths feminine, kind, and compassionate. Of the roughly thirty-six clauses that make up the poem, all but about six of them use the dying man as their grammatical subject or the object in which the sentence references. And of the six clauses that use the daughter as their grammatical subject, two still reference something about the dying man or defines her in relation to the man (e.g. "His daughter is with him, in her kindness, praying/ and holding his hand, though he was a harsh/and bitter man"). The poem's title reproduces this tension, this paradox. It's "Piper's Dad." So while the dying man is referenced in the title by who he is to her (his relation to Piper), it is Piper who is named.

If the poem had ended here, it would have worked best for me. It would have HOWLed less. But it doesn't. There are two more stanzas that interpret this scene, make sense of it in a totalizing way. It is a Whitely, masculine move, one conventional for such poems, perhaps even expected. Chris, like most of us who teach or profess in colleges, cannot escape his own Whiteness and masculine urge to explain the meaning in an objective kind of way, engaging in the habits of a universal, naturalized orientation to the world, and a stance of supposed neutrality, objectivity, and apoliticality. I know these habits myself. I'm guilty of them too. Am I performing that habit now? Most of us professors are guilty of this move. It's kind of expected.

Chris' narrator ends the poem, saying: "Love is a great emptying out and losing." It's a statement about a universal concept, love, and how we all enact it universally. Or rather how love *is enacted apart from the bodies that do that loving* in different places and times. It frames love without the conditions that make love possible, yet paradoxically the poem leans on details, specific conditions.

How is the abstraction of love possible, except ironically in words? How does love exist without people and the material conditions that foster love, except ironically in words? How is it possible for me to talk about "love" as if it were a concept only? Paradoxes. Magic. The poem bewitches.

The poem's setting and details betray its own abstraction of love. The poem moves to abstraction from the details, which is a typical, Western, and Whitely habit of language. It's not a bad one inherently, but it is one of many other kinds of habits possible. In this book, I've purposely avoided this habit in many places, even after editors and reviewers have asked me to make it. And yet, I still do make it, but not just it. I'm kinda doing it now.

Enticingly, the poem moves back to details, which I read as a scene inspired by Chris' own deacon life, the details from which the truth about love arise, or rather the poem presents this very atypical scene to me as one that offers such universal ideas of love. The poem continues: "Love is a rising from a chair. It is a leaning/over a bed. It is a whisper in a room and a word/in a room." These details in their specificity become compelling to me, despite my realizing that this is not a scene I'll likely see in my life. So what truth about love can it really give me beyond the pathos?

I have no father to lean over, to say I love you to. I cannot say that I understand this scene from any of the perspectives given: the cruel father's, Pipers, the narrator's. I will never be a deacon visiting a dying father and his grieving daughter on the day of his death. I will never grieve over the bed of my father. And yet, I am there in the room, sitting next to that man, feeling these feelings as I read.

What I take from my reading of the poem is this: Language is magical, bewitching to me. Love and meanness are in the details. I can be both uncomfortable with what that language is doing, while also knowingly fall for it, be compelled by it. Language is dangerously beautiful if not read critically.

The poem concludes with a statement of fact that seems to tell me only what happened: "The last thing this man/ever said was ugly and vulgar and mean./But this wasn't the last thing he ever heard." It's beautiful, even if it's stated as if it were a universal truth on love, compassion, and death, even if it recenters the poem on the man, not Piper. My agreement with it does not make the statement universal. It's not just what happened or even how to understand what happened. It's Chris' narrator's judgement of things, a truth from a universal, god-tricked perspective. It is not how we all should or can read and judge these details always.

To me, the conclusion of the poem comes off as a Whitely, masculine move to the universal from the particular, even as it is compelling to me because it makes this move so elegantly. I am not immune to this HOWLing. Maybe this critical and resistant reading is what Chris really expects of his readers. He's smart enough, good enough, to do that in his poetry. Maybe he expects me to question the so-called truths that his poem's narrator offers so elegantly. I know that Chris in real life would not force such a reading of life onto me, his friend and former student.

The poem's perspective could be dramatically different and still be "factual." What is so beautiful, for instance, in this woman ignoring the ugly words of her father, or the ugly deeds he committed against her over a lifetime? What's beautiful about denial? What's beautiful about letting a man who behaved so badly get away with it, or not have to confront his evil deeds in his lifetime? How is letting someone avoid their responsibilities to live ethically being compassionate? Why are we focusing on Piper's big, generous, final act and ignoring the many that came before this one? Why must such poems always be about Odysseus and not Penelope? And yet, the poem lets me see Piper as a Penelope. I see her dad as making a sacrifice in war, perhaps a bit of his mind or soul given so that his daughter might be able to live a life of compassion, to forgive him in his many moments of weakness. That's a pretty big sacrifice in my book. The poem is "*Piper's* Dad." The poem is about Piper, which makes it about war, and cruelty, and her dad.

Despite my realizing all this, by not being fooled by the god-trick, by the magic of Chris's languaging, I find myself still wanting to be fooled. My ear bends and mouth savors, "Love is a great emptying out and losing./Love is a rising from a chair." The magic in the habits of Whiteness in my life have often been, as is the case here, paradoxical. I am not immune despite my critical eye and ear. I have been bewitched, wooed. I hate and love. I am repelled by and attracted to it. I, too, am tainted in a lovely and awful way. I am also the dying man saying "you bitch."

The Whitely incantations that have taken me so far from North LV have afforded me a comfortable lifestyle. No need to hold on to Uncle Bill dollars anymore. Ends be meeting like a motha fucka in my house. And ironically, I have made my oppression possible. Or shall we call it my colonization, even as the habits of White language do not easily fit onto the body of a remedial languageling of color? Or do they? I have worked very hard to make them fit.

I should have been able to discern the god-trick during my time at OSU as a grad student, but I didn't, at least not in ways that helped me address the problems of that system. I think most students of color have this problem. At that time, all I could do was feel the problem. I could not articulate it. I could not analyze it nor question it. Maybe it is age. At my current vantage point, I have awakened to more hopeful sunrises and known more disappointing sunsets. Time can give more perspective, more distance, more opportunities to learn and reflect.

Maybe it's the theory. I have more of that now. Maybe I was just too close to my getting out and up. Maybe I was still too hypnotized, too entranced by the Whiteness that I could not see the trick. When Blackness and Brownness in the world seem to only mean poverty and ugly words and stiff stares while Whiteness looks like success, jobs, and validation, what would you choose? All I could see at the time was what the trick offered me, if I could master it. I could not see the trade I made in order to do the trick.

And so, my teaching life would begin to crumble as it began, crumble as I was discovering how much it meant to me, how much I loved helping others come to their language as languagelings themselves.

ABOVE THE WELL

I was in my early 20s and just married. I was learning about my own politics. I was learning how to embody and enact my own agency, and part of this was accepting my birth name and making others accept it too. That is still difficult today for some of my family and long-time friends. Words, once put in our mouths, can be hard to get out. Names are notorious for this. They lodge themselves in our throats and refuse to be pried out. My name, like the versions of English I write and speak, which often are not the same, is simultaneously a political choice and an inheritance that I demand others acknowledge and accept. Of course, these choices come at a cost.

I had to learn about my name, Inoue, on my own. It is a common name in Japan. Many with it have ancestry from Western Japan and the Ryukyu Islands (pronounced: REE-OO-KEY-OO). My name usually has three syllables:

EE-NO-EH, but my family has always pronounced it with two: EE-NOY. So I accept both pronunciations, even though the second is likely an Anglicized version. Inoue means, "above the well."

Asao has a variety of meanings, depending on the Kanji used to represent it (like all Japanese names). Since I wasn't raised learning Kanji, I don't have access to this part of my own name. What I do know is that Asao can mean several things: "is morning cheerfulness," "is clearly husband," "is morning man." A Japanese exchange student once told me that my name likely meant "morning boy." I've always liked this translation, but I love all the meanings of my name. The ambiguity in them set together makes me smile and feel proud in a Toaist dialectical way.

I am morning boy . . . morning cheerfulness . . . clearly husband. The Japanese usually say the last name first when referencing people, so I would be: Inoue Asao. So my name means *Above the well is morning boy . . . is morning cheerfulness . . . is clearly husband.*

Sometimes when I see my name on a piece of paper, I'll say it out loud to myself. AH-SOW EE-NO-EH. And I imagine a version of my biological father that I've seen in pictures from around the time of my birth, 1970. He's lean and youthful with thinning Black hair and wearing a sleepy smile as he looks at me with kind, half-closed eyes, ones I'm sure my mom had a hard time resisting. While I'm older today than he was then, in 1970, I feel like a boy looking at his father, or what I think a boy feels like when he looks at his father.

I can hear him in my mind saying my name. Inoue Asao. Above the Well is Morning Boy. My dad is at the foot of Mount Fuji, which I hear looks a lot like Mount Rainier in Washington, a mountain I came to love dearly after living near its feet for several years, driving towards it every day. My father is standing across from me on the other side of a stone well, looking at me. I can hear the water in the well lapping and splashing. He turns, saying my name again—Asao Inoue—and looks up at the mountain. I'm facing the mountain, leaning over the water in the well. And that's it.

The image means nothing . . . and everything.

I know it's sentimental. I know it's not real. I know it could be telling me about my own unresolved feelings of abandonment by a father I never knew, a father I am disappointed in and paradoxically hold up as something else. He is my connection to Japan. He is the symbol of who I say I am, of the ethnic and racial heritage I claim. On occasion, my mom has told me that my expressions and posture, my smile and stance, are like his, like her remembrances of them. Or maybe I just imagined that she's told me this.

It doesn't help that my mom has always been evasive about him and that part of her life. He is her lucky mistake, one she wouldn't trade for anything, I know.

She's never been derisive toward him, never even said an unkind word about him during all those years without child support checks, the years of poverty. I think she knew the importance of fathers to young boys. My mom always played Penelope well.

I'm told that I was named by my father after a younger brother of his. Asao, the brother, died young, maybe at eleven or twelve. They were close. Asao was my father's favorite brother. And this makes sense to me now, or maybe this is just a story I've invented to make me feel more connected to my dad and my Japaneseness. I don't know, but I've taken this story as real.

My dad was the Black sheep in a family of farmers and bankers in Hawai'i on the big island. They owned land. He didn't want to do those things, didn't go to college either. Instead, he moved to California after serving in the army, or was it at the same time? It was in California where my mom met him. That's what I know, or think I know, of him. Asao didn't have a chance to know his brother, my dad, in all his complexity as an adult. Asao didn't know him in all his goodness and badness. No Asao in his life did.

My dad came from a family that was well off, and he rejected that and went out into the world, married a few times, cheated on wives, had some daughters in Germany, then two sons in California with my mom and cheated on her. I have German half-sisters I don't know. I don't even know if my dad is still alive. He was smart, though, wily. He designed and built drag racing cars, then air conditioning systems for automotive companies, all without a college degree.

My mom seems only to marry mechanics, car guys. I have a picture of my mom standing proudly next to my dad's funny car, a drag racing car. It's a black and white photo with a silvery hue. She is smiling big in the picture with her hand on her large belly, which is holding my brother and me inside. She looks like she's keeping a big, joyful secret. I see my mom and dad both playing out *The Odyssey*, only my dad is not trying to come home. He's trying to get lost, staying out at sea on his adventures. And my mom is not trying to be faithful and loyal. She has let him go. She's trying to survive on her own. She's trying to help her sons thrive or just have a chance at something else.

And of my name in all this? Well, my dad, the self-imposed family reject, had a younger brother whom he loved, and so named me, his second-born of twins, after him. It is a mystery and an honor. What does this say? What does my name really mean? What were the material conditions of the first Asao in Hawai'i? How do I make my life out of a paternal loved one's untimely death?

I suppose I do find some pleasure in the tragic nature of the story of my naming, of the first Asao and his loving brother, my dad. And yet, once I escaped my childhood name, the White name, the nickname, and embraced my birth name, Asao Inoue, my life has not been tragic. It has been a steady climb up Mount

Rainier, with breathtaking vistas and hair-raising cliffs. It's been a beautiful and hard and wonderful and complicated journey over the water and toward the summit. It has been always something beautiful and terrible in front of me. It is looking over a well in the cheerful morning as the sun both rises and sets, and the only shadow is my father.

I'd like to believe that my father gave me my name because he didn't want me to lose my Japaneseness. I'd like to think that he knew the power of names and what names bestow, that my name still holds secrets for me. I'd like to think he consciously avoided the trap that Jugemu's father fell into. Your name is powerful magic, but it can't do everything. Maybe he understood that he wasn't gonna always be there. He knew his own nature. But this name would be there, and it is mine.

I'm sure I have psychological trauma that is associated with my naming, my childhood, and my biological dad, associations and histories that make it easier or more preferable for me to just throw away that childhood nickname into the trash can of my past, but of course, it's not that easy. I still have family and a few old friends who call me by this name from time to time, and I wince inside when I hear it.

Yet, I feel the name in me at times, particularly when I hear it spoken, despite my wanting to reject it. There are some warm memories that come with its sound. But I've made my choice. And the choice is mine. I am the living name on a commemorative stone. I am a time traveler who has been inscribed by his father in loving memory of a little brother who died too young.

Or maybe I am that little brother, reincarnated, living the joyful and painful life he would have lived, yet still without his beloved brother. But that's not true either. I have my beloved brother, Tadayoshi, who is named after my father, so Tad and Asao get to have their lives together after all, just in a different generation. I am that brother and that lost uncle of mine, Asao.

I am Above The Well Is Morning Boy.

CHAPTER 10.

I AIN'T NO HORATIO ALGER STORY

It isn't hard to believe that I've made it, that my life and literacy narrative is a success story. I grew up a poor boy of color in a single-parent home, a remedial English student from North LV who made it, a near flunky with an attitude. Yet I graduated from college, went to graduate school twice, got a master's degree, then a Ph.D. in English, no less. I became a professor of English, directed writing programs, and now am an associate dean in one of the largest and most innovative universities in the US.[1] That's successful. I don't deny this at all.

But as I hope I've shown, I'm not the only hero in my story, and my story is only possible because I'm an exception to the rule for children of color who come from places like I did. My conditions allowed me to be successful, even as they hurt me in other ways. So I'm not a success in the way we often talk about successful people in the US. You know the kind, the rags to riches story, the story of a poor boy who, through his own hard work, determination, and persistence, struggles mightily to achieve great things despite having very little to work with and few helping hands along the way. I do not wish to be read as a Horatio Alger story.

So, as a way to close my literacy story and argument, as a way to ask again how we come to understand the White language supremacist conditions in our lives in order to remake those conditions, I discuss the idea of success and where we in the US seem to get our ideas about it in this closing chapter. This argument about our narratives of success is also an argument about me and how you might understand better what my literacy story means, what lessons you might take from it beyond the ones you likely have already.

THE HORATIO ALGER MYTH OF SUCCESS

Today we all live under the strong and enticing myth of the Horatio Alger story of success, even if you don't know who Alger is. His stories inform much of our discourse about who we are as Americans, what success and hard work means.

---

1   As of 2019, Arizona State University had been named the most innovative university in the US for five years running by *U.S. News and World Report*; see Mary Beth Faller, "ASU Named No. 1 in Innovation For Fifth Consecutive Year," ASU Now, September 8, 2019, https://asunow .asu.edu/20190908-asu-news-number-one-innovation-us-news-fifth-consecutive-year.

His myth of success certainly informed me and how I approached school, even as I slowly grew to criticize the myth. It's a difficult myth to escape.

In 1832, Horatio Alger Jr. was born to Augusta Fenno and her husband, the Unitarian minister Horatio Alger Sr., in Chelsea, Massachusetts.[2] The New England family had esteemed roots, coming from influential Pilgrims like Robert Cushman, who organized and led the Mayflower voyage to the New World in 1620. While his family was far from rich, they were well respected and had some means. Alger Jr. attended Harvard, then bounced around several jobs in the Boston area as an editor and a teacher at a boys boarding school. During this time, he wrote a few serialized books, then a poem, mostly for magazines.

Between 1857 and 1860, he went to Harvard Divinity School, graduated, and took a position as a pastor of the First Unitarian Church and Society in Brewster, Massachusetts, all the while continuing to write stories for magazines. It didn't last though. Just two years into his post in 1866, Alger resigned as pastor and moved to New York City amid controversy in his parish. He had been accused of being "familiar with boys." There was evidence that he had sexually abused several boys. He admitted to it and quit with apparent little remorse.[3]

Horatio Alger is probably best known for his Ragged Dick novels, of which he wrote twelve. Most of Alger's novels were rags to riches stories of boys who make it out of poverty and become successful in some way by their own wit, pluck, and persistence. In many ways, his novels epitomize important narratives of the day, "the Gilded Age."[4] These narratives said that one could do anything as long as one worked hard, was honest, abided by the rules, but mostly, worked hard. These narratives served well the super-rich industrialists and elite of the second half of the nineteenth century, that is, those White men who owned steel factories, oil companies, and railroads. It reassured the working classes that they, too, could be like John D. Rockefeller, Andrew Carnegie, or Cornelius Vanderbilt.

---

2   To read about Horatio Alger and the myth of success in the US, see chapter two of Richard Weiss, *The American Myth of Success: From Horatio Alger to Norman Vincent Peale* (New York: Illini Books, 1988). All of Horatio Alger's books are open access online at https://www.gutenberg.org/ebooks/author/168.

3   To read more about this period of Horatio Alger's life at the Brewster parish, see George C. Kohn, "Horatio Alger: Lover of Boys," *The New Encyclopedia of American Scandal* (New York: Facts on File, Inc., 2000), 6; see also, "Horatio Alger and the 100-Year-Old Secret," New England Historical Society, last updated 2019, http://www.newenglandhistoricalsociety.com/horatio-alger-hundred-year-old-secret/.

4   The term "Gilded Age" comes from the satirical novel by Mark Twain and Charles Dudley Warner, *The Gilded Age: A Tale of Today*, http://www.gutenberg.org/ebooks/3178; the term refers to a time when the US saw immense growth, prosperity, and corruption.

These three industrialists in this order, according to *Business Insider* in 2011, are the richest Americans ever to live, after adjusting for inflation.[5] This included Bill Gates, Jeff Bezos then (who is now considered the richest man alive[6]), and all the tech giants today. In today's terms, Rockefeller's wealth is estimated at $336 billion, Carnegie's at $309 billion, and Vanderbilt's at $185 billion. Meanwhile, Bill Gates was fourth on this list, with a net worth of $136 billion. Jeff Bezos, who recently announced he would step down as the CEO of Amazon.com, is currently estimated to be worth $150 billion.[7]

If they were alive today and had their fortunes, Rockefeller or Carnegie could give away the equivalent of Bezos' wealth and still be richer than Bezos currently is.[8] So the narratives that Horatio Alger offered in his novels for young boys would be very enticing, especially if your world was limited and filled with hard labor that paid very little. If all you saw around you was poverty, hard luck, and even harder work for little pay, you needed to believe that you had access to the life of a Rockefeller or Carnegie or Vanderbilt. Even today, most want to believe that they can be the next Bezos, even though they cannot.

Most agree that Alger's stories of boys making it on their own by hard work and persistence have always been fantasies. They simply are not the way life really works most of the time. They aren't how our current capitalist systems and economies are built. To be successful, to have your hard work pay off in the right

---

5   Gux Luban, "The 13 Richest Americans of All Time," *Business Insider*, April 17, 2011, https://www.businessinsider.com/richest-americans-ever-2011-4/.

6   Robert Frank, "Jeff Bezos Is Now the Richest Man in Modern History," CNBC, July 16, 2018, https://www.cnbc.com/2018/07/16/jeff-bezos-is-now-the-richest-man-in-modern-history.html.

7   It should be noted that net worth and wealth are difficult to calculate, as often such super-rich families have many different kinds of holdings that are not easily tabulated unless they are sold, so total net worth is a slippery figure. However, three other lists of the richest men in the US to have ever lived list these three men in the top three places in the same order: John D. Rockefeller, Andrew Carnegie, Cornelius Vanderbilt; see Christine Gibson, "The American Heritage," *American Heritage*, October 1998, https://www.americanheritage.com/american-heritage; Peter W. Bernstein and Annalyn Swan, *All the Money In The World* (New York: Knopf, 2007), 17.

8   It's worth noting that over the years, the Rockefeller fortune has been divided and trusted to numerous family members and descendants, and it is very difficult to estimate the family wealth today. The *Motley Fool*, a blog on nasdaq.com, estimates today's Rockefeller family fortune to be worth around $10 billion; see, Sean O'Reilly, "How Rich Is the Rockefeller Family Today?" *The Motley Fool* (blog), September 1, 2016, https://www.nasdaq.com/articles/how-rich-rockefeller-family-today-2016-09-01. In his last years, Andrew Carnegie gave his vast wealth away to charities, doing things like establishing thousands of libraries. Carnegie famously said, "The man who dies rich, dies disgraced." See, Chloe Sorvino, "The Gilded Age Family That Gave It All Away: The Carnegies," *Forbes*, July 8, 2014, https://www.forbes.com/sites/chloesorvino/2014/07/08/whats-become-of-them-the-carnegie-family.

ways, you have to have a lot of conditions in your favor along the way. No one person controls all or most of these conditions. They are networks and systems, structures in our society, schools, jobs, and languages.

But the myth that hard work always equates to success lets poor folks dream of a better tomorrow. It democratizes success. It gives everyone access to success, even if only in their dreams. It keeps the working poor, like my mom, working hard, and allows the rich, who own the places and companies in which the poor work, to get richer. And of course, paradoxically, to have any success, even a modest amount, does require hard work. But it's easy to believe the fallacy that if I want to be richer or more successful than I am today, all I gotta do is work harder. It's an ever-sliding scale that offers an ever-retreating success.

Richard Weiss, who researched Horatio Alger Jr., also examined this myth of American success, explaining that its roots can be found in "early American Puritanism," that is, seventeenth-century New England, namely in the sermons of ministers like Robert Cushman and Alger's family.[9] Even as early as 1879, Mark Twain criticized the Horatio Alger success story in his own short, satirical story, "Poor Little Stephen Girard." In Twain's version, Little Stephen is not saved by a rich banker despite his honesty and hard work. Instead, he is chastised and left worse off. Upon showing the banker the bounty of his silent toiling, of picking up pins from the front steps of the bank, the banker responds: "Those pins belong to the bank, and if I catch you hanging around here any more [sic] I'll set the dog on you!"[10] The experience of Twain's Little Stephen is more like that of most in the US then and now. But statistically, it's even more so for people of color.

One way to see just how the Horatio Alger myth of success works against people of color is to consider the wage gap for Black women in the US. If everyone works hard and persists, then we should all be making about the same amount of money with the same qualifications. But that is not the case. In 1967, three years after the passage of the Civil Rights Act of 1964, Black women made 43 cents for every dollar made by White men.[11] Fifty years later in 2015, that gap was at 63 cents on every dollar made by White men. It didn't even matter if Black women had college degrees. They still made $1,000 less a year than their White male counterparts. Similarly, Black women with master's degrees only got 64 cents for every dollar a White man with the same qualifications got.

---

9   Weiss, *American Myth*, 4.

10   Mark Twain, "Poor Little Stephen Girard," *Carleton's Popular Readings*, ed. Anna Randall-Diehl, (New York, 1879, 183–84; repr., http://historymatters.gmu.edu/d/4935/).

11   This and the following statistics come from Kayla Patrick, "For Black Women, Hard Work Doesn't Always Pay Off," National Women's Law Center, July 27, 2017, https://nwlc.org/blog/for-Black-women-hard-work-doesnt-always-pay-off/.

Hard work, grit, and pluck have never paid off in the same ways for women of color. And if you've bought into the myth, then you likely blame yourself for not making it, not getting the promotion, not making enough money, not working hard enough. I mean, the Alger narrative of success says if you work hard and long enough, you'll be successful. And if you don't, well, then you only have yourself to blame. Now, if you are one of the lucky ones and have made it and are looking at all those who haven't, you might accuse them, those Black women for instance, for not being as hard working or diligent or smart as you. I mean, c'mon, you made it, right? Why can't they?

Both views are false conclusions that come from accepting the Alger myth, or not thinking it through carefully. And our judgements of other people and their language practices as well as our own are implicated in this myth of success. We often use language as a marker of how successful people are or will be. We substitute judgements about how someone writes or speaks with how smart or capable they are, as I discussed in chapter 5. Why else would teachers grade your languaging?

So when we accept the Alger myth completely, the victim is victimized thrice: first by the system that feeds all of us the Alger myth of success, assuming in the HOWLing that tells us we all have the same kind of access to the same things; second by each other, each of us blaming the other for the unfair conditions in which we all work and that benefit some more than others by systemic default, thinking in a hyperindividualized way that everything, including our own success, comes from within ourselves only; and third by ourselves, beating ourselves up for not being able to achieve success like those we think we see around us, thinking in fast-fashion that what we see is all there is, missing the systems and structures that afford some more than others, systems that are so present they are invisible and seem neutral and even fair.

Now, there is an alternative way to see things. We could accept the idea that working hard is good and preferable without believing that it will always result in success, security, or the rewards we initially seek. We could see success as a function of one's material conditions *and* labors, just like our literacy that we inherit and use. This is not as an attractive narrative, though. It suggests that if you don't like how things are working out, how little your labors and grit pay off, it's not simply a personal matter.

It ain't just about fixin' yourself. It's a systemic issue, a problem with the conditions and systems we work in that determine what your hard work and determination are worth. It's not about the signs of God's election, nor about the markers that show to everyone your supposed value in society. It's about understanding the value of the system itself and what it is capable of. This alternative way of seeing success suggests change, maybe revolution. It suggests that surely different systems, ones that do not place so many boundaries and limitations on most people, are possible.

In his novels, Alger is thinking in Puritanical terms. As the late nineteenth- and early twentieth-century German sociologist, philosopher, and political economist Max Weber (pronounced MAUX VAY-BER) explains it, according to Puritanism, the best way to see one's election into heaven, or know that you are predestined by God, is through the material markers of his grace,[12] that is, things like money, expensive clothes, nice homes, and big families. This isn't foolproof, of course. The signs of election are not always clear. But according to most Calvinist doctrine, no one earns their way into Heaven, and the "elect" who go to Heaven are already predetermined. Weber offered a useful theory to explain not only how Puritanism agrees with the values of capitalism but how the two systems produce something else.

Weber explains that the "spirit of Capitalism" favors profit for profit's sake. When you insert Calvinist doctrine into a capitalist society, you get values that promote making profits as the highest good, both for the individual and society. It's surely a perversion of Calvinism, but that's partly Weber's point. The two systems, Calvinism and capitalism, make something new in the US, make a new spirit or set of guiding values. Profit is a divine calling. It proves you are good and valuable to society. Part of the logic is: God has given you this, so it must be good. Money, then, is the sign of election and success. In one sense, it is "trickle-down" economic theory.[13]

Data scientist Cathy O'Neil offers lots of contemporary evidence for the phenomenon Weber describes, from finance to college rankings. In banking and the places where big data is used to manipulate people, which turns out to be every field and industry these days, she explains:

---

12   Max Weber, *The Protestant Ethic and the "Spirit" of Capitalism and Other Writings* (New York: Penguin Books, 2000), 19–21.

13   Trickle-down economic theory has roots dating from the turn of the twentieth century in U.S. politics, but it was made popular by President Reagan and was called "Reaganomics." In the mid–1980s, Reagan's economic policies focused on the supply-side of the economy, lowering a variety of taxes for corporations and the super-rich with the assumption that the money saved there in the system would trickle down to everyone else. That trickling down never happened, but this kind of economic policy has been a staple of the Republican party. In the early 2000s, President George W. Bush had similar economic policies. The language then was around providing money to "job creators" so those savings would trickle down to everyone else. Again, there was no evidence that money would actually trickle down. To read about trickle-down economics and Reaganomics, see, William A. Niskanen, "Reaganomics," The Concise Encyclopedia of Economics, 2002, https://www.econlib.org/library/Enc1/Reaganomics.html. To read criticisms of Bush-era "job-creator" tax cuts, see, Rick Ungar, "The Truth about the Bush Tax Cuts and Job Growth," *Forbes*, July 17, 2012, https://www.forbes.com/sites/rickungar/2012/07/17/the-truth-about-the-bush-tax-cuts-and-job-growth/#1e1bba507463.

> Whether in finance or tech, the message they've [college
> graduates from elite universities] received is that they will be
> rich, that they will run the world. Their productivity indicates
> that they're on the right track, and it translates to dollars. This
> leads to the fallacious conclusion that whatever they're doing
> to bring in money is good. It "adds value." Otherwise, why
> would the market reward it?

> In both cultures, wealth is no longer a means to get by. It
> becomes directly tied to personal worth.[14]

These are not old-fashioned, archaic ideas that we see only in movies. They aren't ideas relegated to antiheroes, like Gordon Gekko, telling us that "greed is good."[15] Weber's "spirit of Capitalism" infects us all in tacit ways. And what is one of its central logics? Hierarchy. People are ranked and graded. Colleges are ranked and graded. Stocks and mortgages are ranked and graded. The rankings and grades end up being used to determine the value of people and decisions in systems. The ranks and grades become a surrogate for merit.

Just a few years before Weber published his ideas, Thorstein Veblen, an American economist and sociologist, offered a similar theory of the leisure classes in the US. Veblen explained that those who can afford to engage in "conspicuous consumption" do so because it shows their alleged value. They buy expensive food, clothing, houses, jewelry, and other things not because they need them, but because those obvious material things are signs of wealth and success.[16] In effect, conspicuously consuming expensive things means you are good and successful. Veblen was criticizing the practice, of course. You have value to society, even if your good to society has not been proven. The theory of conspicuous consumption says that we all peacock around because, well, we think it is important to show everyone our value and worth, even though "worth" is understood in this system only in monetary terms.

Veblen's work reveals that we don't have to think in terms of Calvinist or Puritanical doctrine that interprets markers of wealth as God's favor. We justify our ideas about wealth and spending through other means too. And, this kind of behavior implicitly reinforces the social, economic, and racial places we all are born into in society since it ignores the way the system sets up some groups to succeed more easily and more often than other groups.

---

14   O'Neil, *Weapons*, 47.

15   Gordon Gekko was played by Michael Douglas in the movie *Wall Street* (1987) in which he spoke the famous line: "Greed is good."

16   Thorstein Veblen, *The Theory of the Leisure Class* (New York: Houghton-Mifflin, 1973), 64.

Some of us are born into families that conspicuously consume, while others are born into ones who cannot. As O'Neil shows in her book, the cycle feeds itself. This means that worth in such systems is inherited, like our languages and names. These conditions allow us to blame people too easily for who they are, where they come from, and how they use language under the guise of promoting personal responsibility, hard work, and persistence. It uses the Horatio Alger myth against people of color, working class folks, and the poor.

ALGER AIN'T TALKIN' BOUT BLACK BOYS

Of course, the success narrative isn't just about careers and jobs. It's also predicated on living a life free from harassment, living a safe life, one that affords everyone the chance to work hard and persist. It's about having equitable chances to life, liberty, and the pursuit of happiness that we say we all get in the US. But you do not have such chances when your risk of police violence upon you is statistically much higher than your White peers. Success and persistence requires the freedom to exercise such things in your life.

These inequitable life chances can be read in Twain's Little Stephen story, and in George Floyd's death in Minneapolis in May of 2020. It can be seen in the apparent murder by hangings of Robert Fuller and Malcolm Harsch, two Black men in California just 50 miles apart.[17] We can also see it in the hundreds of other Black citizens killed by police every year in the US, which have become more and more difficult for local governments and police agencies to justify recently.[18]

A recent study by researchers at Rutgers University using federal data found that Black men were 2.5 times more likely to die at the hands of police than their White peers.[19] It is a leading cause of death for Black males. This means that "1 in 1,000 Black men and boys in America can expect to die at the hands of police." Since 2015, police in the US have killed on average 1,000 people a year. The death rate of Blacks killed by police are three times what they are for Latine, and four times the rates for Whites.[20] In the US, Black men and boys do

---

17 Sandra E. Garcia, "Families Challenge Suicide in Deaths of Black Men Found Hanging From Trees," *New York Times*, June 14, 2020, https://www.nytimes.com/2020/06/14/us/robert-fuller-malcolm-harsch-deaths.html.

18 "Controversial Police Encounters Fast Facts," CNN, June 4, 2020, https://www.cnn.com/2015/04/05/us/controversial-police-encounters-fast-facts/index.html.

19 Amina Khan, "Getting Killed by Police Is a Leading Cause of Death for Young Black Men in America," *Los Angeles Times*, August 16, 2019, https://www.latimes.com/science/story/2019-08-15/police-shootings-are-a-leading-cause-of-death-for-Black-men.

20 Mark Berman, John Sullivan, Julie Tate, and Jennifer Jenkins, "Protests Spread Over Police

not have equitable chances for life, liberty, and the pursuit of happiness. They usually do not even get the chance to be a Ragged Dick.

Consider De'Von Bailey, a 19-year old young, Black man who was shot in the back by a White police officer in Colorado Springs, Colorado, as he ran away on August 3, 2019.[21] The same officer, Sergeant Alan Van't Land, shot and killed another man in 2012.[22] Colorado Springs has a population of 472,688, and just 6.2 percent of that number are Black residents. The overall poverty rate in the city is 12.6 percent, but that same rate for Black residents is 20.17 percent, and it's 22.02 percent for Latine residents. Meanwhile, White residents' poverty rate in the same city is at 9.35 percent.[23]

Why tell you this? These statistics matter to the narratives we tell ourselves about those around us or those over there, in the "bad part of town." They make up a part of our material conditions that we all use, including the police, to make decisions, especially quick ones, ones we don't have time to ruminate over, the kind of fast thinking that Daniel Kahneman researched.[24] The narratives associated with Black men and boys are not like Ragged Dick. They are of a different sort that we often set against Ragged Dicks. They are an even crueler, more fatal version of Twain's Little Stephen Girard.

The title of the *USA Today* story on August 13, 2019, about the shooting of De'Von Bailey reveals these narratives of young, Black men in the US. The title of the article is: "De'Von Bailey Was Shot in the Back and Killed by Police, his Family Says. They're Rallying for 'Justice.'" By ending the first sentence with the qualifier, "his family says," it appears as if the police may not have shot and killed him. It would appear this detail is in question, but it is not at all. The police body camera footage clearly shows Sergeant Van't Land shooting an unarmed Bailey. So we know exactly who killed whom. But you might not know this from the *USA Today* coverage, as it doesn't even name the officer.

Shootings. Police Promised Reforms. Every Year, They Still Shoot and Kill Nearly 1,000 People," *Washington Post*, June 8, 2020, https://www.washingtonpost.com/investigations/protests-spread-over-police-shootings-police-promised-reforms-every-year-they-still-shoot-nearly-1000-people/2020/06/08/5c204f0c-a67c-11ea-b473-04905b1af82b_story.html.

21 Vandana Ravikumar, "De'Von Bailey Was Shot in the Back and Killed by Police, His Family Says. They're Rallying for 'Justice,'" *USA Today*, August 13, 2019, https://www.usatoday.com/.

22 Karu F. Daniels, "Colorado Cop Who Killed Unarmed De'Von Bailey Has Past of Brutality, Still Honored," The Root, September 8, 2019, https://www.theroot.com/colorado-cop-who-killed-unarmed-de-von-bailey-has-past-1837967840.

23 "Colorado Springs, Colorado Population 2019," World Population Review, accessed October 29, 2019, https://worldpopulationreview.com/us-cities/colorado-springs-co-population.

24 Kahneman, *Thinking*; also, I provide more details about fast thinking in the section called "Our Fast Thinking and Mindbugs" in the appendix essay found in this book.

In the news article, there is no racialized body of a White police officer shooting yet another young Black man in the back. Here's the article's second and third paragraphs:

> The family of a Black Colorado man who was fatally shot by police this month in Colorado Springs are rallying to demand an independent investigation into his death.

> Surveillance video obtained last week by The Gazette newspaper in Colorado Springs appears to show 19-year-old De'Von Bailey running away from two officers before being shot in the back and falling to the ground.[25]

In this account, no agent, no police officer, pulls a trigger—not grammatically. The first paragraph uses the passive construction to erase the subject doing the shooting: "a Black Colorado man who *was fatally shot* by police." Who fatally shot him? The police? Who in that organization did it? Do bullets just come out of "the police"? No, a police officer has to make a judgement, draw a gun, and pull a trigger. Furthermore, a police system has to train such an officer to make those kinds of decisions. Laws and policies of local governments and agencies have to be made in order to protect all those police officers when they make a judgement, pull a gun, and shoot. Instead, this sentence and paragraph makes De'Von into only a "Black Colorado man" whose primary characteristic is being "fatally shot by police."

The sentence that makes up the second paragraph uses another passive construction that erases Sergeant Van't Land. He's not even at the scene, apparently. De'Von is just shot in the back. It's almost as if it doesn't matter who did it, only that it was done. But it does matter when the one who did it is supposed to protect the citizens of Colorado Springs, all of them, not kill some more than others for running away unarmed. That's no reason to draw a gun, no reason to pull a trigger, no reason to kill anyone. No one is in danger, except the young, Black man—that's probably why he ran.

Furthermore, putting "justice" in quotation marks in the article's title can create a sarcastic tone. Who doesn't want justice? Do the parents have some perverted notion of justice? No, we all want justice. Justice is supposed to be the rule of law. Justice is what everyone expects here. So why quote "justice" in the headline if not to call it into question? The reason is: When justice is what a Black family wants, it is suspect. A Ragged Dick De'Von is not imagined to be in this story, at least not to the *USA Today* writers and editors, and perhaps not to many of their readers.

---

25   Ravikumar, "De'Von Bailey."

And this news outlet should know better. They deal in words, circulate headlines on social media, which is where I found the news article first. They know how Twitter and headlines work. They know that many often do not read them carefully. Many people only read the headlines and do not look at the story itself. So we can say that the *USA Today* knows what it's doing when it comes to the words they tweet or circulate. They know this story calls into question not just De'Von but his family, who are all victims. They know a reader can read this headline with some sarcasm. They know the headline erases the bad decisions of a White police officer, and bad policies and laws. These words protect bad systems, racist ones. They are working with the narratives of Black boys in the US as thugs, as always guilty and dangerous, as always suspect, even their family's words.

The story is so common. Black boys are just shot by "police." Justice has already been meted, apparently. No one is to blame, really, not when a Black kid gets shot. The bottom line is: Black boys are no Ragged Dicks. They don't get to be a part of the Horatio Alger story of success.

EXCEPTIONALS THAT LIFT US UP AND KEEP US DOWN

I'm in a room with about fifteen university administrators and staff, mostly from offices in the administration building and the marketing communications department. They're interviewing me for a communications position. It's a technical writing job of sorts with some marketing in it. The room is dark, quiet, but friendly enough. Most in the room smile or seem interested in what I've said up to this point.

"Don't you think that your image and face on university marketing materials would encourage other Asian Americans and minorities to succeed in college, or to go to college? How do you feel about being a role model for other students of color?"

I feel awkward in the moment, a moment I'm sure decided for those in that room my inability to do the job, at least not in the manner they were looking for. The question is sincere and honest, even kind sounding. It is meant to help me see the error of my logic in a parental fashion. Earlier in the discussion, the committee implied that I might be asked to "participate" in marketing campaigns, to be on "marketing collateral" that advertised the university. How did I feel about this? I am not enthusiastic about it.

I talk about a time that I'd refused a similar offer from another educational institution, a community college. It doesn't feel ethical to me. It feels dishonest to be a part of that. I think that they understand my sense of morality in this intimate question. As we continue, they ask me more questions, and the session turns into an examination of sorts. It all starts to make sense.

I was invited to this interview by one of them, asked to apply for this job. I had some background that applied. I had a good portfolio of work that a few had seen in another context. I am known by several in this particular hiring committee as a "strong candidate." But I am also there to put "color" into their hiring processes. The university and the town it is situated in is a very White place. Candidates like me are at a premium.

They are testing me: Will I be a good token? Will I accept their notions of "diversity" and "multiculturalism"? In the moment, I want to tell them that by implication, any marketing material that uses people of color to sell a university to prospective students at a school that has barely any students of color on its campus is dishonest and unethical. The tactic constructs people of color as part of an exotic scenery for the vast majority of White students who come to the school.

I want to ask them if they know that at the time, 44.1 percent of those who identified themselves as "Asian Americans" 25 years old and older had a bachelor's degree while only 26.1 percent of White people had the same degree.[26] Why do we need urging to go to school? We are already going to school. We are achieving higher rates of graduation than any other racial group identified on the US Census. I want to tell that committee, "Look, I should not be a role model." And, if I'm to represent students of color at large, I am still no role model. I am an exception. Exceptions should not be used to prop up the rule, to justify how good the system is doing. I actually illustrate the opposite.

As problematic as it is, I am a "model minority." And paradoxically, my story is more complicated than this myth allows. There are intersectional dimensions that make for my successes and failures: class, economics, language, geography, gender, and of course, race. I also have privileges that make being a model problematic, especially for such a broad grouping of students, like students of color.

Instead of saying any of this, I say, "Hmm, I see, but I feel it's more complicated. I'm just not sure." And then I tell them with a smile that I understand my racial designation as political and that I cannot knowingly allow it to be used in that way. From their puzzled looks, even by the African American and Filipino committee members, I can tell they do not understand. They cannot see why I am so against the idea. They cannot see that the message of me is false on their marketing materials if it suggests that there is now more opportunity for students of color.

---

26   Kurt J. Bauman and Nikki L. Graf, *Educational Attainment: 2000*, U.S. Census Bureau, U.S. Department of Commerce, (Washington DC: U.S. Census Bureau, August 27, 2003), http://www.census.gov/prod/2003pubs/c2kbr-24.pdf.

Some smile, some nod, but no one says a word. They just scribble on their yellow tablets. Maybe they think I am a bitter, little, Brown man, seething with anger, inscrutable. Maybe they can't put the logic together because of their investment in the school, its multicultural agenda, their personal commitments to institutional diversity, because they really care about diversity and encouraging students of color to come and succeed. Maybe they really think that displaying bodies of color for White students to see is a good idea, that it ain't some kind of conspicuous multicultural consumption. Maybe they think pictures of Brown students is the antiracist structural work that will change things?

This is how these kinds of exchanges have always gone down with me. They are collegial, pleasant, usually non-confrontational, and encouraging, friendly, and explicitly about tolerating "different voices" and "celebrating diversity." They are about lifting up the exceptionals of color. But I leave always wondering: Does lifting up an exceptional put down everyone else?

~~~

While it's easy to see how the Horatio Alger story is false, especially for people of color, it's equally easy to see elements of it in any success story that gets told in the media. But don't let these exceptionals fool you. One can believe in the ethic of hard work without accepting the entirety of the Alger myth of success, namely that all hard work always pays off in the same way for everyone, regardless of your material conditions, who you are perceived to be racially and morally, or where you come from and how you talk.

The problem is that most success stories are told because they are spectacular and exceptional. We want to be like those exceptional people. But in the same way that Alger's novels functioned in the Gilded Age to keep the working classes working for very little, so too do narratives of bootstrapping and success work today. In fact, most of us likely believe we are the exceptions. Our hard work will pay off, even if we don't always see it around us. Holding up exceptionals too often keeps people satisfied with their current conditions, ironically by making them itch for more, a more that is possible. Exceptionals do not inspire us to change the system. They anesthetize us so that we leave it alone, broken. We see what the system has produced for the exceptional, and we want that for ourselves too.

Do you hear the contradiction in this logic? We know they, the models placed in front of us, the Ragged Dicks of the world, are not the rule, yet we think all of us are above that rule. Each of us likely thinks that we are above the statistics. We are the extraordinary ones. A Ragged Dick in each of us. At the same time, exceptions do happen. It's nice to dream, to shoot for the impossible. Why can't we all achieve our dreams, be Ragged Dicks making it in our own ways in the world? It should be the rule. There should be room for that. But what should our narratives tell us? What rules of the system should we hang our hats on?

In our current economic circumstances, we need such dreams, something that helps us believe in a better tomorrow. I needed such things to create my dreams as I climbed out of the ghetto, struggled through college, always looking for markers of conspicuous success. This is why we have lists of these exceptionals published in magazines like *Inc* and *Entrepreneur* and on the Business Insider website, with each exceptional's net worth attached.[27]

If they were not so rare, if they didn't make so much, the lists would be uninteresting. They'd be of our neighbors, friends, and family. The people would be common in their successes. Success itself would be typical, un-newsworthy. These people and their success have to be rare and spectacular. How else does a Brown kid make it as a remedial reading student in North LV or through the blinding Whiteness of Corvallis, Oregon? Does he have to be an exceptional? Is that an unfair ask of him?

The lists are framed as ways to "inspire" us, or "blow our minds." Of course, we only need inspiration if we know that the chances of success are rare. Here is a list of just a few of the Alger-like descriptions from these articles:[28]

- "Starbucks's [CEO] Howard Schultz grew up in a housing complex for the poor . . . Net worth: 2.9 billion"
- "Born into poverty, Oprah Winfrey became the first African-American TV correspondent in Tennessee . . . Net worth: $3 billion"
- "Legendary trader George Soros survived the Nazi occupation of Hungary and arrived in London as an impoverished college student . . . Net worth: $24.2 billion"
- "Ed Sheeran dropped out of school and slept in subway stations . . . net worth of $110 million"
- "Leonardo DiCaprio comes from a drug-torn town outside of Los Angeles . . . net worth is upwards of $245 million"

What we find among the successful, if we bothered to look at the total—all of the successful people in the world—is that there are far, far more stores of

---

27   The articles I'm referring to are: Jacquelyn Smith and Rachel Gillett, "17 Billionaires Who Started Out Dirt Poor: When in Need of Inspiration from Real Life Rags-to-Riches Tales, Look to These CEOs," *Inc.*, August 5, 2015, https://www.inc.com/business-insider/; AJ Agrawal, "These 5 Rags-to-Riches Stories Will Inspire You," *Entrepreneur*, September 29, 2016, https://www.entrepreneur.com/article/282092; Erin McDowell, "20 Rags to Riches Stories That Will Blow your Mind," Business Insider, July 5, 2019, https://www.businessinsider.com/.
28   The first three come from Smith and Gillett, "17 Billionaires"; the last two come from McDowell, "20 Stories."

rich and successful people who make it because life has dealt them a really great hand. Conditions create millionaires and billionaires, not hard work. They get a few extra cards up their sleeves, or a few more pulls from the stack. They were made for success, birthed into it. The game is set in their favor, much like my college friend Erik. It ain't his fault. He's playing the hand he is dealt. It doesn't help to blame the exceptional, or those the system favors. The system is to blame.

Race, the White card, is the good card dealt in this game. It trumps most other cards. Most of these exceptional people may have worked hard, done wonderful things—the Elon Musks and Bill Gates of the world—but they are as successful as they are because of the help they got from their families, connections, from their particular material conditions that allow people like them to succeed in the ways they do. But let's think more carefully about these lists of exceptional and inspirational figures, the Ragged Dicks in front of us.

There are few people of color on these lists. The typical story is not, Brown kid makes it big by his own hard work and grit. No. Ragged Dick is a White kid, one who, despite his rough exterior and flaws, is honorable and noble inside. He just needs a bit of pushing, or direction. That's the normal story. In the first chapter of the first novel, Alger offers this exposition at its end as a way to set up the story of Ragged Dick, the boy who will go from rags to riches:

> I have mentioned Dick's faults and defects, because I want
> it understood, to begin with, that I don't consider him a
> model boy. But there were some good points about him
> nevertheless. He was above doing anything mean or dis-
> honorable. He would not steal, or cheat, or impose upon
> younger boys, but was frank and straight-forward, manly
> and self-reliant. His nature was a noble one, and had saved
> him from all mean faults. I hope my young readers will
> like him as I do, without being blind to his faults. Perhaps,
> although he was only a boot-black, they may find some-
> thing in him to imitate.[29]

Unless we are talking about the rare, truly exceptional among exceptional stories, this is not the image of most Black or Latino boys on TV, in films, or on the news. It's not how De'Von was framed in the *USA Today* story. In Alger's novel, Ragged Dick is poor and homeless, smokes cigars, and spends what little money he has by day's end, but he doesn't "steal or cheat." He is "manly and

---

29 Horatio Alger, *Ragged Dick; Or, Street Life in New York with the Boot-Blacks*, (Salt Lake City, UT: Project Gutenberg, 2004), n.p., https://www.gutenberg.org/files/5348/5348-h/5348-h.htm.

self-reliant." His nature is "a noble one." But mostly, he is White. He has potential. He is worth a second chance, or a third.

The problem isn't that White Ragged Dicks get second and third chances, get help. The problem is that when we believe without evidence to the contrary that everyone gets these same kinds of chances in our systems, we can then blame those who do not succeed for their failures and misfortunes. The failures and misfortunes, like De'Von's essence as just a Black man who was shot by police, are not attributed to the system but to people only.

The presence of Oprah Winfrey, Michael Jordan, Barack Obama, or any other Black exceptional seems to suggest that De'Von is to blame for his own death, for his lack of worth. This is the danger of the model minority myth. It uses exceptionals as the rule. And our systems support such uses, like those college marketing materials that yearned for my image. Systems, like police, schools, and language itself, seem to be neutral, but they are not. If you have rules and other structures that make up a system, then you have bias in the system. Focusing too much on exceptionals hides the system's biases.

It's not that I think these magazines and websites or their editors do not want to show people of color who are good, moral, and successful, who work hard and are rewarded for it. There is no evil conspiracy here. There are people of color on their lists. By my count, the previous lists have Oprah Whinfrey, Shahid Khan, Do Won Chang, Lakshmi Mittal, Li Ka-shing, and Halle Berry. The rest of the individuals are White.

Of the approximately 30 business people and entertainers listed in these articles, just six are people of color. That's about 20 percent, but these lists, while clearly U.S. centric, are international too. Li Ka-shing is from Hong Kong, JK Rowling (who is on the list too) is a U.K. citizen, Lakshmi Mittal is from India. And there's only one Black woman, Oprah, no Black men. These numbers don't seem to square well with the world's population.

As of this writing, the estimated world population is about 7.8 billion people. The largest three ethnic groups by number are the Han Chinese (1.315 billion), Arabs (450 million), and Bengalis (230 million) from India.[30] That's almost 2 billion people of the 7.7 billion. That's 25 percent of the world's population that is not White, and we've not counted most of the world yet, the continent of Africa, South America, or places like Japan, Korea, Vietnam, or Thailand, not to mention the US or any of the countries in Central America, like Mexico and Panama.

---

30   For a rolling calculation of world population, see "World Population Clock," Worldometer, accessed January 10, 2020, https://www.worldometers.info/world-population/; a graphic map of world populations over time is available at World Population History Project, accessed January 10, 2020, https://worldpopulationhistory.org/.

So it's safe to say that 20 percent of the world's population is a fucking low number for Ragged Dicks of color, if we think everyone has equal access to hard work that pays off in similar ways, and equal access to grit and persistence in their efforts toward success. If we think this and accept that 20 percent as accurate, then how does one account for such low numbers? People of color should represent something like 60 to 70 percent of the Ragged Dicks on these lists. But they never do.

Are people of color just not as smart and hard working as White people? Of course not. The problems are structural, in the systems. Many don't get the chance to work hard or pursue things, and most of those people proportionally to their numbers are of color. People of color in the US have to work for less, but often do the same job better than their White peers. And if you think, "Well, there are many people of color who have success in the world. It is just that the U.S.-based magazines don't show us those people because they are less meaningful to a U.S. audience. We've never heard of all those millionaires in China or Brazil. The list wouldn't be interesting," then you're missing something. This logic points to another face of the problem I'm showing.

Why are exceptionals of color less interesting to a U.S. readership when seen en masse? Why would a list more representative of the world, perhaps one with more Chinese, Indian, Latin American, and Arab millionaires, be less interesting, less inspiring? Why not include someone like the Nigerian billionaire Aliko Dangote, who is the richest Black person in the world?[31] He's worth almost three times what Oprah Winfrey is. His net worth was over $8 billion in 2020. Then again, Jeff Bezos, the former White CEO of Amazon, is worth almost 20 times what Dangote is, or about $153 billion.[32] Apparently, White and Black exceptionals are not the same.

And who are these lists really pointed at? Who are they really meant to inspire and uplift? We've all bought into the Horatio Alger story of success. And when we show ourselves lists of Ragged Dicks, we want to imagine ourselves like those people on the list, or rather what is projected on the lists is a White imaginary reader or viewer who then imagines themselves as one of the Ragged Dicks on the list. Do you see the difference? The second instance is structural in nature, not personal. It's not a story about an individual making it in the world. It's a story about a world making certain kinds of people into exceptionals in order for the system to continue. Bezos, not Dangote. Lists of exceptionals lift up White people by pushing down or away Black and Brown people.

31　Mfonobong Nsehe, "The Black Billionaires 2019," *Forbes*, March 5, 2019, https://www.forbes.com/sites/mfonobongnsehe/2019/03/05/the-Black-billionaires-2019/#149a4d936795.
32　Gibson, "American Heritage."

THE MYTH OF THE BLACK PREDATOR

The Alger myth of success and inspirational lists of Ragged Dicks do not circulate in a vacuum. In Western cultures, something or someone must be Ragged Dick's opposite. That's how the HOWL of clarity, order, and control works. Think of the urban Black boy in the imagination of the U.S. today. He is likely a scary individual, a thug, maybe a gangster or drug dealer, seemingly unredeemable. This is the way Trayvon Martin, the 17-year old Black boy, was understood by his killer, George Zimmerman, a 28-year-old community watch coordinator in 2012.[33] Black boys are not seen as needing guidance, but punishment.

Apparently, "justice" is always suspect when we are talking about killing this kind of boy. He may have deserved it. We don't know what he was up to. He doesn't deserve the benefit of the doubt or a second chance like Ragged Dick. There's no bright spark in him, no White essence just needing some polishing to show itself. What he needs is a bullet in the back. The root of this unequal vision of people of color is an historical White racial fear.

There is no surprise here, really. The US has a long history of demonizing Black men and boys—and of being unjustifiably frightened of them. Black males have been viewed as worthless and indolent, as well as dangerous savages. They need supervision or they'll rape White women. Wasn't that the fear behind the 1955 brutal killing of Emmett Till, a fourteen year old Black boy who allegedly whistled at a White woman in Mississippi?[34] Wasn't White racial fear of the Black body who would rape White women the central message of the infamous silent film, *Birth of A Nation*?[35] In the eyes of White people in the US, Black men and boys have always been imagined as dangerous predators.[36] This is seen in White fears over slave revolts before 1865, when slavery was abolished.

The *Virginia Gazette* from January 25, 1770, offers a detailed account of one such unsuccessful revolt by slaves in which a White steward of one plantation's

---

33 For an account of how Martin was portrayed in the media and the 911 call that Zimmerman made the night he killed Martin, see the introduction in Ersula J. Ore, *Lynching: Violence, Rhetoric, and American Identity* (Jackson, MS: University Press of Mississippi, 2019).

34 For an account of Emmett Till, see "Emmett Till is Murdered," History, last updated August 28, 2020, https://www.history.com/this-day-in-history/the-death-of-emmett-till; or "The Murder of Emmett Till," Library of Congress, accessed March 12, 2021, https://www.loc.gov /collections/civil-rights-history-project/articles-and-essays/murder-of-emmett-till/.

35 *The Birth of A Nation*, was originally called *The Clansman*, and was directed and produced in 1915 by D. W. Griffiths. It was a commercial success and was the first film in the US to be screened at the White House by President Woodrow Wilson at the urging of a college friend, Thomas Dixon Jr., the author of the book from which the film was based.

36 For discussions of the Black male in the U.S. imagination, see Takaki, *Iron Cages*, 113–116; see also chapter 6 of bell hooks, *Black Looks: Race and Representation* (New York & London: Routledge, 2015).

slaves was overcome and "beat severely." The slaves then assembled in a barn and attempted to take on those who would rescue the now bound steward.[37] The story, like many others of the time and afterwards, reveals the White anxieties over slave rebellions, anxieties rooted and attached to the Black male body, adult or child, who would revolt over seemingly the smallest slight. The narrative neglects the fact that the steward was the guy with the whip, the one doling out lashes daily. There was, no doubt, a long history of violence against the Black slaves in the account from the *Virginia Gazette* before the incident occurred. Instead, the news account favors the innocent White victim, even though the only people killed are Black.

But we don't have to go that far back to see how narratives of dangerous Black males continue to be circulated in the White American imagination. The term "superpredator" captures this White fear well. The term was first popularized by Hillary Clinton when she was First Lady in 1996. She got the term from John J. DiIulio Jr., a professor of economics and political science at Princeton University (now at the University of Pennsylvania). William J. Bennett, DiIulio, and John P. Walters use the term in their 1996 book, *Body Count: Moral Poverty—And How To Win America's War Against Crime and Drugs*.[38] The book uses the term to help define their theory of "moral poverty," which they say explains the rise in crime and drug problems in the US from the 1960s to the early 1990s.

These problems were predominantly in poor, Black and Latine communities. They explain that "the poverty of being without loving, capable, responsible adults who teach the young right from wrong" was central to the rise in rates of drug use and criminal activity. It wasn't economic poverty, they say, that causes such rise in rates of dangerous criminality.[39] It isn't the structural problems in Black and Latine communities. It isn't the outcomes of historical racism inherited by those communities, like redlining practices or restrictive covenants. It is moral poverty, they say. Moral poverty occurs when kids don't have parents, guardians, relatives, or teachers around to provide important

---

37   The *Virginia Gazette* article is reproduced on *The Geography of Slavery* website, accessed March 21, 2021, http://www2.vcdh.virginia.edu/gos/index.html. For a fuller account of several famous slave rebellions, see Henry Louis Gates, Jr., "Did African-American Slaves Rebel?" PBS, accessed March 12, 2021, https://www.pbs.org/wnet/african-americans-many-rivers-to-cross /history/did-african-american-slaves-rebel/. For an annotated list of sources that discuss the fear of slave rebellions, see Jason T. Sharples, "Slavery and Fear," Oxford Bibliographies, last modified November 29, 2018, https://www.oxfordbibliographies.com/view/document/obo-9780199730 414/obo-9780199730414-0308.xml.

38   William J. Bennett, John J. DiIulio Jr., and John P. Waters, *Body Count: Moral Poverty— and How to Win America's War against Crime and Drugs*, (New York: Simon & Schuster, 1996),

39   Bennett, DiIulio Jr., and Waters, 13.

moral lessons and capacities to them, capacities like feeling "joy at others' joy; pain at others' pain; satisfaction when you do right; [or] remorse when you do wrong."[40]

Bennett, Dilulio, and Waters claim this moral poverty creates the superpredator. And here is one description of this superpredator that the authors offer:

> Based on all that we have witnessed, researched and heard
> from people who are close to the action . . . America is now
> home to thickening ranks of juvenile "superpredators"—rad-
> ically impulsive, brutally remorseless youngsters, including
> ever more preteenage boys, who murder, assault, rape, rob,
> burglarize, deal deadly drugs, join gun-toting gangs and create
> serious communal disorders.[41]

It would seem that these young ones are inherently bad, unredeemable. So severe are their behaviors that they have no morality. They are brutal, animalistic, savages. They are predators. This is the image that is placed onto young, Black boys like De'Von. They are not Ragged Dicks. This description could be voiced from the anxious mouth of a colonial slave owner in Virginia, or a KKK Grand Wizard in Mississippi, or the former governor of Alabama, George Wallace, yelling in his 1963 inaugural speech, "segregation now, segregation tomorrow, segregation forever."[42] Why else would one segregate if not to keep savages and predators away from the innocent? Everything works from a Black vs. White binary. Superpredators vs. Ragged Dicks. Savage vs. Civilized. Dangerous Black predators vs. innocent White citizens.

Obviously, I see moral poverty theory as deeply flawed, ignoring the structures that enable choices available to those in poor communities, ones I've lived in. Unlike White, middle-class suburbs, places I've also lived in, the communities in question do not have the same access to the kinds of things that the authors of *Body Count* say make for morally upstanding boys and men, Ragged Dicks. In effect, this theory, like Alger narratives of success, blames the Black and Latine victims for bad choices made among too many other bad options.

The theory too easily lets us assume that people have innate morality and behaviors. It falsely claims that our material conditions have little effect on developing either our morality or behaviors, except for good parents who are

---

40   Bennett, Dilulio Jr., and Waters, 14.

41   Bennett, Dilulio Jr., and Waters, 27.

42   See, "'Segregation Forever': A Fiery Pledge Forgiven, But Not Forgotten," NPR, January 10, 2013, https://www.npr.org/2013/01/14/169080969/.

present or not. It neglects the reasons for why some parents are absent, as if we all have the same choices, the same proximity to the things they say make us all moral. This argument and theory HOWLs like no other.

Beyond the assumed binary that artificially orders bodies in the world by color, it also assumes a universal proximity to such things as safety, health, education, language, and a freedom from police harassment. My mom had to work three jobs. How could she be present, how else could she make ends-meat? How else is one to be moral and responsible to their children if not by working and providing for them?

Years later, DiIulio himself would recant his idea, saying, "'If I knew then what I know now, I would have shouted for prevention of crimes."[43] What DiIulio knows now is that violent and property crimes since 1993 have sharply declined. For instance, between 1993 and 2018, violent crime rates dropped 51 to 71 percent, depending on which sources you use, while property crimes dropped 54 to 69 percent. Meanwhile, typical U.S. views of crime did not track with these lowering rates of crime. A Pew Research Center survey in 2016 revealed that 57 percent of registered voters felt that crime continued to worsen since 2008. And numerous surveys by Gallup, conducted between 1993 and 2018, found that 60 percent of Americans felt crime was worse than the year before.[44]

Why do Americans have an inability to see declining rates of crime? Part of the answer could be that we make a false conclusion from what appears to be evidence of criminality in many Black people. It's our availability heuristic operating, a mind bug, fast thinking. I'm talking about the increase in incarceration rates generally, and most notably, the even higher increase in Black incarceration, which many people conclude means crime rates are increasing. But the truth is: crime has decreased over the last 25 or 30 years, even as the prison systems have prospered, swelled.[45] The swelling prison population is due to the increase in

---

43   Elizabeth Becker, "As Ex-Theorist on Young 'Superpredators,' Bush Aide Has Regrets," *New York Times*, February 9, 2001, https://www.nytimes.com/2001/02/09/us/as-ex-theorist-on -young-superpredators-bush-aide-has-regrets.html.

44   Crime statistics and surveys of opinions on crime can be found in John Gramlich, "5 Facts about Crime in the U.S.," Pew Research Center, October 17, 2019, https://www.pewresearch. org/fact-tank/2019/10/17/facts-about-crime-in-the-u-s/. To read more about the connections between the term "superpredator" and young Black men, see Rachel Leah, "The 'Superpredator' Myth Was Discredited, but it Continues to Ruin Young Black Lives," Salon, April 2, 2018, https://www.salon.com/2018/04/21/the-superpredator-myth-was-discredited-but-it-continues -to-ruin-young-Black-lives/.

45   For statistics on incarceration rates, see "Fact Sheet: Trends in U.S. Corrections," The Sentencing Project, June 2019, https://sentencingproject.org/wp-content/uploads/2016/01/Trends-in-US -Corrections.pdf. To see prison profiles and statistics, see, "United States Profile," Prison Policy

"three strikes" laws, mandatory sentencing laws, and the criminalizing of crack cocaine that began in the 1990s.[46] The ones who have paid most dearly for this massive expansion of structures, of biases in the police and justice system, are Black males and Latinos.

Michelle Alexander offers a trenchant and careful look at the way the US prison system has become "the new Jim Crow." In fact, all that has really changed is the language we use. She explains:

> The current system of control permanently locks a huge per-centage of the African American community out of the main-stream society and economy. The system operates through our criminal justice institutions, but it functions more like a caste system than a system of crime control. Viewed from this perspective, the so-called underclass is better understood as an *undercaste*—a lower caste of individuals who are permanently barred by law and custom from mainstream society. Although this new system of racialized social control purports to be colorblind, it creates and maintains racial hierarchy much as earlier systems of control did. Like Jim Crow (and slavery), mass incarceration operates as a tightly networked system of laws, policies, customs, and institutions that operate collec-tively to ensure the subordinate status of a group defined largely by race.[47]

Thus, I think, we are conditioned to see only that which we can see, hear only what the systems around us prepare us to be able to hear. The narratives that we tell ourselves, or that circulate in our culture, prepare us to see and hear particular things, things that the systems are set up for us to notice. These narra-tives are the grounds by which Kahneman's availability heuristic and confirma-tion bias work. These fast judgements are shaped by narratives like the ones that Horatio Alger, DiIulio, and others circulate.

De'Von is no anomaly. He is the rule, the anti-Ragged-Dick. Further evi-dence can be seen in the many deaths of innocent young Black men and boys, all assumed much more dangerous than they were, all surely not deserving of death: Michael Brown, John Crawford III, Ezell Ford, Laquan McDonald, Akai

---

Initiative, accessed March 12, 2021, https://www.prisonpolicy.org/profiles/US.html. For a dis-cussion of trends in crime and incarceration rates in the US, see Campbell Robertson, "Crime Is Down, Yet U.S. Incarceration Rates Are Still Among the Highest in the World," *New York Times*, April 25, 2019, https://www.nytimes.com/2019/04/25/us/us-mass-incarceration-rate.html.

46   See chapter 3 in Michelle Alexander, *New Jim Crow*.

47   Alexander, 13.

Gurley, Freddie Gray, William Chapman, Jeremy McDole, Jamar Clark, to name just a few of the many.[48]

White racial fear structures our world, our theories of crime, our news stories, our narratives, our very language. That's the enemy here. It's not the police officers. They too are victims, although not as innocent and not as victimized as those they kill. We are all victims of the Horatio Alger myth of success and the White racial fear that comes from the myth of the Black predator. These narratives work in concert to criminalize, dehumanize, and demoralize the Black body and to a lesser extent the Brown body. In this historical context, why would we not remind ourselves that Black Lives do Matter?[49] We already know and tell ourselves that White ones do. I mean, the morality embedded in the Alger stories is nothing less than "White Lives Matter." And today, it appears they matter at the cost of Black lives.

The narrative of success that began with Puritanical ideals of hard work and Horatio Alger myths of persistent Ragged Dicks pulling themselves up by their own bootstraps hides the reality of systemic unfairness. It's a convenient excuse to hoard the few riches available to the working masses, to divide and conquer working people of all races, economic standings, and Englishes. It keeps us from seeing the way we are all oppressed, feeding us the idea that all we have to do is work hard, perhaps harder than the guy next to you. That's it. Just keep working and good things will come. Don't worry about others. If we all just take care of ourselves, everything will be a'right.

Your job is to take care of yourself. Get you yours! But if you ain't visualized as a potential Ragged Dick, you are more likely to end up shot dead on the street. Of course, there is always an element of truth in such myths of hard work. Working hard ain't a bad way to go through life, but don't use it as a method to get rich or successful. Don't hang your hat on it. It may be better to work hard because you find meaning and value in working hard.

TURTLES GET HELP

A few years after finishing my master's degree at OSU, I found the man of color I could trust, a Brown languageling like me. He would end up being my mentor

---

48   One way to see this problem is to consider the Mapping Police Violence project at https://mappingpoliceviolence.org/. The web site shows a map of the frequency of police violence and offers several graphs that distill the data. For instance, the site shows that Blacks are three times more likely than Whites to be killed by police in the US. It also states: "Police killed 1,147 people in 2017. Black people were 25% of those killed despite being only 13% of the population."

49   In 2013, Alicia Garza, Patrisse Cullors, and Opal Tometi, three radical Black organizers, created the Black Lives Matter (#BlackLivesMatter, or #BLM) movement. See, "Herstory," Black Lives Matter, accessed March 12, 2021, https://Blacklivesmatter.com/herstory/.

and eventually place the doctoral hood on me, symbolizing the "habit" of a Ph.D., renaming me Dr. Inoue. My mentor was Victor Villanueva. He has been my academic father since. I owe much to Victor.

In his acceptance speech for the Conference on College Composition and Communication's Exemplar Award in 2009, its highest accolade, Victor ends with an image of a turtle on a post. He says, "The former president of our university once said to me that when you see a turtle on top of a post, you know it didn't get there on its own."[50] Of course, he's thanking all those who made his learning, languaging, and career possible. He's saying, no one does language on their own. No one succeeds on their own merit and work. Victor's own literacy narrative, his award winning book, *Bootstraps: From An American Academic of Color*, is all about how the bootstrap myth in the US is false, how race plays an important part in the myth, among other things.

For years, when I would write emails to him, I would accidentally write, "Dear Victory," then change it. I was typing too fast, fingers slipping on the keys. I didn't want to look bad in front of the one professor I really respected. Now, I want to chalk this up as a Freudian slip, or a *parapraxis*, which in Latin means, "contrary practice." These are slips in our languaging that read as revealing hidden or unspoken intentions or meanings. They are the words we mean to say when we think we are trying to say something else.

Victor was a Victory to me. He was the rare gem in the mountain of rocks in my education. I don't mean to devalue or put down Chris or any of my other teachers up to that point. I've had many great ones. They made me ready to do the work in my doctoral program. They all are important to my story, and I'm grateful for them, especially Chris. But I was thirty-one years old when I left for graduate school the second time to get my Ph.D. in Rhetoric and Composition. It was the first time in my life that I had a teacher of color, the first time. In all the eighteen years of formal education before that, I never walked into a classroom or office where the teacher was a person of color, let alone a man of color. So yes, Victor was a Victory for me.

I still remember the first class session I took with Victor. It was a rhetoric course, fall semester of my first year in the doctoral program. I got to class five minutes before it started, and the room was already full of students. A room that seated maybe 30 people had 35 or 40 people in it. I had no seat. There were students standing along the walls of the room. I was one of them.

---

50   Victor Villanueva, "2009 CCCC Exemplar Award Acceptance Speech," *College Composition and Communication* 61, no. 3 (2010): 581–582, https://library.ncte.org/journals/CCC/issues/v61-3/9961.

Victor came in and smiled, and I thought I saw him give me a side glance. He said, "Okay, if you're not registered officially for this course, you have to give up your seat to students who are." It took a few minutes, but I got a seat in the front row. It's what I wanted. I'm sure he was thinking of me. He had the roster. There were only 15 or so people registered in the graduate seminar. I was the only student of color. We'd already had meetings. He knew me. I thought, he's looking out for me. It was the first time in all of my schooling that I felt truly comfortable, truly at ease in a class. It was the first time I felt really connected to my teacher. I sat in that class glowing every day throughout the semester, smiling, basking in all of it. I thought, this is what I have been missing, what has been denied me. I will make the most of Victor.

Like my parapraxis, Victor's last name is meaningful to me too. Victor is Puerto Rican, grew up in Bedford-Stuyvesant, New York. His last name, Villanueva, is Spanish in origin, likely originating in the eleventh century in Catalonia (northeast Spain), and literally means "new town." How appropriate for my new mentor, the one who would show me new, fertile ideas, not forests, as wonderful as they are, but more cultivated farm lands of theory. New town. A new place to live and grow as a languageling of color. New career. New name. New town.

I knew I needed Victor when we moved to this new college town, Pullman, Washington, the home of Washington State University, but I never could have imagined in what ways. When we got there in the summer of 2001, it was hot. We were coming from Oregon, the Willamette Valley, a cooler place. In Pullman, many days it was in the low 100s. We didn't have air conditioning in our rented house, so sometimes we'd go to nearby Moscow, Idaho, and sit in the cool, air conditioned mall.

We had no money. I was now on teaching assistant (TA) wages, which actually hadn't started yet and wouldn't amount to much. About a month after we got there, I received a letter from WSU. It said that my dependents, my wife and two small children, would no longer be covered on the health insurance that the school provided me for being a TA. Kelly was just six or so months past the birth of our youngest child, Takeo. And our oldest was just three years old. All three needed medical care. They needed to have regular check-ups. In fact, Kelly was on some medication that needed refilling.

This news was devastating. My first thought was, well, I guess I'll have to quit grad school and get a job. My second was, maybe I can work a deal with someone, work somewhere, do the TA gig, and do grad school all at the same time. That would be very hard to do and graduate in a timely manner, or at all. We were already taking some loans to afford things. Every additional semester it took to finish meant not only living in poverty longer, but increasing our debt.

A few months later, we'd go on food stamps and WIC. Our savings, which was mostly a small cashed out retirement account, would also get spent quickly. I went to see Victor. He was the chair of the English Department as well, so the TA benefits were his purview.

"I don't know what to do, Dr. Villanueva."

I was on the verge of crying in front of this man I'd just met but knew and respected by reputation. I had asked him months before on the phone if he would work with me if I came to WSU to do the Ph.D. He said, of course. No hesitation. I didn't know at the time that I was a cohort of one—that is, I was the only Rhetoric and Composition Ph.D. student coming in that year. Victor would be all mine to work with. I wouldn't have to share him with other grad students in my same year of the program. What luck! That would be a big leg up, especially when it would come time to go on the job market, apply for jobs. And now, I was coming to tell him that I may have to leave the program before I even took a class.

I showed him the letter. We were sitting at his conference table in Avery Hall on the second floor where the English Department has its main office. I put the half-folded letter on the table between us. I looked up. I remember feeling hopeless and lost. I thought: just someone, please, throw me a life preserver, a piece of driftwood, something, anything. I'll do anything. I want this Ph.D., but I need my wife and children to be healthy.

I looked out the window at the entrance of the Bookie, the university book-store. There was a flow of students coming and going through its doors in their pre-fall semester exuberance. They were all White students, probably 18 or 19 years old, and happy. A second later, Victor sighed. He placed one finger on the letter, then opened a drawer near him, pulled out his checkbook, and wrote a check to me.

"Look, you came here under the assumption that your babies and wife would have health insurance. They will have that."

I was speechless and grateful and stunned and happy and relieved. At that moment, I knew there was nothing I would not do for this man. In many other ways, Victor has helped me pull on bootstraps in my career. Turtles on posts, the two of us. And he is smart enough to see that once you're on the post, part of your job is to help other turtles get to their posts, which he has done for many others. I feel this same honor of posting turtles myself today.

I suppose I should have expected this treatment from him. I mean, the year before, when I was deciding to apply and go back to grad school, I started reading books I thought I'd need to know in a Ph.D. program in Rhetoric and Composition. His was the most striking one, the one that resonated with me. It was a big part of my going to WSU. I read Aristotle, I. A. Richards, James Kinneavy,

I Ain't No Horatio Alger Story

Edward P.J. Corbett and Robert Connors, all influential "must read" scholars in the field, all White guys. None really grabbed me.

I mean, the rhetoric was interesting. I always liked words, but it wasn't until I picked up Victor's book, *Bootstraps*, that I saw and heard what seemed like something I could do, something I wanted to do. It was rhetoric alive. It wasn't a disembodied voice trying to be neutral and objective. It was a ragged voice of color, words trying to *situate* themselves in a real world. It was a Ragged Ricardo of color. It was a real turtle on a post. And I got this sense from the subtitle itself: *From An American Academic of Color.*

But it was more than the personal and subjective way that Victor wrote that grabbed me. If the book were just personal and reflective, it would be another version of Chris' beautiful White prose. It was clear by this point in my life that was not enough. It was the theory that he interlaced into the personal. Theory shows the structuring, the history, the racism that was still unnamed by me at the time, although felt constantly.

In his opening prologue, Victor names the themes of race and language, of systems of racism and dominant language expectations, that he explores in the book. This is not an individual exploring his forest. It is more cultivated than organic, and it is passionate. It is explicitly political and material. It speaks of systems. It is about the conditions that make a man like Victor, or me, or someone else of color.

He explains that his "views are grounded in experience, elaborated upon by theory, and tested in research."[51] That would be the general pattern, the outline of the book. The theory he speaks of is Gramsci's Marxian theory. He quotes Gramsci:

> Autobiography can be conceived "politically." One knows that one's life is similar to that of a thousand others, but through "chance" it has had opportunities that the thousand others in reality could not or did not have. By narrating it, one creates this possibility, suggests the process, indicates the opening.[52]

The book showed me how Ragged Dicks are made and unmade, how turtles help turtles onto posts, and how structures in history, society, and education work to keep some turtles from their posts by providing ramps for others. I, too, have had opportunities that hundreds of others on Statz and Pecos did not. Who am I to squander that? How irresponsible that would be, how selfish!

---

51 Villanueva, *Bootstraps*, xvii.

52 Antonio Gramsci, *Selections from Cultural Writings*, ed. David Forgacs and Geoffrey Nowell-Smith, trans. William Boelhower (Cambridge, MA: Harvard University Press, 1985), 132, quoted in Villanueva, xvii.

Victor annotates Gramsci's words, saying "Perhaps in narrating, the exception can become the rule—boots for everyone, strong straps."[53] There is hope in this book—boots for everyone—without forgetting the real material conditions of people of color, I think. Victory feels knowable and possible for perhaps the first time in my life.

In chapter 3, Victor describes his family moving to Los Angeles, California, just a few years before my parents would meet in that same place, make love, and have twin boys in Inglewood. Victor's family settles in Compton, just a few miles southeast past the 110, very close. In the chapter, he describes his time at Manuel Dominguez Senior High School, the drafting class. I wonder, how is it possible Victor and I could be so alike? I was a technical drafting specialist (81 Bravo) in the U.S. Army National Guard right out of high school. It's a career that isn't possible anymore because of computers and software like AutoCAD. I was trained to draft on old drafting boards with pencils and rulers. Like Victor, it is a past that I've discarded.

Victor tells of his dropping out of high school around the time of the 1965 Watts riots. At the same time, he meets a friend at Dominguez: "Tifft was an Okie, alone, not living in Bell Gardens with the other Okies, a California minority, alone. Later there would be *The Grapes of Wrath*. Later still, there would be the realization that *The Grapes of Wrath* describes the victims of neo-colonialism, the dispossessed because of economics, though blamed on dust."[54] It's a subtle nod to Gramsci's economic and cultural theories and the theories of John Ogbu,[55] which Victor discusses in the previous chapter.

In that earlier chapter, Victor explains Ogbu's theory of three kinds of minorities. "[C]astelike" minorities "are those who are regarded primarily on the basis of some particular birth ascription, in this country, race or a particular ethnicity, like Latinos." Autonomous minorities are "those who are subject to ethnic or religious distinctiveness yet manage to accommodate the mainstream, even if not assimilate," such as Jews and Mormons. Finally, the immigrant minority, such as Italians, while still distinctive in some ways, are "not excluded from the mainstream."[56] There is something in Tifft, a "California minority" but White. That still makes him a minority. He is not a castelike minority. That's certain. But perhaps there is something of both the autonomous and immigrant minority in him.

---

53   Villanueva, xvii.

54   Villanueva, 38.

55   John Ogbu, *Minority Education and Caste: The American System in Cross-Cultural Perspective* (New York: Academic, 1978).

56   Villanueva, *Bootstraps*, 30.

I hear in Victor's words a paradox: There is reason to build a relationship, to keep this White friend. The compassion resonates with me. We have some shared oppressions. I also knew this anxiety. More in common.

The chapter goes on. During the riots, Victor is in the mobile home of Tifft with Tifft's dad: "Tifft, the father, sits with a rifle across his lap. Says, 'Might have to kill us some niggers.' And somewhere inside, Papi, Victor, is hurt, frightened, confused. He can't let on that something within him is also a nigger."[57] It's the old paradigm of "at least I'm not Black." You could be a poor, White, Okie in a trailer on the edge of Watts, but at least you ain't no N-word.[58]

Black folks get shot. Tifft's dad would have cause, so he rationalizes. It's a version of De'Von's story before De'Von was born. When a Black person is shot, no one is to blame. There's always doubt, always a justifiable cause to do it, always quotation marks around "justice." If we have no theories to help us, no histories, we are doomed to repeat our terrible narratives. Or worse, we will not see how they control us, shaping what we think we see and hear and feel. It's fast thinking, implicit biases that help maintain White language supremacy. We don't see how they make only certain views of people available to us, like Black boys as savage criminals needing a bullet in the back.

This is how we come to understand the White language supremacy in our lives in order to remake those conditions. We see the languaging in our lives as racialized. We understand where it all came from with theories that allow us to experience our conditions differently, that make us feel our languaging from two steps back. Doing that, stepping back, can help us understand how our worlds make us and how we might remake our languaging in more socially just ways.

This racial friction that Victor shows in his book is how the oppressed are divided and conquered. The trouble comes from another set of narratives. These center on a term, "herrenvolk republicanism," or the idea that a republic like the US should be run by a "master race," a *herrenvolk*.[59] This herrenvolk republic is set up and visualized as a hierarchy in which, naturally, social and economic pressure is thrust downward on those groups who are seen as occupying the lower rungs of society. It's what Alger myths of success and focusing on exceptionals

---

57   Villanueva, 38.

58   My practice at this point in my life is to not use the N-word, because of its particular history, one I do not wish to contribute to, even though regretfully I have used this word in my life. Since I know that all U.S. readers will understand my reference, I see no reason to use the word here. I have left the word intact in the previous quotation because it is what was published.

59   To read about herrenvolk republicanism and its connections to race, I suggest Pierre L. Van Den Berghe, *Race and Racism: A Comparative Perspective*, 2nd ed. (New York: Wiley, 1978); and David R. Roediger, *Wages*. For a similar account of how the US has been structured along such racial herrenvolk lines, see Ronald Takaki, *Iron Cages*.

and imagining all Black men as predators do in our systems of language and judgement. It's a racial hierarchy built with language.

And as I've shown in this book, race has been an easy hierarchy to structure such a herrenvolk republic in language standards. And White people, like Tifft's dad, see themselves nearer the top of the herrenvolk republic, worthy of its narratives of success. He too, like his son Tifft, could be the next Ragged Dick if they just keep working hard enough, if they just let the system see their pluck and perseverance. And the gun in the lap is an assurance that the Alger myth of success will be theirs and not given to those Blacks in Watts.

A page later, Victor discusses Signithia Fordham's theory of "racelessness," "the decision to go it alone" in life as a person of color.[60] He's talking about his reading of Richard Rodriguez' autobiography, *Hunger of Memory*, another literacy narrative of an exceptional man of color, but not like Victor's or mine, and yet all three of us are literacy exceptions.[61] Rodriguez says he's left, given up, his Latino-ness. He's now reborn, renamed, an American only through his own success as a writer and student. His literacy has made him an American. He likes his standardized English, as he should. It is a great English, like Chris' English. It's enticing, mesmerizing, magical. But I think, maybe, Rodriguez let it bewitch him too much.

The book was a favorite of mine just a few years before reading Victor's. Victor disagrees with Rodriquez strongly. His success acceptance of a Standard English is not what makes Rodriquez famous, he says, not what gets his book read in classrooms. It is that he is understood as a Mexican American author. One cannot simply proclaim one's escape from their castelike minority status. It's not how the system works. You keep that for a lifetime. It's not a choice. It's a structure, an inheritance. White people decide your membership in the club, man. Don't forget it. There are bigger things that run deep and overlap each other at work. Biases in systems. Victor explains in a compassionate way, even as he disagrees with Rodriquez:

> What he [Rodriguez] did—what I did in that tension-filled
> moment in Tifft's mobile home, have done in the years prior
> and since—is fall back on that painful, confusing strategy that
> people of color who succeed employ: what Signithia Fordham
> calls "racelessness." It is the denial of other-cultural affiliation,
> a denial of the collective, any collective; it is the embracing of
> America's dominant ideology, the ideology of individualism.[62]

---

60   Villanueva, *Bootstraps*, 40.

61   Villanueva, *Bootstraps*, 39.

62   Villanueva, 39–40.

Ah, Alger's success narrative tricks us into accepting the ideology of individualism. Ragged Dick is the language vehicle in which these ideas travel. And this is what I realized that year before I went back to grad school to learn with Victor. I learned a little bit of how Whiteness in literacy works in schools and colleges. I began to learn about White language supremacy, although no one was calling it that. I started to figure out the bias in all of our systems—schools, news media, business, and religions.

As writers, no one gets a stance of neutrality and objectivity. When you put ideas in words, you cannot have a voice that plays god-tricks on its readers if you are gonna tell something meaningful, truthful (not the "Truth"), and ethical. We do not just walk through our own forests of words discovering truth and meaning, as seductive as that sounds.

The forest was already planted, engineered for certain truths by particular people in history. Our path and what we might discover on it was excavated before we walked it. And someone or something else put you in that forest in the first place. A student of color like me or Victor or Rodriguez cannot go it alone in school or life. We do not transform ourselves into unhyphenated Americans through our own will and persistence. We do not get to be Ragged Dicks. We are turtles on posts, the exceptionals. And that ain't nothin to brag about.

Horatio Alger's myth of success and the bootstrapping myth in the US reinforces the idea that stories like mine, ones of a person of color succeeding despite poverty, *can be* the norm in societies. But our society is subtly and carefully designed to maintain such color and poverty lines. Part of this structural problem has to do with how we judge language and the people who use different forms of English. My story is meant to offer nuance and paradox. It is a story about systems, conditions, not my own exceptional pluck and willpower.

If there is one thing you take from my literacy narrative, I hope it is that literacy ain't exactly what we usually say it is. It ain't just words and grammar. It is also a lifetime of experiences. It's Fred in the trailer park blaming you for things you couldn't possibly have done, but you look like the kind of boy who does that stuff. It's a second grade teacher urging you to say the N-word. It's winning a reading contest in that same class when you have no food in the cupboards at home. It's making "ends-meat," not "ends meet." It's the negative wealth of far too many Black households and the wealth gap of Black women who work harder than most only to be raggedy. No Horatio for them. It's one in every thousand Black males killed by police. It's the others around you letting you in the circle, sort of, and you finding out only later that you never really were in the circle. They thought you were a Mr. Yunioshi, and they smile and laugh as they sing The Vapors. It's a veteran breaking down in front of you, unable to make sense of his own words and life. It's the love of a forest of voices, even with its impassable brambles of Whiteness, and the man who showed it to you, your beloved friend.

It's about finding your first mentor of color in your 30s, a man who shows you the roots of the forest you've been walking. He says, stop looking up so much. Dig motha fucka, Dig! There's more underneath those trees that can tell you how they grow, how they were watered, what fruit they bear and who can eat it. This is how you change the forest. You dig at the roots. It's the superstructure that holds all this shit together. Both the trees and the roots are important. And so really literacy is about help, lots of help, and chances, and systems, lots of systems. Necessary and ugly and historical biases. None of us do literacy alone or in a vacuum.

The point is, do not mistake my story of apparent language success as some kind of Horatio Alger story. My story is more than a poor, fatherless kid from the ghetto of North Las Vegas making good as a university professor and associate dean, a multi-award winning academic author. I did not pull myself up by my own wit, gumption, and bootstraps. I am no Ragged Dick. I am Above the Well is Morning Boy. I am the exceptional who ought to be the norm. I am a turtle on a post trying to help other turtles onto their posts.

CHAPTER 11.

ANOTHER ENDING, OR LET ME SAY THIS ANOTHER WAY

Words can be acts of violence. And I'm not speaking just metaphorically. What I hope this book has argued well to you is that words ain't never been just words.

Sticks and stones *may* break our bones, but words, they can wound our psyches, break our spirits, and harm us in ways that keep hurting long after the exchange is over. Words make us as much as we make them. This means they also hurt and help us, wound us and salve the wounds that need healing. Words are the weapons of a racist war we've been fighting for centuries.

Most of the time, though, our intentions for our words are good, or we want them to be good. We don't mean harm. And yet, harm happens every day, everywhere, to everyone. So I wonder, how meaningful or useful or productive is it to use our intentions for our actions and words as a yardstick by which to measure their worth or goodness or fairness? Let me state it plainly: A person's intentions to be fair do not matter when it comes to reproducing racism and White language supremacy in the world. Our intentions about our actions or language really only help us sleep better at night by ignoring the pain and hurt that our words, race-judgements, and ideas about language and intelligence do to others. Our intentions allow us to wage a tacit racialized language war against others, against those whom we say we wish to help or don't want to harm.

Because we do not control most of the variables and conditions in our lives, we hold on to our good intentions. We control those, but our good intentions do not control the outcomes of our actions, language, and judgements. If this is true, we should stop using personal intentions as the main measure for whether we engage in or contribute to racism and White language supremacy in the world. This does not mean we don't need good intentions or can't see the value they provide us. In other words, I don't want to ignore the good intentions of people, White, Brown, or Black. I want to separate our intentions from how we measure the appropriateness and effectiveness of our actions and words, of our institutions and classrooms, of our policies and guidelines, of our language standards and how those standards are used against people.

The problem is that in systems of scarcity, hierarchy, competition, and singular linear standards for language use—systems that are predicated on a few winners and a lot of losers, where most decisions are ones about who is right and who is wrong, what is true and what is false, what is professional sounding and what sounds unintelligent—helping ourselves ends up harming others because of how those systems use and circulate our decisions.

Let me say that more simply. Too often, helping yourself harms others. In systems of limited resources, helping yourself usually means keeping something from others or denying them something that you want or allegedly deserve more. It's usually a zero-sum game. Either you win (and they lose) or you lose (and they win). The system of grades and GPAs works this way. But I don't think our systems have to be this way. We can change systems.

One difficulty in applying any lessons you might take from this book about White language supremacy, about fighting structures that hurt us all, is that it is too often very difficult to imagine alternatives. What alternatives are there to grading by a single standard in writing classrooms, or to a single standard of English for U.S. news anchors on TV programming, or the English offered in all grammar and style guides, or the English used in international business settings? How do we as individuals change our habits of language and judgement so we do not unconsciously reproduce White language supremacy yet still communicate effectively with one another? How do we simultaneously change the systems that demand, use, and reward only one standard of English? How do we create a world where it doesn't require a rare exception like me to get what I have, to achieve what I have?

Not easy questions to answer. Much of the difficulty is because we are talking about systems that need changing, not one, not two, but many all at once.

I'm not gonna try to offer a list of systemic changes for schools, or language tests, or language practices for business settings, or media. I cannot. These are things everyone must figure out together. I'm also resisting trying to answer these questions because that rehearses a HOWL that experts and professors have been enacting for a long time that reproduces their conditions of language and judgement as if they represent universal conditions for language and its judgement. I don't know all the conditions or answers.

People like me giving THE answers to complex problems that affect lots of people not like me in places I do not know, speaking languages I do not speak, is how we got in this mess in the first place. Conditions and people, places and languages, are multiple and context-specific. We all have to do this changing with each other, for each other, in our ways together.

So I'll end this book a second time with a fable, a futuristic-fantasy-tale of anti-structural magic, a made-up story that's also about White language supremacy and systemic change. It's a fable about you, a future you, or someone like you, or not you, or who could be and cannot be you. It's about the places that make you and unmake you. It's about languaging—that is, those places and you and what you do. And it's about not your languaging, not your places, not what you do, and not you. It is not a blueprint for what we should do today or tomorrow, but it points in the directions we might go, directions that offer ecological freedom without denying that we always create the boundaries of the places where we live and commune.

I'll leave it up to you to decide what my fable means and what to do with it. It's not the answer, but if we care about addressing the systemic problems of White language supremacy in our world, we shouldn't ignore such possibilities. The possibilities of a world without White language supremacy are painful and wonderful and everything in between and outside these things. I offer the fable not as a solution to follow or figure out but as a bit of languaging that I hope instigates, prods, pokes at us all, gives us cause to language more and perhaps do some non-languaging as well. We are the languages we do in the places we do that languaging with the people there. Our languaging are the structures we need to rebuild and celebrate, to make new places, people, and practices for a more socially just tomorrow and today.

It's tempting to end this book with the previous chapter. It would make this book an even ten chapters. It would bring many of the ideas in the book back full circle. It's about me, not something more seemingly abstract, like a fictionalized fantasy fable. But ending on chapter 10 would be exercising a habit of White language that I'm trying to avoid, so I cannot end it there. This is my story, but it ain't just my story. I must resist the hyperindividualism of that urge to end on me, since I don't think you should leave this book thinking about me alone. Instead, I end with an odd chapter, a prime numbered chapter, one that is meant to be a kind of critical counterstory, a fictional fable of a make-believe world that I want. I hope it urges you and makes you uncomfortable. I hope it is more than a story.

A FABLE ABOUT WHITE LANGUAGE SUPREMACY

On a clear, bright day, much like today, everything changed. Hundreds of thousands of visitors came from somewhere, maybe space, another dimension. They appeared floating around us. Gravity meant nothing to these visitors, neither did objects nor the alleged laws of physics. At first, everyone was scared of them. They were frightening, translucent beings of nothing and everything, floating in the spaces between objects and through things, walls, buildings, tables, cars, everything.

They moved through matter as if none of it was there, yet was. The closer and longer you looked at one of them, the more infinitely filled their jelly-like translucent bodies seemed, filled with everything—the universe, sticks and shiny objects—and nothing, like clear running water, moving but not. Some of them were two and three stories tall at the same time—impossible. Others were the height of an average walking cane. All had no mouths or noses or arms or legs, just a body, like a stock of moving clearness, always moving, with three dark spots that moved around their column-like bodies, sometimes fast, sometimes slow, growing and shrinking.

They said that they didn't believe in physics or science as we knew them, said they could talk the fabric of space and reality, so moving in time and space, being and not being, was nothing more than thought or word. At least, "That's how you might think of it," they said to us. "We know your languaging because we have been in your places," they told us. Distances were not important to them. How things are typically done wasn't important to them. Nothing seemed important to them. They seemed so foreign and untouchable, so unusual, that no one knew how to approach them. So people waited.

It took 48 hours before they reached out to everyone on the planet, all at once.

They called themselves a series of clicks, column gestures, and scents that smelled like rain on roses. "In your languaging," they said, "you may call us 'The Doers.'" Everyone knew this instantly, the minute they communicated in a silence that was as loud as anything could be because no one could escape the messaging. They said that they have attended to all of our knowledges, languages, sciences, arts, histories, religions, everything. They know all we know, have done all we have done. They said they wanted to commune with us before it was too late, before we destroyed each other with the way we hear and see others' words. "There is everything here," they said. "You are missing it all. These are your choices."

It was the hierarchies, categories, and rankings by the "reifications of race" that everyone inherits, that's how they worded it. *Racial reifications you have inherited.* These are the organisms, they told us, in the DNA of our languaging and judging that we have used to hierarchize, categorize, and rank everything and everyone. They explained that we do this ranking even when we say we are not, that it is in all our languaging. It is in how we think and make decisions, how we make our world and each other. It makes us think we see everything there is, but really it hides more than it shows.

We are doing race in all that we do, in all that we say, in all that we think. And we don't have to, and we must. It's how we unequally make ourselves from the material of difference, they explained. It appears that we come by this naturally, but it is not natural, not necessary. Nothing is natural. We control our naturals, they told us.

They said that we must move past the "virus of White supremacy, of single standards for things." Once you or something you've built is infected, you cease to see the virus as a virus. It seems to be normal, part of you or the process or the thing built, as well as the ideal, what is accepted and expected. They ended their message by saying, "Every place has a legitimate claim to reality. Language openly your way through." And we knew in our bones that they were not speaking of individuals doing, or feeling, or intending to do by themselves. It was communal action. It was the actions of structures around and of us all.

People were stunned, unsure what was happening. And yet, many people felt The Doers had always been there. It was like recognizing something right in front of you anew. It was like gazing upon something you had seen every day of your life dramatically differently, like a picture of your mother as a child after the day she dies and now that picture isn't a reference anymore. It's not a decoration, a wall-hanging. It's a window into love, and sorrow, and tears, and smiles, warm safe hugs, and sacrifices of the small important things that make us and unmake us each day.

The picture becomes your mother in a past that recedes ever faster by the minute, but it's not just a fucking picture. It's symbolic. It's real to you, more real than any picture has ever been. It's not a reference to a person. It's not a memento. It's all you have left of your mom, all you have left of the first nurturer who showed you the world with soft warm hands, who spoke your name to you for the first time, then again and again until you were made with that word. This was the feeling many people had about The Doers. They were knowable and mysterious, beloved and feared. People felt in ways to know more.

The Doers' technology was so advanced that it didn't make any sense to people on Earth. It looked like nothing. It was just small stones, various scents, waving stalks, and whispers. Sometimes it appeared to be nothing. Some people said they were gods, had superpowers. The Doers said, "No, we are not gods. We do not have superpowers. You just don't have the proximity to us, to what we do. You are not from our places to understand us on our terms."

They said they'd long since abandoned what we called technology. Ideas about things that might help us do what we need to do is old fashioned to them, they said. They said that it's all in how you language and let language do. It's all in how you realize where you become and what your languaging already is becoming. "We are all becoming," they would say. Everyone can become in all that they can, and that is all that is needed.

The Doers said they are making the world and themselves "always and already simultaneously." "We do it all," they said, "and we don't do any of it. It just is, and we accept that." And yet, they said, "We control it all in its uncontrollableness. We hope you will become to accept in your ways."

They explained that once you realize this idea, there are no such things as impossible and astounding, exotic or same, difference and conflict, good and bad, right and wrong, hierarchy and levels. There are so many other ways than ranking things by some kind of yardstick that make the kinds of futures and landscapes you yearn for. All these things are just constructions, thought-systems that are us and not us, that are out there and not real at all yet also so very real and inside us and everything in between these places.

They said that you may come to see how Whiteness has made you simultaneously sharp, dull, round, square, prickly, smooth, wet, dry, fire-hot, ice-cold, and so very, very limited. In a soft, compassionate way, they explained that we were like a child in a playpen, you and me. You walk in circles in a small enclosure for weeks with your eyes to your feet, telling yourself how much you are learning and experiencing of the world, and call it a transcontinental hike. This has been our conditions, all of us.

The Doers told us that all these thought-systems are becoming. Whiteness is becoming. Blackness is becoming. Brownness is becoming. All your languaging is becoming. "The places in between these locations are becoming," they explained. "They are all necessary and disposable."

Someone important, a national leader, asked them on the fourth day why they had come to us. What were their intentions? The Doers were perplexed. They answered in unison from all over the globe.

"Our intentions? We are here for the doing. We are beyond intentions, at least in the way you mean it."

"But surely, you have some purpose or goal for your visit, some outcome you hope to achieve? Do you intend to wage war on us, to enslave us, to colonize us?"

"We do not wish to be evasive," they said. "We have come to do language with you. This is our way. We want nothing from you but to nurture our connections, our interbeing-ness with you. We only want to become with you on your terms and ours."

The leader was confused.

"From across the universe," The Doers said, "we felt your suffering and sorrow. It moved us to commune with you, to become our shared tangled destinies." And then, they made the offer: "If you are ready, you can do from your places too."

The leader was still confused.

"It will take time to become," they said. "Time is what we have."

Many people were suspicious of The Doers. None of it made sense. You don't travel across the expanse of space and time and other dimensions of existence just to be with someone else, to communicate for no reason. There are always reasons and purposes for communicating, right?

But many people, especially the disenfranchised—the poor; most people of color; those in countries ravaged by poverty, or under the boot of dictators, or struggling under the historical weight of colonialism and the theft of their lands, labors, languages, and lives; women of all stripes and temperaments; transgender people just trying to walk in worlds that take their legs away—these were the first peoples who felt a kind of connection to The Doers. They were the first to see the systems and their oppressions because the systems and languages hadn't worked for them ever. They were the first to try to give up the judging of languaging, to feel languaging in its differences and be okay with it all. They attended to themselves and those around them in a world that does not ask for attending but only listening. They took in and gave up many things that most of the White people with power on the planet saw as important.

The Doers said, "Let us become with you. It's not really a demonstration, but you may think of it as such. It will help us do together, but you must agree to become." So the disenfranchised went, group by group, first cautiously, then as word got around from those returning, they went in rushes, by the millions, as if their lives depended on it.

The Doers took these groups of people on one-second trips to faraway planets in distant galaxies with civilizations that were based on the exchange of hugs or the weaving of what only could be described as hair, but it wasn't hair. It was more than that. It was each being's destiny and inheritance and other things that have no human expressions for them but are understandable if you are there weaving hair that is not hair.

Or they went to places that were so ancient that those there no longer had need for their origin tales or the need for emotions like envy or selfishness. They went to planets just born, rich with new foliage and life starting to understand itself. The people would come back completely changed. They'd say, "I was there for years. I watched the first word invented by a tribe of beings with eyes behind their heads. They lived on the edge of a milky river that ran both ways. I cried because I knew them in this way. How can I live the way I have after having experienced this thing, that word? I am not me anymore. My eyes are behind me."

The people who'd travelled had not aged either, and only a second went by on Earth. Most who didn't travel were White and didn't believe in the travels, said it was a hoax. The Doers were drugging people, or maybe it was an elaborate mind-trick. The disenfranchised want to believe these things. "It's like a religion," the White doubters said. "They want to believe liberation or freedom or the answer to their problems is in something so simple as a one-second trip," the White doubters argued. "They just need more patience and perseverance," the White doubters said.

But too many had gone, too many came back a second later and told long tales of other words and worlds and people and places and languages and ways of understanding, and they learned all these things. These different ways of doing things, of languaging, and of understanding the world and themselves, came from people who were not known to be creative or inventive or to lie about such things. They even came from those few growing numbers of White people who left for a second. Every last one of them was now of these places and people. That's what they said, "I am now of another place." But still, the White doubters who had not travelled were stubborn.

So the Doers took more people on trips, but this time it was trips in time on Earth. Some went to Arles in southern France on the day that Van Gogh at thirty-five found yellow and sunshine and the beauty of sunflowers in the fields, and they wept with him as he saw yellow like no one had seen it before, and felt his sorrow and pain as he expressed it on canvas after canvas, throwing each one aside only to grab another, subtly dying of joy and grief, screaming in his head, "How yellow the flowers are!" with paint on his fingers and face. "I wish some-one could feel the yellow like I feel it."

And the travellers came back stunned and shocked in jubilant despair.

Some went to the moment when Basho first discovered that he loved poetry on a street in Edo and dedicated himself to mastering how to do poetry with as few words and as much love as possible, and they felt in their bellies the light-ning and fire of the world and everything in it, the connections of disconnected things, toads and water, a word and the screams of every person who had died in all the wars that had ever been fought, each scream clearly articulated and exclaiming the life that that person had lived and wanted to live.

And they all came back with a calm sense of knowing and speaking of these things that made everyone around them at peace with an itch that needed to be scratched.

Some went to the death bed of Marie Curie in a hospital in Passy, Haute-Savoie, and could see the lack of blood cells not being created by her bone marrow because of all of the radiation she'd been exposed to, without which she'd never have been awarded her two Nobel Prizes, one in physics and one in chemistry, and they followed across the globe the path of radiation parti-cle-waves from a tube that contained an isotope she kept in her pocket, passing through people and things, witnessing the ionizing of particles in its wake that made up people and things, and it seemed like tragic magic, a wonderful phe-nomenon that is so clearly not what we think it is, and they experienced the elation and joy of millions of people cured and the pain and angst of millions more killed by that particle-wave, and then they spoke with her words as she told one doctor after another, "No, it is not the radiation. I know radiation, radiation knows me. We are bedfellows. We will live our lives together. We do not get to live apart!"

And they returned in subtle awe of insignificant things.

Some travelled to the last ceremony in a small cave in Argentina on a starry night, where a tribe of unnamed dark, beautiful people danced at a wall in that cave by firelight. They watched as the tribe screamed and hooted, sang unknown songs of beauty and tragedy, then one by one, the members of the tribe dipped their hands and feet into a pot of warm blood just emptied from a four-legged, horned creature long-since extinct and placed them on the wall, hand by hand, foot by foot. An elder in leaves and vines cried and dusted each hand and foot with a White powder, and the members each went off to the shadows of the cave and made love to each other as if the universe depended on their love-making. And they saw the future of this tribe after the Portuguese and Spanish colonizers would come and take it all away with iron and crosses, calling their ceremonies hedonistic and devil-worshipping, then whipping them, enslaving them, and making them say words they did not know, or die.

And the travelers returned in shame of past deeds done with a hope of rebuilding and making love like the universe depended on it.

Still more went to the last buffalo hunt of an Apache tribe who did not use the word "Apache" in the North American plains before the knowledge of White Europeans changed them, before they'd slowly lose the sacred practice of buffalo hunting, before the hoop of stars in the sky stopped talking to them, before it all stopped, and they experienced the hunt with the hunters, riding their proud horses, standing on the plains in bare feet in the same way that thousands of their ancestors had done before them exactly like that, and they saw the beauty and horror and mundaneness in it all in a flash, and they realized that they were the plains, and the buffalo, and the arrow, and the axe, and the feet of the hunter and his ancestors, and the hoop in the sky, and the grass, and the sun and moon, and the words spoken and unspoken between us all.

And everyone returned and wept in ecstatic sorrow and excruciating joy at all they had not seen while looking straight at it.

Others went to the moment that an African slave who had survived the transatlantic slave route on a leaky boat with a slave master named "Hicks" had lost his name because Hicks said it was not important anymore. They followed that slave as he survived the voyage and stepped his first foot on North American soil as the brilliant sun crested over a faraway mountain, and they squinted through his slave eyes that saw more than anyone around him did in ways no one could see or has ever seen since, and they felt his sea and home sicknesses deep in his belly, felt his brilliance and determination to live and be human and be all that he was, felt his deep humanity and love for all things around him. They felt his words in his chest that could free nations and open minds and reveal so much in the world that was needed, so much that the world begged for at the time, and they saw his eyes and strong body that had withered on the voyage to America but knew that he would rebuild himself and come to be the most important philosopher and artist ever to have lived that was never known because he was a slave and would die at 27 years old because he had spilled his master's wine on a new rug.

And everyone came back and bowed their heads in shame with the courage to look at such things in their faces and call them what they are.

And then, after days of the travels, after every last person on Earth had travelled somewhere, after people became other places, The Doers vanished. They said nothing in parting. But everyone knew why, and everyone knew what needed doing. And everyone realized how much they could do and what they'd been squandering. They realized their own compassion and need for each other and their differences. And they got to tearing down and remaking everything. They remade everything from scratch. It seemed the only answer.

They didn't do away with race, or Whiteness, or Blackness, or Brownness. Instead, they let those constructions be on their own made up terms as self-identified, self-conscious things that were useful in the world as ways to know one's self in community and to become community. They created new structures that did not hierarchize or rank or use one's place as a synecdoche for all places. They gave up overly simple and selfish ideas, like grades, and first place, or second, or winners and losers. They chose to build collaborations and walked away from competition. They chose to build systems and machines and ways of walking on the Earth that smiled at failure and confusion, and they reached out their hands to hold others softly. These new structures were not sacred or natural. They were not more important than people but important to people in innumerable ways.

Each person became to feel and experience their us-ness on landscapes of us-es. They became to language the presence of many standards that are not standards, only local norms. They felt it not as the loss of rigor but as the presence of people, ideas, words, knowing and unknowing, discernable, and confusing. A single standard inflicted on all, Whiteness as the standard place, was understood as irrelevant and someone's beauty. Standards were replaced. In their place always was the sacred place of communion, of what we do in the places we are at with those there. They became to build the sacredness of their places as multiple.

Most important of the remaking from scratch was how they remade their own languaging, becoming rainbows of their own minds and judgements and habits of languaging. They did it in such a way that even those generations after the travels and the visit from The Doers, people understood and saw and heard and felt their worlds in ways that allowed for the multiplicity of paradoxical words. People began to speak and hear the Aurora Borealis. They began to hear the color yellow and feel their feet on the earth, placed in the footprints of everyone who had come before them. The sacred hoop in the sky began to talk. And some even made love as if the universe depended on it.

It didn't take long before people on Earth began to float, then they seemed almost translucent with everything inside of them and nothing. The so-called laws of physics and all the other impossible ideas and constructions that limited them and their lives just wasn't, and it was. Everything was becoming.

And they came to continually realize in innumerable ways that the point of languaging isn't to make others understand you, or to win, or persuade, or even encourage or inform. These things happen when they happen. Languaging is always doing, communing, suffering with, becoming in communities of becoming. And everyone in their ways became languagelings, bright as the sun, dark as the cosmos, clear as running water, and always and already simultaneously.

AN ARGUMENT AND METHOD FOR DEEP ATTENTIVE READING

Today we are not encouraged to listen carefully, compassionately, or thoughtfully to each other. Our culture in the US doesn't provide many examples or opportunities to practice deep listening to those around us. Generally speaking, the way we interact on social media, such as Facebook, Instagram, and Twitter, is a good example of this. We post something, collect "likes," and many call this being heard. But what does that act of being heard look and feel like to the listener? Do we even think in terms of *listening* when we think of those who like a social media post? What were the last three things you liked or interacted with on whatever social media platforms you use? Can you remember what those interactions were about? Are you sure? If you can't remember the details, or even the posts or tweets, then how can we say we've really listened to those messages, those people?

The title of this essay could also be called: *You can't skim a book if you want to really understand the argument*. A big reason for this is that a lot of what we tell each other may sound initially counter-intuitive, wrong, or opposed to what we've known to be true or correct. Others' ideas may just be hard to hear carefully because of what you already believe about, say, language and judgement and how strongly you feel about those beliefs. Our feelings about our beliefs often can get in the way of being open minded or listening carefully to others' ideas. I know, I work on this daily in my own life and teaching.

In fact, you may initially hear something else in my words than what I'm actually saying. For instance, when I say that standards of English when used in classrooms to grade are racist, what is your response? Do you think I'm saying that good grammar is racist? Many with particular views about language and race do, but I'm not saying that at all. These kinds of misunderstandings are quite natural, because you wouldn't believe what you do if you didn't have some good reasons or experiences to back up those ideas and because you likely have strong feelings about those beliefs. Therefore, if I said, "learning standard English in school is not vital to success in the business world," you might respond by disagreeing directly with that claim, too.

But why exactly are you disagreeing? Are you disagreeing because you've seen firsthand how Standard English is directly or indirectly vital to success in business settings? Have you really seen it? And if you have, how do you know that your experiences are a good sample of all experiences in all business settings? How many business settings have you operated in that demonstrate this claim? What experiences do you have with English usage and business settings precisely? What experiences do you have, or have access to, that may actually disprove your ideas about the use of English in business settings? That is, can you imagine a world where success is not determined by how one uses a particular kind of English? Could we not be living in some version of that world?

In short, why do you think your experience and knowledge are enough to answer this kind of question? Why do we see what we want to see so often? Why is it so hard to see others' views and ideas of things as reasonable? The short answer is that we do a lot of fast thinking. Our judgements of many things, especially those that have emotions and other commitments of ours connected to them, are not made from facts. Well, they are always made from facts, but they are often just our *personal* facts. It's a mindbug[1] we all have. It's fast thinking.

OUR FAST THINKING AND MINDBUGS

We all do fast thinking all the time, much of the time out of necessity. We don't know enough about everything on which we have to make judgements and decisions, yet we still have decisions to make. The flaw in much of this reasoning, however, is that we usually don't have a lot of information to go on, and what we do have, we tend to overestimate its explanatory or supportive power. Numerous brain studies show that our brains use our initial beliefs and feelings about a topic to create a coherent story to back up our ideas about, say, the importance of learning "proper English." Psychology researchers have studied various versions of this judgement phenomenon. It's a system that our brains use to make fast judgements, ones that come to us quickly and copiously throughout each day.

One such judgement system is described by Daniel Kahneman, a Nobel Prize winning psychology professor from Princeton. In *Thinking, Fast and Slow*, Kahneman describes this judgement system as the "availability heuristic," or a system our brains use to make judgements about any number of things. Here's how he says it works: Our brains make decisions based on the information available to us or the information we can readily retrieve in our minds that relates to the question or problem at hand, and because this information is readily

---

1   I get this term, "mindbug," from chapter 1 of Mahzarin R. Banaji and Anthony G. Greenwald, *Blind Spot*. In the chapter, the authors discuss visual mindbugs, memory mindbugs, and social mindbugs. Each mindbug is a different way for our brains to trick us or make flawed sense of complex data.

available to us, we bolster its strength as proof of our initial ideas—that is, having only this information in mind, we assume it is all we need to make a decision in the present case.

The availability heuristic reveals how our brains often substitute the question at hand with an easier, more accessible, question, one we are able to answer. So instead of answering, "how important is Standardized English to success in business settings?" Many of us answer a question like, "how important *do I see* Standardized English being in business settings?" The second question is more accessible to us, but it is not the same question initially asked.

Doing this substitution and thinking you have a good answer to a question like this is equivalent to turning on ESPN, watching several hours of sports programming about the NBA, then concluding that women do not play professional basketball. For all you know, women do not, but that's only because you don't have enough information in front of you. Your sample is limited and biased. There wasn't any coverage of the WNBA league when you watched, or you've never looked for it in the past.

The first question about Standardized English in business requires a lot more data to answer, as does the women and basketball question, and it is not wise to answer either question based solely on one's own experiences alone since the nature of the questions are broad-reaching and beg for a large amount of data that one person often cannot experience by themselves. Our own literacy narratives and what they might tell us are similar in nature. They are not what they too often appear to be. And so, you'd have to do a lot of research to find out the answer to questions like mine about the need or usefulness of a particular kind of English, or even questions such as: what did I learn about language in school, how did I learn it, and what does it tell me about myself and the world around me?

Now, technically speaking, the WNBA example is actually an illustration of what Kahneman identifies as the WYSIATI heuristic, another kind of fast thinking that causes errors in judgement. It is similar to the availability heuristic. Both mind bugs use limited information to make a decision. The WYSIATI or "What You See Is All There Is" heuristic occurs when you only take into account what you see, thinking mistakenly that what you see in front of you is all there is to consider when making the judgement you are currently trying to make.[2]

But we have more mindbugs. Our brains often look for information that confirms our initial hypothesis about our beliefs, like those around Standardized English and business settings. Some might call our initial beliefs—or the

---

2   Kahneman, 85–88.

ideas we search for evidence to confirm in our minds—*bias*, thus activating another system of judgement in our brains that leads to errors in judgement, "confirmation bias."[3] This typical judgement phenomenon has been researched extensively by psychology researchers. Shahram Heshmat, an emeritus associate professor from the University of Illinois at Springfield provides this coherent definition:

> Confirmation bias occurs from the direct influence of desire on beliefs. When people would like a certain idea or concept to be true, they end up believing it to be true. They are motivated by wishful thinking. This error leads the individual to stop gathering information when the evidence gathered so far confirms the views or prejudices one would like to be true.
>
> Once we have formed a view, we embrace information that confirms that view while ignoring, or rejecting, information that casts doubt on it. Confirmation bias suggests that we don't perceive circumstances objectively. We pick out those bits of data that make us feel good because they confirm our prejudices. Thus, we may become prisoners of our assumptions.[4]

So not only do we need to slow down our thinking about what we believe yet have very little actual data to support, but we need to be on guard against confirmation bias, or the way our brains try to support our initial assumptions about certain ideas, such as our beliefs about language and the goodness of language standards, which in the process ignores other possible ideas, answers, and interpretations of our world and the people in it. We need to be careful that we don't just pick those details, ideas, and evidence that back up our initial ideas and ignore the details, ideas, and evidence that suggest contrary judgements and conclusions.

Confirmation bias and the availability and WYSIATI heuristics remind us to be careful and to slow down. We must be vigilant and not selectively hear what we want to hear. These judgement errors show us that we must be attentive to what we don't find initially appealing as we read something, like the text you

---

3   Kahneman, 80–81. For more about confirmation bias, see also Daniel Gilbert, "How Mental Systems Believe," *American Psychologist* 46, no. 2 (February 1991): 107–119, https://doi.org/10.1037/0003-066X.46.2.107. For a definition of confirmation bias, see Encyclopædia Britannica, s.v. "confirmation bias," last updated October 9, 2019, https://www.britannica.com/science/confirmation-bias/additional-info#history.

4   Shahram Heshmat, "What Is Confirmation Bias," *Psychology Today*, April 23, 2015, https://www.psychologytoday.com/us/blog/science-choice/201504/what-is-confirmation-bias.

have in front of you, perhaps. Knowing how our minds are bugged is the first hurdle in being really attentive, the first hurdle to reading carefully and compassionately. It can also help us understand how our language and standards easily become racist.

As if these potholes in judgement weren't enough to guard against, we also have a lot at stake when it comes to language and arguments about language. If you are like most everyone else, you care about your identity. Part of who you are is how you talk, your language, and the particular system of symbols you use to communicate, make sense of the world, connect with others, and understand who you are. So, one might say that our beliefs about language are personal. They are emotionally charged. There is a lot at stake for each of us.

Our emotional responses, however, can get in the way of hearing other ideas carefully and attentively. Sometimes we call these emotional potholes in discussions or social settings "triggers"—that is, the ideas, words, and images that trigger a strong emotional response in some people. But it is usually never the trigger that is the problem. It's usually what made the trigger a trigger that is worth paying attention to.

Emotional triggers are actually helpful in attending to others more carefully and deeply. If we can notice our emotional responses to ideas, people, or their language, then we might better understand when our emotions halo onto the judgement we are making at the moment. This is called the "halo effect," and Kahneman discusses it in his book, too.[5] The halo effect occurs when people take their feelings (good, bad, or otherwise) about a person or idea and use them, usually unconsciously, to make a judgement on a new instance dealing with that person or idea.

In short, our previously charged emotions about a person or idea often affect our future judgements about that person or idea. This may be why many take it personally when I call standards for English racist. What they hear is me calling them racist. It feels like a personal attack, because the statement is easily wrapped up in other ideas that we each have stake in, that we care and feel deeply about. The idea of so-called "proper English" can be emotionally charged because our past emotions about people and ideas halo onto our present discussion.

What complicates many discussions, like those about race or language, are our attitudes and beliefs about race or language more generally. For instance, many linguists discuss our attitudes about language as "language ideology," or "a system of beliefs, assumptions, presuppositions, ideas, values, and attitudes

---

5   Kahneman, *Thinking*, 3–4.

about language."[6] Language ideology is a term used to identify something important about language: We all have beliefs (and feelings) about language, what it means to us, and what it signifies. When I use the word "ain't" in this book, some readers hear that as unintelligent or unschooled. Others don't. This is language ideology at work.

We use our ideas about language to make sense of language and other people. Our beliefs about language help us make judgements about what it means when we see or hear some people using language in particular ways and others using it in other ways. What makes discussions about language so difficult is that the topic of language and its standards are also wrapped up with emotionally-charged ideas and biases (prejudgements) that deal with the idea of language itself and other kinds of languages. These problems of fast thinking, mindbugs, and language ideologies are overlapping and make it hard for differently-minded people to engage compassionately and meaningfully with each other—that is, to mindfully attend to others' words.

If we all want to make the best decisions possible for us and those around us, then we need the most information possible. That means being open to other ideas and information. Being open minded is vital to healthy, good, and ethical decision making. This also means that we gotta do our research before we make decisions about things, and we have to deeply listen, attend to others' words. Thus, it is good for all of us to listen carefully, attentively, and compassionately to those with whom we may initially disagree, to be wary of how our emotions may be haloing onto our current thinking, to be careful that we do not simply confirm our original biases, and to search out information that helps us ask good questions and answer the real ones in front of us meaningfully and ethically—even if those answers make us uncomfortable.

DEEP ATTENTIVE READING

So when you find yourself feeling angry or irritated at others' words, say mine, you might pause and engage in a quick mental practice that can offer a way for you to separate what you know from what you feel, or to distinguish the details of my arguments from how they make you feel. That is, I think using an easy mindful reading practice, what I call *deep attentive reading*, can help you make sense of the ideas and concepts you encounter and your own reactions, biases,

---

6   Minglang Zhou, "Language Ideology and Language Order: Conflicts and Compromises in Colonial and Postcolonial Asia," *International Journal of the Sociology of Language* 2017, no. 243 (2017): 100–101, https://doi.org/10.1515/ijsl-2016-0047.

and feelings about them, regardless of what conclusions you ultimately make about my argument or any argument you're reading.

What I'm proposing is one form of a common contemplative practice that can be found in various forms in a number of spiritual traditions on the planet, but I draw my inspiration from Christian and Buddhist traditions.[7] At those moments of concern or when you find yourself upset, angry, or even excited and joyful because of what you're reading—when you find yourself triggered—do the following:

1. Pause for at least ten seconds, and take three deep, slow breaths.

2. As you breathe, notice how you feel and where those feelings are located in your body.

3. Tell yourself: "I am feeling _____, but that feeling is separate from what I'm reading on the page."

4. Return to your reading.

This practice centers on the breath. It helps readers slow down, pause, notice our reactions to a text, locate those emotions, and separate them from our ideas in order to see both our emotions and ideas more clearly. This is not to suggest that our emotional responses are not important to our judgements; instead, it is to help us see when our emotions might be keeping us from understanding the fullness of our habits of language and the ways our emotions are part of our judgements. There is plenty of research and many cultural and spiritual traditions that use the breath to calm down, focus, and cultivate habits that help people do a range of things in mindful ways, ways that are self-compassionate. James Nestor's recent book, *Breath: The New Science of An Old Art*, offers some of that history and suggests practices that are worth considering.[8]

---

7   For the Christian tradition of *lectio divina*, or "divine reading," see Christine Valters Paintner, *Lectio Divina - The Sacred Art: Transforming Words and Images into Heart-Centered Prayer* (Woodstock, VT: Skylight Paths Publishing, 2011); for Buddhist versions of contemplative practices that read or listen to the world and others, see Thich Nhat Hanh, *Peace is Every Step*; or Thich Nhat Hanh, *Being Peace* (Berkeley: Parallax Press, 1987); for a range of contemplative practices applied to a range of disciplines in higher education, see Daniel P. Barbezat and Mirabai Bush, *Contemplative Practices in Higher Education: Powerful Methods to Transform Teaching and Learning* (San Francisco, Jossey-Bass, 2014); for a theoretical look at mediation and contemplative inquiry, see chapter seven of Arthur Zajonc, *Meditation as Contemplative Inquiry: When Knowing Becomes Love* (Great Barrington, MA: Lindisfarne Books, 2009); for another version of a similar kind of deep attentive practice that is meant to address racial microaggressions in everyday life, see Ijeoma Oluo, *So You Want To Talk About Race* (New York: Hachette Books, 2019), 175–176.

8   James Nestor, *Breath: The New Science of A Lost Art* (New York: Riverhead Books, 2020).

As you do this practice, do not try to figure out your feelings or emotions or even try to understand them too finely. Just notice them in a non-judgemental way. It is normal and okay to have whatever emotional reaction you do, but don't project the cause of those feelings away from you, although this is reflective work that you might do if you wish to pursue deeper thinking about these issues. For instance, if you wanted to do that deeper work, you might ask: Why do certain ideas, and even words, trigger me and make me so angry, upset, sad, or happy? Where did I get those ideas or information? How did I come to feel so strongly about such ideas or words? What makes the trigger a trigger for me here?

While this reflective work is important, it may be too much to do while also trying to hear and understand a text, like this book, carefully. If your purpose for reading something is to understand the argument on its own terms, then focus on trying to read and understand it rather than responding to all the ideas that may trigger you. That can come afterwards. Again, this is not easy reading. We don't usually practice listening to each other on the other's terms or listening to change ourselves. I often have a hard time doing this, but I find the pausing and noticing how I feel to be helpful and ultimately rewarding.

As you practice deep attentive reading, also resist the urge to make reasons for your emotional or other responses. That is, resist thinking things like: "Well, what he said here made me angry because . . ." or "I'm upset because he is wrong and isn't considering . . ." This kind of response mixes your intellectual response with your emotional one. It's easy at these moments to engage in mindbugs, that is, engage the availability or WYSIATI heuristics, confirmation bias, and the halo effect. To avoid them at this crucial mindful moment, resist making reasons for how you are responding to the text.

Try to view these emotions and thinking as if from a third-person perspective, or as if you are floating above them, just observing them happen. When I slow down my thinking, pause, and become more mindful of how I am feeling and what I am thinking, I become a more critical and compassionate reader, more able to engage meaningfully with what or who is in front of me.

We can never fully separate our emotions and thoughts, but if we want to understand an opposing argument, we have to be able to distinguish these two things from each other and work hard to not project them onto others and their words. Your anger is *your* anger, just as my anger is mine. It is my response to something I hear or see. And that's okay, but my anger, irritation, or emotions may have to do with other things than the strength of someone else's argument or the data they bring to bear on the question at hand.

I will have a very hard time knowing this without first pausing, noticing, and separating my feelings *about* what I hear from *what* is being said to me. I'm sure we have all experienced times when we didn't like the truth presented to us because it was painful or it was costly or it made us realize that we were wrong or needed to change, yet it was the truth. It was only later when we had some distance from the initial contact with that truth that we were able to see that our emotional response was getting in the way of our acceptance of or engagement with the truth.

This also means you can have any kind of response possible to opposing ideas, people, or words. You don't have to be angry or upset. You might be curious or inquisitive. Disagreement does not have to mean a fight or a battle. It can mean a collaborative moment where we work together to understand each other. So, you might ask: How could someone who is trying hard to understand how language works and find ways toward a more peaceful world, someone who has done decades of research on this subject, come to these ideas in front of me? How can he think or be so different from me? You are not locked into your first emotional response, as important as it is to who you are, but it may not be necessary to who you might become.

More importantly, this reading practice is compassionate, critical, and difficult. Deep attentive reading is a practical way to read so that you can separate or detach your emotional responses to words and people from those words and people, at least long enough to hear the ideas distinctly. The practice is meant to help a reader attend deeply to other's words on the other person's terms, not yours, in order to discern what they are saying and what you are feeling about those ideas. This can help you better understand what they say and better understand your emotional responses to those ideas and words. This ultimately means you will better understand your own ideas, too.

Deep attentive reading is not asking you to ignore or put aside your emotional responses. Actually, it helps us pay attention to them, to get to know them, but not let them override or overly control our ability to sit compassionately with others' words, to attend to difficult ideas deeply on the other's terms. While all of our emotional reactions are human, valid, and normal, they can often shade or affect our intellectual responses to other's words and ideas. Deep attentive reading offers a way to pay attention to both.

Some might say that I'm saying that our emotions "get in the way" of our reasoning and logical natures, but that's only half true. By necessity, our emotions filter our reasoning and our logical responses. They give color or texture to our otherwise logical responses to things, the arguments we make about why we believe or judge things to be the way we see them. So we have both an emotional response and an intellectual one to our world for good reasons. And we can use both to help us make sense of things, to figure out the best, ethical, responsible, and sustainable answers to complex human problems.

I don't think it's wise to neglect our emotional responses to words, but it is important to distinguish between emotions and ideas. You might think of the practice of deep attentive reading as a way to separate how you feel about something you read from how you think about what you read in order to see how those two dimensions are related and might work together (or against each other).

It is in the separation of these two dimensions of our experience with others' ideas, words, and even bodies—one dimension that is mostly cognitive (what you think) and one mostly affective (how you feel)—that can help us make deeper sense of things, perhaps more compassionate sense of things. This kind of reading can help us treat others ethically and with the respect we all deserve as human beings. I know, this sounds like a weird way of reading, but it is only because our culture and society do not encourage us or offer many opportunities to pause consciously and notice our emotions and separate them from our ideas. Deep attentive reading can help you do this.